TEXTILE ASCENDANCIES

AFRICAN PERSPECTIVES

Kelly Askew and Anne Pitcher
Series Editors

Textile Ascendancies

Aesthetics, Production, and Trade in Northern Nigeria

Elisha P. Renne and
Salihu Maiwada, Editors

University of Michigan Press
Ann Arbor

Published in the United States of America by the
University of Michigan Press
Manufactured in the United States of America
Printed on acid-free paper
A CIP catalog record for this book is available from the British Library.
Library of Congress Cataloging-in-Publication data has been applied for.

First published April 2020

ISBN: 978-0-472-07444-0 (Hardcover : alk paper)
ISBN: 978-0-472-05444-2 (Paper : alk paper)
ISBN: 978-0-472-12663-7 (ebook)

Publication of this volume has been partially funded by the African Studies Center, University
of Michigan.

Digital materials related to this title can be found on the Fulcrum platform via the following
citable URL: https://doi.org/10.3998/mpub.10176049

For the northern Nigerians who have worked as weavers, spinners, indigo dyers, cloth beaters, designers, embroiderers, tailors, traders, cotton pickers and farmers

CONTENTS

Digital materials related to this title can be found on the Fulcrum platform via the following citable URL: https://doi.org/10.3998/mpub.10176049

ACKNOWLEDGMENTS

We are indebted to many people in Gwarzo, Kaduna, Kano, Minjibir, and Zaria, in Kaduna State and Kano State, Nigeria, and in the United Kingdom and the United States. While they are too numerous to mention individually, we would like to thank Alhaji Shafi'u Abdulkadir, Hajiya Zaineb Abdulkadir, Alhaji Sa'idu Adhama, Mr. Muhammed Buhari, Alhaji Aminu Alhassan Dantata, Mr. Gordon Hartley, Alhaji Sani Hunkuyi, Mr. Wuese Iyorver, Alhaji Usman Kayyu, Professor Murray Last, Alhaji Isyaku Shittu, Alhaji Ya'u Tanimu, and Mr. Alhassan Abdulkarim Umar for their cooperation and helpful interviews. In addition, we thank Mr. Ashiru Abdullahi, Mr. AbdulMajid Maiwada, Mr. AbdurRahman Maiwada, Malama Binta Sani, and Hajiya Hassana Yusuf for their research assistance. At Ahmadu Bello University, the kindness of six vice chancellors over the years has reassured us of the value of this long-term collaborative project, while colleagues at Ahmadu Bello University in Zaria, and at Bayero University and the Federal College of Education–Kano—both in Kano—have been most generous with their time and advice. At the University of Michigan, we have benefited from the comments and suggestions of faculty colleagues. We would also like to thank his Royal Highness, the Emir of Zazzau, Dr. Shehu Idris, CFR, for granting permission to conduct research in Zaria City and to his Royal Highness, the Emir of Kano, Alhaji Muhammadu Sanusi II, CON, for his support for this research project in Kano, Minjibir, and Gwarzo.

In addition, the exceptional help of librarians at the University of Michigan, at the Herskovits Library–Northwestern University, at Ahmadu Bello University, and at the Bodleian Libraries–Oxford University; museum curators at the Museum of Science and Industry, Manchester; archivists at Arewa House at the Nigerian National Archives, and at the Kaduna State Ministry of Information—all in Kaduna—all have greatly facilitated this study. Finally, this long-term research on the history of textile aesthetics, production, and trade in northern Nigeria would not have been possible without funding from various sources, which include the Department of Anthropology, the Department of Afroamerican and African Studies, the Advanced Study Center of the International Institute, and the Humanities Institute—all at the University of Michigan—as well as the Fulbright U.S. Scholar Program, the Pasold Research Fund, and the John Simon Guggenheim Memorial Foundation.

We are likewise grateful to the editor of the University of Michigan Press, Dr. Ellen Bauerle, to Anna Pohlod, our editorial assistant, to the design staff, and to the three manuscript reviewers, whose kind but firm comments regarding the manuscript's organization facilitated the publication process. Professors Kelly Askew and Anne Pitcher, senior sponsoring editors for the African Studies series at the University of Michigan Press, continue to provide outstanding support for African studies research.

PREFACE

The collaboration on which this edited volume is based began informally in September 1994, when Elisha Renne, a Fulbright fellow, met Salihu Maiwada and Dakyes Usman in the Department of Industrial Design at Ahmadu Bello University, Zaria, in Kaduna State, Nigeria. Because of their shared interest in and appreciation of Nigerian textiles, they met on several occasions to discuss future research possibilities. Over the following years they continued to meet when Renne was in Zaria. In 1999, Usman and Renne coauthored a paper on everyday Hausa aesthetics that focused on bicycle decoration, which was published in the journal *African Arts*. Maiwada and Renne's collaborative research on textile aesthetics, production, and trade began in 2005 when they interviewed hand and machine-embroiderers in Zaria City and asked about changes in the hand-embroidery of the large Hausa robes known as *babban riga*. Their coauthored article was published in the journal *Textile History* in 2007. They subsequently received a grant from the Pasold Foundation in 2009 to continue their research on textile history in northern Nigeria, this time focusing on the history of the first textile mill, Kaduna Textiles Limited, that was established in Kaduna. This project, which included interviews with Mohammadu Waziri, a contributor to this volume, was carried out in 2010–2011 and was published in *Textile History* in 2013. Research funds from the Center for African Studies, University of Michigan, also enabled Maiwada, Renne, and Usman to organize materials for an exhibition, "Sir Ahmadu Bello and Kaduna Textile Limited," which was held at Arewa House, Kaduna, in November–December 2012.

In 2014, Maiwada and Renne continued their study of northern Nigerian textile history with additional funding from the Pasold Foundation. Maiwada conducted research in the rural town of Gwarzo, in western Kano State, where he interviewed hand-weavers about *mudakare* textiles, while Renne conducted interviews in Kano with Chinese textile manufacturing representatives. There she met Hannatu Hassan, a graduate student of Dr. Maiwada, who helped her to make connections with northern Nigerian textile traders whom she later met in Guangzhou, China (the Guangzhou research was published in 2015 in the journal *Textiles: Cloth and Culture*). An additional grant from the African Studies Center, University of Michigan, in 2015, enabled Dakyes Usman to interview former designers from Kaduna textile mills on the digitization of pattern reproduction and Hannatu Hassan to interview Nigerian textile traders in Kantin Kwari market in Kano about the impact of Chinese textiles imports. Abdulkarim Umar DanAsabe joined the project at this time and followed up on his extensive research on the history of traders and textile manufacturing in Kano.

In November 2015, Maiwada, Usman, and Hassan traveled to the United States to participate in an exhibit, "Textile Trade Ascendancies: Nigeria, UK, China," at the University of Michigan. They also met with Renne to discuss preparations for this edited volume. Subsequently, the entire group of contributors met several times in Zaria and Kano in the following years, with final meetings in January 2018. The complete set of chapters was submitted to Ellen Bauerle at University of Michigan Press in February 2018. Since then, they have kept in touch by e-mail and phone.

It has been almost twenty-five years since Salihu Maiwada, Elisha Renne, and Dakyes Usman began conferring about textile production, embroidery, and cotton print designs in Northern Nigeria. This edited volume is a testament to the virtues of long-term research collaboration and friendship. That Abdulkarim DanAsabe, Hannatu Hassan, and Mohammadu Waziri later joined the group has been an additional benefit.

Introduction

ELISHA RENNE AND SALIHU MAIWADA

In northern Nigeria, textile aesthetics, production, and trade have historically been reflected in the distinctive dress of men and women, which revealed local tastes and social identities. Many of the textiles they wore derived from an elaborate system of textile production that flourished in nineteenth-century northern Nigeria as women, men, and children worked as cotton growers, spinners, weavers, indigo dyers, cloth beaters, designers, embroiderers, tailors, and traders, in a system facilitated by the establishment of an independent Islamic state, the Sokoto Caliphate, in 1808 (Candotti 2015; Kriger 1988, 1993; Last 1967; Shea 1975). While some European textiles and silk yarn were brought from trading towns such as Egga in the confluence area of central Nigeria (Johnson 1973) and from North Africa via trans-Saharan trade routes to the city of Kano, the textile, weaving, and dyeing metropolis of northern Nigeria (Johnson 1976; Lydon 2009), these imported textiles and yarns only added to the repertoire of textiles available for use rather than diminishing local textile-related production. Various changes occurred with the imposition of British colonial rule in the early twentieth century, which ended the Caliphate system of governance. There were increased imports of European textiles, both plain and printed cotton material, although handweaving, embroidery, and cotton production continued. Toward the end of the colonial era and with the establishment of an independent Nigeria in October 1960, industrial textile mills were built in Kaduna and Kano, the two largest cities in northern Nigeria. Some earlier patterns of textile-related work persisted, while some were modified. The hand-embroidery by men of the large prestigious robes known as *babban riga* continued, although they no longer used locally handwoven narrow-strip cloth, which was replaced with a type of imported cotton damask for their work. However, by the 1970s in Zaria, many men had left hand-embroidery for machine-embroidery, while women who had previously embroidered men's caps filled this specialized economic niche (Guyer 2004; Maiwada and Renne 2007; Renne 2004). The long-standing practice of distributing a hierarchy of embroidered robes during Islamic holidays and for political appointments, as well as the importance of these robes for representing a Hausa-Fulani identity and the social status of their wearers, supported this continued demand (Northern Region of Nigeria 1954).

By the early twenty-first century, however, this constellation of textile production, gift distribution, consumption, and trade had changed. While the machine- and hand-embroidery of robes and caps persists, most domestic textile mills are closed, and handweaving is all but abandoned (Maiwada and Renne 2013). Textiles have become mere commodities, with the social contexts and processes of production disconnected from those consuming them (Kopytoff 1986). Traders in the famous Kantin Kwari market in Kano, where textiles are sold to buyers throughout Nigeria and beyond, now mainly sell manufactured textiles from China, which has become the primary source of textiles for northern Nigerians. This edited volume examines these changes in textile aesthetics, technologies, and social values in order to place this extraordinary shift in textile demand, production, and trade within its historical, sociocultural, political, and economic context. Textile manufacturing has declined elsewhere as well. For example, in the United States, mills have closed throughout the Carolinas (Minchin 2013). Textiles and apparel are mainly imported from China, while Chinese manufacturers are buying US grown cotton (Tabuchi 2015).[1] Yet the history and decline of the US textile industry differs from the Nigerian experience. For it was in 1793 that the manufacture of cotton thread began in Pawtucket, Rhode Island; the first cotton textile mill was introduced in Waltham, Massachusetts, in 1813. Although rural New England women during the nineteenth century took up hand-spinning and handweaving, as the name for this period—"the age of homespun"—suggests, more and more factory-manufactured textiles were being produced (Ulrich 2001).[2] Indeed, increasing urbanization and ideas about modernity associated with "city ways" ended the widespread use of handwoven textiles as dress and bedding in the northeastern United States by the century's end. And while US textile manufacturers had access to increasingly sophisticated textile production equipment, competition from foreign textile manufacturers and apparel producers with equally up-to-date equipment and lower labor costs were able to overtake the US market.

Thus, while the decline in the northern Nigerian textile production—both mill-manufactured and handwoven—occurred more than a century later and reflects certain similarities, particularly the rejection of handweaving as an outmoded occupation inconsistent with modern social life, it differs in two important ways. First, the machinery used in the early Nigerian textile mills was soon outdated and until recently was not replaced, while the electrical power grid to run the mills was failing. Second, the enduring importance of traditional rulers and local ethnic identity in northern Nigeria has supported the continued use of particular handwoven textiles because such associations are too important to be entirely forgotten (Weiner and Schneider 1989). Nonetheless, the production of textiles has largely come to be separated from those who are consuming them.[3] The contributors to this volume consider precisely how the distinctive aesthetic evaluations and social values associated with cloth, along with weaving and trade, have changed over the past two centuries in order to explain why textile-related production has declined in northern Nigeria.

This larger question concerning why textile-related production— handweaving, the hand-spinning of cotton thread, indigo dyeing, and industrial textile manufacture—declined in the twenty-first century is approached by considering three related questions. First, how have the material qualities of textile materials, cloth, and clothing historically been assessed, defined, and valued, and how is the re-evaluation of an aesthetics of materiality related to changing individual and social identities? For example, those involved in the indigo dyeing of cotton textiles could vary the depth of color by the number of times a cloth was dipped in the dye vat, and they could vary the blue-black sheen by the amount of indigo paste that was beaten into a dyed cloth.[4] The social worth and personal qualities of those wearing cloths displaying these differences in color intensity and sheen—as well as traces of indigo dye on people's skin—would be judged accordingly by astute viewers. Such visual and material distinctions also had socioeconomic consequences. In Kura, the town near Kano famous for *dan* Kura black indigo turbans, "it was estimated that out of a population of approximately 8,000 residents, there were 2,000 dyers and 80 cloth beaters in Kura" in 1909 (Shea 2006). More recently, changing aesthetic tastes for fabrics of lighter weight that are color-fast have reduced the demand for indigo-dyed cloths so that in Kura at the beginning of the twenty-first century, only one dyeing center was still operating there (Ibrahim 2016).[5] The blue tinge left on the skin and on other garments are no longer considered to be signs of beauty and wealth.

Second, how have changing textile production processes and associated technologies affected textile qualities, their availability in northern Nigerian markets, and consumer tastes? During the colonial era (1903–1960) in northern Nigeria, British colonial officials promoted the importation of British cotton baft—both unbleached (*akoko* or *alawayyo*) and bleached (*zauwati*)—which led to their being used in the making lighter weight hand-embroidered robes and kaftans. Printed cotton textiles (known locally as *atamfa*) were also imported and were worn as wrappers by well-to-do women, while village women made do with locally resist-dyed *adire* cloths of varying quality. With independence and the establishment of textile mills in Kano and Kaduna in the 1960s, a wide array of plain and custom-printed textiles became available to northern Nigerians, who also commissioned textiles for political parties and family events. Thus, the wearing of cotton printed textiles became widespread as women and men sought to include them as fashionable dress. Their easy availability during the early 1960s enabled Ahmadu Bello, then the premier of Northern Region of Nigeria, to distribute cotton textiles manufactured and printed in the newly established mills in Kaduna during his tours of the Northern Region (Paden 1986).

Third, how have textiles produced in northern Nigeria acquired a distinctive "social life" as they were exchanged for other things such as kola, given as gifts by emirs to maintain their subjects' loyalty, and used as "envoys" to establish diplomatic and working relations? (Fee 2002). During the nineteenth century, European travelers in northern Nigeria frequently remarked on the particular textiles they gave to chiefs and village heads to ensure safe passage, sometimes lamenting when they did not have appropriate textiles to give (Barth 1857; Staudinger 1990 [1899]). More recently, with most textiles in the market presently imported from China, northern Nigerian traders have come to rely on a range of electronic means for buying and selling textiles. Thus, textile traders in Kano rely on the Internet and FedEx to obtain cloth samples from Chinese companies, and Kano traders in Guangzhou, China, rely on smartphones to send images of textiles to confirm orders from buyers in Nigeria (Renne 2015). How have the "social lives" of these textiles been affected by the speed of these new trading practices such as the digitization of business orders and shipping? While the Internet of Things—the connectedness of devices, vehicles, and building using programmed sensors and Internet connections to exchange information and to control things—will doubtless be interpreted in particular ways appropriate to the infrastructure of northern Nigeria, it has possibilities for textile production and trade in future industrial sites there (Giginyu 2014).

SHIFTING ASCENDANCIES OF PRODUCTION AND TRADE

In order to address these questions, the volume's authors focus on several different aspects of textile aesthetics, production, and trade—textile names, indigo-dyeing terms, and social meanings; cotton print textiles and an aesthetics of wealth and beauty; industrially woven textile manufacturing in Kaduna and in Kano; the growth of Kantin Kwari market in Kano and the impact of Chinese textile imports; and new technologies of production and trade—mainly in Zaria and Kaduna (both in Kaduna State) and in the metropolis of Kano and Gwarzo Local Government Areas (both in Kano State). The topics are considered in the context of different periods of governance, under Fulani-Islamic governance associated with the Sokoto Caliphate (1808–1903); under British colonial rule (1903–1960); under democratic/military rule after independence (1960–1999), and finally under democratic rule during the twenty-first century (2000–2017).

There has been extensive research conducted on textile production and use during the period of the Sokoto Caliphate, on handweaving, indigo dyeing, robe production, and dress, as well as textile trade and distribution, based on Caliphate documents, traveler accounts, museum collections, and archival files. Marisa Candotti (2015) and Colleen Kriger (1988, 1993, 2006) have documented handwoven textile production, which included the increasing use of luxury materials such as silk thread (Douny 2011; Kriger 2010), as the textile production and trade expanded under the relative security that Caliphate rule provided (Candotti 2010; Last 1966; Philips 1992). An example of "bigger is better," the economic advantages of scale—in sources and preparation of materials, in weaving workshops, in indigo-dyeing practices, and in trading caravans—also contributed to the prosperity that supported robe production (Shea 2006). The making of large embroidered robes was part of Caliphate governance, with sumptuary conventions regarding the wearing of silk robes and embroidery delineating the social and political standing of those associated with emirate courts. By the end of the nineteenth century, Kano Emirate officials sent one thousand robes annually to the Caliphate treasury in Sokoto (Candotti 2010, 201) while the Zaria Emirate sent robes and slaves to Sokoto as tribute (Last 1967, 105).

This extensive production of handspun cotton and silk textiles as well as indigo-dyed robes, wrappers, and turbans is reflected in the plethora of names of particular types of cloth, garments, and indigo-dyeing terms. Heinrich Barth (1857, 1:510), who visited Kano in 1851, noted the enormous quantities and varieties of cloth that were produced in the Kano area:

KANO FROM MOUNT DALA.

Fig. 0.1. Etching of Kano, seen from Dala Hill, 1850, from Heinrich Barth (*Travels and Discoveries in North and Central Africa*, vol. 1, New York: Harper & Brothers, 1857, p. 500.)

The principal commerce of Kano consists in native produce, namely, the cotton cloth woven and dyed here or in the neighboring towns, in the form of tobes or rígona (sign. ríga); túrkedí, or the oblong piece of dress of dark-blue color worn by the women; the zenne [*zane*] or plaid, of various colors; and the ráwani bakí, [black turban, dyed and beaten with indigo] or black lithám [veil].

Indeed, he mentions more than fifteen specifically named cloths, which include:

"Fari-n-zénne," the white, undyed one; "zénne déffowa," of light blue color; "fessagída," with a broad line of silk; "hammakúku," with less silk, . . . "zelluwámi," a peculiar zénne with a silk border; "jumáda," another similar kind; "da-n-katánga," . . . with red and black silk in small quantity and a little white; "albássa-n-Kwára," . . . a kind of zénne with three stripes of mixed colors. (Barth 1857, 1:510n).

As is discussed in chapter 1, the many names for cloths that Barth observed underscores the multitude of textiles produced in the mid-nineteenth century in the Kano Emirate.

The processes of production in the Kano of dark-blue cloth and shiny black turbans and wrappers (*rawani baki* and *zane*) mentioned by Barth were examined by Philip Shea (1975), whose work on indigo dyeing examines the innovations that the widespread demand for these textiles encouraged. Through the use of large cement-lined indigo dye vats, dyers in the Kano area, particularly in the town of Kura, were able to lower production costs and prices, combining aesthetics and economics, to increase demand for Kano indigo-dyed cloths that were traded throughout West Africa.

During the colonial period, Kano-area textile production and trade continued, even with increased British textile imports and colonial officials' efforts to send Nigerian raw cotton to textile manufacturers in Manchester, England (Hogendorn 1995; Johnson 1974).[6] The demand for handwoven narrow-strip textiles continued, in part because they were more durable and in part because the appearance of narrow-strip seams was considered to be both visually attractive and was associated with a northern Nigeria social identity. Thus even when British plain-weave cotton cloth was used for indigo dyeing, tailors would sometimes sew false seams to give the appearance of narrow-strip cloth, thus confirming a cloth's authenticity.[7] Yet despite the importance of narrow-strip seams for some, there was also a shift in men's handweaving in the early 1950s, associated with the development of wide-width-strip looms that enabled weavers in the Gwarzo area to weave wider cloth known as *mudukare* for Fulani consumers (Maiwada 2013) as is discussed in chapter 3.

The increasing imports, not only of plain white cotton baft and shirting materials (known by a range of names denoting their material qualities) but also of cotton print textiles, grew in popularity. While white continued to prevail as the preferred color for men's robes and kaftans, women began to wear wrappers and outfits made with printed British and Dutch cotton textiles as well as locally made *adire* indigo-dyed cloths when they could not afford imported cotton prints (see chapter 2). Yet men also exhibited shifting fashion tastes during the postwar years, when lighter weight manufactured cotton print (*atamfa*) and damask (*shadda*) textiles became stylish. The latter came to be particularly important for men's robes as the import of Singer sewing machines expanded the tailoring profession (Maiwada and Renne 2007; Pokrant 1982).

This reliance on manufactured textile imports changed toward the end of the colonial period, when northern Nigerian political leaders, such as Ahmadu Bello, sought to bring industrial textile manufacturing to the North. Beginning in 1957 in Kaduna, several large textile mills were established with backing from foreign textile manufacturers, such as the British firm, David Whitehead & Sons, Ltd., and the Hong Kong-based firm, the Cha Group (Onyeiwu 1997). This industry grew after independence, with six large mills opened in Kaduna in the 1960s; by 1985, there were nine mills in Kaduna and nineteen small-to-medium-size mills in Kano (Andrae and Beckman 1999, 82). In the *1991 United Nigerian Textiles PLC Annual Report*, the chairman, Dr. Cha Chi Ming, stated that "the Company has now become the first textile manufacturer in Nigeria to record a turnover of over N1b (one billion Naira) during the past year" (Renne 2019).

Industrial textile production began earlier in Kano with the opening of the Kano Citizens Trading Company mill in 1952, which was founded with capital provided by wealthy local businessmen. Its opening was followed by other privately owned mills, which specialized in a range of products: plain cotton cloth, towels, bedsheets, uniform material, and cotton-knit garments. At the height of their production in the 1970s, textiles manufactured in Kaduna and Kano mills were sold in several countries in West and Central Africa.

By 2007, however, with a faltering infrastructure, outdated weaving equipment, and increasing imported textiles from China, most of these mills were closed. There have been several efforts to revive the industry, although various factors—lack of electricity and water, insufficient sources of raw cotton, problems of customs control of imported, less-expensive textiles, and the ending of the World Trade Organization Multifibre Arrangement in 1994— have all made these plans difficult to implement (Agbese et al. 2016; Taylor 2007).[8] Dr. Abdul Alimi Bello, president of the Kaduna Chamber of Commerce, Industry, Mines and Agriculture, cited these factors and observed that "We are members of WTO . . . we are a signatory to it," so the importation of industrially woven textiles should continue (Agbese et al. 2016).

What has distinguished textile production in the twenty-first century in northern Nigeria, however, is that handweaving has significantly declined, which had not been the case for most of the twentieth century. For even as British textiles were imported into the country, northern Nigerian handweavers continued to make cloth (United Nations 1968), although indigo dyeing was beginning to decline (Shea 1975). Nonetheless, various forms of kaftan and cap embroidery as well as tailoring and textile trade continue to play a critical role in Hausa-Fulani social life. Despite the use of imported textile materials—lightweight damask cotton and synthetic silk thread—in new styles of embroidery (referred to as *mai rumi* in Zaria and *passamenterie* in North Africa; Vogelsang-Eastwood 2010, 20; Renne 2018), the importance of projecting a northern Nigeria (Arewawa) identity, whether it reflects a distinctly Hausa or Fulani ethnicity, persists.

MATERIALITY, AESTHETICS, AND SOCIETY

This volume contributes to recent research on the materiality of things in that it seeks to bring together two previous approaches to the study of materiality. In the first—an art historical approach—the focus has been on materials themselves, for example, cotton and indigo, and the ways their transformation into things or aspects of things (thread, cloth, or colors, shiny finishes) attract aesthetic responses. The second—an anthropological approach— examines what Arjun Appadurai (1986) has called "the social life of things," which refers to the ways things such as textiles take on a social life of their own, for example, as they are received as tribute and distributed as gifts, bought as commodities, used to denote regal status, and kept as inalienable objects with valued ties to the past (Weiner and Schneider 1989). As Joanna

Sofaer (2008, 3) has suggested, "These two approaches to materiality—what one might broadly categorize as the aesthetic and the social—are not necessarily mutually exclusive. Indeed, it is in the intersection between them that some of the most fruitful ground may lie." Thus, in addressing the question of how to explain the particular trajectory that the decline of textile production and indigo dyeing has taken despite the continued demand (by some) for handwoven strip textiles and indigo-dyed turbans, this dual approach is quite useful. For it is the material qualities of wide-strip *mudukare* textiles with inlaid geometric patterns or of narrow-strip *turkudî* textiles—made with cotton or indigo-dyed thread with seams that attest to their traditional status and authenticity—that provoke an aesthetic associated with either a Fulani pastoralist ethnic identity or a particular prestigious past of Hausa-Fulani emirate power and royal dress.

While the social and political context in which the use of material things such as handwoven strip textiles has changed, they have taken on an heirloom quality, much as textiles such as coverlet and quilts produced during the nineteenth-century "Age of Homespun" have in US society (Ulrich 2001). Handwoven cloths and hand-embroidered *babban riga* robes may be worn during traditional functions to evoke a sense of the past. While shiny black turbans, dyed with indigo and beaten with indigo paste (*shuni*) textiles may also be worn at such events, indigo-dyed garments are no longer in fashion and the former dyeing centers (*karofi* or *marina*) found in towns and villages throughout the North have largely disappeared (Ibrahim 2016). The faster production of industrially printed and dyed textiles provides a different context in which indigo-dyed textiles cannot keep pace. While a man in nineteenth-century Kano might bring a worn white robe (*riga*) to a dyer who would renew it by dipping it in indigo dye pits, and could later return with the dirty blue robe to have specialists beat it with indigo paste to make it into a shiny, new-looking black *kore* robe (Ferguson 1973, 308), a man in twenty-first-century Kano would be more likely to give an old robe out and to buy a new robe or even replace it with a simple kaftan. As Appadurai (2013, 262) has noted, objects such as elaborately hand-embroidered robes and more recent machine-embroidered kaftans with minimal designs are situated within a particular context: "design and fashion, in this changing world, become the infrastructure through which the demand of objects for contexts becomes channeled and stabilized to some extent." In other words, the temporal context thus contributes to the aesthetic response to the materiality of things such as locally produced robes and indigo-dyed textiles, which have largely been replaced with quickly changing, patterned textile fashions manufactured and designed elsewhere.

A more personal sense of the way an aesthetics of materiality intersects with changing socioeconomic and political contexts of textile production, use, and trade may be seen by focusing on particular textiles. By considering how northern Nigerian women and men experience these changes through their relationships with particular types of cloth, shifts in what is considered fashionable as well as accessible are more clearly seen. For example, the peacock (*mai ɗawisu*, literally, owner of the peacock) pattern, which was popular among women in Zaria, Kaduna, and Kano in the 1960s and 1970s, reflected their pride in owning cotton print textiles that depicted what was considered a beautiful and prestigious bird. Alternately, *mudukare* cloth handwoven on wide-width-strip looms in the area around Gwarzo, in Kano State, is not worn by the Hausa men who weave it. Rather it is sold to Fulani men and women who have their own aesthetic sensibilities (Maiwada 2013). In some ways, the biographies of such cloths parallel the textile histories of particular people, places, and times.

In this volume, we intend this focus on production of textiles as a corrective to the emphasis on the study of consumption (Dilley 2004). For it is not simply processes of commodification that figure in here but also processes of mechanization. George Orwell ([1937] 1958, 205) has observed the impact of machines on material preferences and on social life: "Mechanisation . . . leads to the demand for more machine-made articles and hence to more mechanisation. . . . But in addition to this there is a tendency for the mechanisation of the world to proceed as it were automatically, whether we want it or not." One can hardly blame northern Nigerians for wanting to wear industrially manufactured textiles and seeking to obtain machines to make such textiles themselves.

A TEXTILE HISTORY OF ASCENDANCY AND DECLINE

There have been several studies of the history of handwoven and industrial textile production in the United States: in the Carolinas and Massachusetts (Freeman 2018; Minchin 2013); in England; in Lancashire and Manchester (Singleton 1991; Williams 1992); in India (Mohota 1976); and in Japan (McNamara 1993). Studies of African textiles have tended toward an aesthetic approach although historians such as Candotti (2015), Kriger (2006), Leeb-du Toit (2017), and Shea (1975) have examined social and political aspects of textile production and use. This volume builds upon their work by taking a *longue durée* approach, through a focus on textile production and indigo dyeing during the period of the Sokoto Caliphate to the establishment of industrial textile mills in northern Nigeria and the subsequent decline in textile production and dyeing by the second decade of the twenty-first century. In this way, these chapters contribute both to studies of specific aspects of African textile history and to studies of processes of textile handweaving, industrial production, and manufacturing decline in other parts of the world. In a parallel fashion, this volume also examines efforts to revive textile manufacturing as a source of both employment and creativity. New forms of textile production, in particular the possibilities of Chinese-Nigerian textile manufacturing collaboration, while not the focus of this volume, relate to earlier Chinese-Nigerian textile collaboration at the United Nigeria Textiles Limited and Finetex mills in Kaduna. Such collaboration as well as the continued operation of smaller, more specialized textile mills in Kano suggest some of the ways that such collaboration may move forward in the future.

This volume is divided into three sections, with chapters that examine the historical particularities of ascendant textile regimes in northern Nigeria and the more general consequences of the mechanization and digitization of textile production there. In part 1, the material qualities of textile materials, cloth, and clothing produced by hand and by machine are historically assessed, defined, and re-evaluated in three chapters. In the first, Elisha Renne focuses on the names of the many different types of textiles produced and traded in the Sokoto Caliphate, based on dictionary entries devised by G. P. Bargery (1993 [1934]). While many of these terms were documented during the early colonial period, most were still in use, although many are no longer known in the twenty-first century. These distinctively named handwoven cotton cloths defined by Bargery are discussed, along with those relating to indigo-dyeing practices. Similarly, the use of *babban riga* robes as tribute, as gifts, and as diplomatic "envoys" is also considered. In chapter 2, Renne examines the manufactured textile trade and changing dress fashions during the colonial era, focusing mainly on one particular type of textile—printed cotton textiles (*atamfa*)—which were imported during the first half of the twentieth century. As part of this development, an indigo-dyed and patterned cotton cloth, known as *adire*, came to be made in Zaria and Kano. How these textiles were obtained, valued, assessed, and used is considered as well. One particular pattern, known as peacock (*tsuntsun Maka* or *d̃awisu*), which was thought to be especially beautiful, suggests the basis of aesthetic judgments regarding these printed and dyed cloths. In chapter 3, Salihu Maiwada discusses past handwoven textile production as well as current production and marketing practices in Gwarzo Local Government Area and in Minjibir Local Government, both in Kano State. His findings reveal the ways that aesthetic tastes, mechanization, and the social context of handwoven textile production may intersect. For while older men handweavers he interviewed noted that demand continues for handwoven wide-width-strip textiles by Fulani men and women, handweavers in Gwarzo are finding it increasingly difficult to find young men interested in pursuing handweaving work. Yet young men in Minjibir continue handweaving along with their elders, raising the question of how these different responses to handweaving can be explained.

In part 2, the ways expansion of local textile manufacturing and the increasing mechanization of cloth production have affected textile qualities, availability, and consumer tastes are considered. In chapter 4, the authors discuss the growth of the textile manufacturing industry in Kaduna. Two of the chapter's authors, Mohammadu Waziri and Salihu Maiwada, who formerly worked in Kaduna textile mills, discuss their own work experiences and the logistics of textile production, as well as the smuggling of Chinese textiles into Nigeria. In chapter 5, the history of Kano textile manufacturing, which began with the opening of Kano Citizens Trading Company mill in 1952, is examined by Abdulkarim DanAsabe. Since textile manufacturing in Kano was largely based on investments from local businessmen, its origins differed from the Kaduna textile industry. But like Kaduna, most—but not all—of the Kano mills had closed by the end of the twentieth century.

In part 3, the authors consider how changes in textile production have affected the "social lives" of cloth, the shift from cloth as a product locally made with local materials—either by hand or by machine—to a commodity produced and digitally designed elsewhere. In chapter 6, Hannatu Hassan examines the background of textile trading and marketing in the large Kantin Kwari market in Kano, initially dominated by Kano-based Lebanese traders and subsequently by a range of Kano traders. She then discusses the entry of Chinese textiles into the market as well as several recent controversies associated with the Chinese presence in Kantin Kwari market. She concludes the chapter with a consideration of the possible Nigerian-Chinese textile manufacturing collaborations in Kano. Nigerian-Chinese textile connections are also considered by Dakyes Usman, who in chapter 7 discusses the practice and uses of screen and digital printing. The digitization of communications and design printing have increased the speed of devising new, fashionable textile prints, which has facilitated the rapid manufacture of Chinese printed textiles that appeal to northern Nigerian textile tastes. In chapter 8, Maiwada and Renne consider how the intersection of textile aesthetics, production technologies, fashion tastes, and changing socioeconomic and political contexts have contributed to the decline in textile production in northern Nigeria. While "being in fashion" affected the elaboration of hand-embroidered robes during the nineteenth century, the painstaking craftwork involved in their production—the hand-spinning of thread, the handweaving and sewing of narrow-strip textiles, the embroidery work, tailoring, and beaten finishing— was mirrored by the stately and careful slowness associated with the dignity of traditional rulers and the heaviness of robes made with handwoven materials of cotton and silk. The imported lighter-weight imported cotton cloth and later locally manufactured cotton textiles, which became commonplace in the twentieth century, were used to produce machine-embroidered robes and kaftans that kept pace with more quickly changing fashions. Yet despite the allure of industrial textile production and manufactured cotton print cloths as signs of modernity and development, the demand for some types of handwoven textiles persists, just as some older, named patterns continue to be embroidered on new kaftan fashions, reflecting the enduring nature of northern Nigeria's long textile history.

NOTES

1. The dearth of available cotton for producing manufactured textiles in Chinese mills has led to the use of synthetic thread for weaving some textiles that are sold in Nigeria. Such cloths, which have a shiny, rubbery texture, are referred to as *roba* (in Zaria) or *yar da atamfa* (in Kano; see chapter 6).

2. Prior to the nineteenth century, handweaving in colonial America had been a men's occupation (Ulrich 2001, 4); see Renne (1995), and Schneider and Weiner (1986) for a discussion of the implications of gender and handweaving.

3. We have adopted the definition of "production as the act or instance of the manufacture of things (broadly conceived) from a set of raw materials (again, broadly conceived): that is, the act of bringing things into existence" set out by Dilley (2004, 799).

4. See chapter 2 for a discussion of how dyers sometime sought to reduce the amounts of indigo used. Shea (1975, 173) also describes the specialization associated with the beating of indigo paste (*shuni*) into cotton textiles, noting that fine differences in the amount of paste used and in the beating process resulted in cloths with distinctive sheen.

5. Present demand is sustained mainly by Tuareg men who wear *dan* Kura cloths as turbans and veils (Murphy 1964).

6. These efforts were used to support the presence of British colonial officials in Nigeria. For example, the 1927 film, *Black Cotton* (British Instructional Films Ltd.), later released as *Cotton Growing in Nigeria*, which was presented to British audiences, showed Nigerian cotton growing and textile production processes to explain the benefits of British cotton-marketing improvements and Nigerian cotton exports for Great Britain.

7. Colleen Kriger (1993, 365) notes the importance of such seams in ensuring that a *bakin rawani* (black turban) was authentic.

8. With the implementation of GATT rules in 2005, trade restrictions on textile exports and imports were eliminated (see the World Trade Organization website, Textiles Monitoring Body (TMB): The Agreement on Textiles and Clothing, 2015).

REFERENCES

Agbese, Andrew, Christiana Alabi, Maryam Ahmadu-Suka, and Francis Iloani. 2016. "Why Textile Industry Remains Dormant Despite FG's N100bn Bailout." *Daily Trust* (July 3), https://www.dailytrust.com.ng/.

Andrae, Gunilla, and Björn Beckman. 1999. *Union Power in the Nigerian Textile Industry*. New Brunswick NJ: Transaction Publishers.

Appadurai, Arjun. 1986. *The Social Life of Things*. Cambridge: Cambridge University Press.

Appadurai, Arjun. 2013. *The Future as Cultural Fact*. London: Verso.

Bargery, G. P. 1993 [1934]. *A Hausa-English and English-Hausa Dictionary*, 2nd ed. Zaria: Ahmadu Bello University Press.

Barth, Heinrich. 1857. *Travels and Discoveries in North and Central Africa*, vols. 1–3. New York: Harper & Brothers.

British Instructional Films Ltd. 1927. *Black Cotton* [*Cotton Growing in Nigeria*], http://www.colonialfilm.org.uk/node/1322.

Candotti, Marisa. 2010. "The Hausa Textile Industry: Origins and Development in the Precolonial Period." In *Being and Becoming Hausa: Interdisciplinary Perspectives*, edited by A. Haour and B. Rossi, 187–211. Leiden: Brill.

Candotti, Marisa. 2015. "Cotton Growing and Textile Production in Northern Nigeria: From Caliphate to Protectorate, c. 1804–1914." PhD dissertation, SOAS, University of London.

Dilley, Roy. 2004. "The Visibility and Invisibility of Production Among Senegalese Craftsmen." *Journal of the Royal Anthropological Institute* 10, no. 4: 797–813.

Douny, Laurence. 2011. "Silk-Embroidered Garments as Transformative Processes: Layering, Inscribing and Displaying Hausa Material Identities." *Material Culture* 16, no. 4: 401–15.

Fee, Sarah. 2002. "Cloth in Motion: Madagascar's Textiles Through History." In *Objects as Envoys*, edited by C. Mullen Kreamer and S. Fee, 33–93. Washington DC: Smithsonian Institution Press.

Ferguson, Douglas. 1973. "Nineteenth Century Hausaland Being a Description by Imam Imoru of the Land, Economy, and Society of his People." PhD dissertation, University of California, Los Angeles.

Freeman, Joshua. 2018. *Behemoth: A History of the Factory and the Making of the Modern World*. New York: W. W. Norton & Company.

Giginyu, Ibrahim. 2014. "Why We Embarked on the Kano China Town Business Project." *Daily Trust* (December 14), https://www.dailytrust.com.ng/.

Guyer, Jane. 2004. "Niches, Margins and Profits: Persisting with Heterogeneity." *African Economic History* 32: 173–91.

Hogendorn, Jan. 1995. "The Cotton Campaign in Northern Nigeria, 1902–1914: An Early Example of a Public/Private Planning Failure in Agriculture." In *Cotton, Colonialism, and Social History in Sub-Saharan Africa*, edited by Allen Isaacman and Richard Roberts, 50–70. Portsmouth, NH: Heinemann.

Ibrahim, Yusha'u. 2016. "Karofin-Kura: A Tale of 800-Yr-Old Dyeing Centre." *Daily Trust* (July 3), https://www.dailytrust.com.ng/.

Johnson, Marion. 1973. "Cloth on the Banks of the Niger." *Journal of the Historical Society of Nigeria* 6: 353–63.

Johnson, Marion. 1974. "Cotton Imperialism in West Africa." *African Affairs* 73, no. 291: 178–87.

Johnson, Marion. 1976. "Calico Caravans: The Tripoli-Kano Trade After 1880." *Journal of African History* 17: 95–117.

Kriger, Colleen. 1988. "Robes of the Sokoto Caliphate." *African Arts* 21, no. 3: 52–57, 78–79, 85.

Kriger, Colleen. 1993. "Production and Gender in the Sokoto Caliphate." *Journal of African History* 34, no. 3: 361–401.

Kriger, Colleen. 2006. *Cloth in West African History*. Lanham, MD: AltaMira Press.

Kriger, Colleen. 2010. "Silk and Sartorial Politics in the Sokoto Caliphate, 1804–1903." In *The Force of Fashion in Politics and Society: Global Perspectives from Early Modern to Modern Times*, edited by B. Lemire, 143–63. Surrey, UK: Ashgate Publishing.

Kopytoff, Igor. 1986. "The Cultural Biography of Things: Commoditization as Process." In *The Social Life of Things*, edited by A. Appadurai, 64–91. Cambridge: Cambridge University Press.

Last, Murray. 1966. "An Aspect of the Caliph Muhammad Bello's Social Policy." *Kano Studies* 1: 56–59.

Last, Murray. 1967. *The Sokoto Caliphate*. London: Longman.

Leeb-du-Toit, Juliette. 2017. *Isishweshwe: A History of the Indigenisation of Blueprint in Southern Africa*. Pietermaritzburg: University of KwaZulu-Natal Press.

Lydon, Ghislaine. 2009. *On Trans-Saharan Trails: Islamic Law, Trade Networks, and Cross-Cultural Exchange in Nineteenth-Century West Africa*. Cambridge: Cambridge University Press.

Maiwada, Salihu. 2013. "The Assessment of Fulani Society and Traditional Dress in Northern Nigeria." *Journal of International Academic Research for Multidisciplinary* 1, no. 8: 97–108.

Maiwada, Salihu, and Elisha Renne. 2007. "New Technologies of Machine-Embroidered Robe Production and Changing Work and Gender Roles in Zaria, Nigeria." *Textile History* 38, no. 1: 25–58.

Maiwada, Salihu, and Elisha Renne. 2013. "The Kaduna Textile Industry and the Decline of Textile Manufacturing in Northern Nigeria, 1955–2010." *Textile History* 44, no. 2: 171–96.

McNamara, Dennis. 1993. "Association and Adjustment in Japan's Textile Industry." *Pacific Affairs* 66, no. 2: 206–18.

Minchin, Timothy. 2013. *Empty Mills: The Fight Against Imports and the Decline of the U.S. Textile Industry*. Lanham, MD: Rowman & Littlefield Publishers Inc.

Mohota, R. D. 1976. *Textile Industry and Modernisation*. Mumbai: Current Book House.

Murphy, Robert. 1964. "Social Distance and the Veil." *American Anthropologist* 66, no. 6: 1257–74.

Northern Region of Nigeria. 1954. *Report on the Exchange of Customary Presents*. Lagos: Government Printer.

Onyeiwu, Steve. 1997. "The Modern Textile Industry in Nigeria: History, Structural Change, and Recent Developments." *Textile History* 28, no. 2: 234–49.

Orwell, George. [1937] 1958. *The Road to Wigan Pier*. New York: Houghton-Mifflin Harcourt.

Paden, John. 1986. *Ahmadu Bello, Sardauna of Sokoto: Values and Leadership in Nigeria*. Zaria: Hudahuda Publishing Company.

Philips, J. E. 1992. "Ribats in the Sokoto Caliphate: Selected Studies 1804–1903." PhD dissertation, University of California, Los Angeles.

Pokrant, R. J. 1982. "The Tailors of Kano City." In *From Craft to Industry: The Ethnography of Proto-Industrial Cloth Production*, edited by E. Goody, 85–132. Cambridge: Cambridge University Press.

Renne, Elisha. 1995. *Cloth That Does Not Die: The Meaning of Cloth in Bunu Social Life*. Seattle: University of Washington Press.

Renne, Elisha. 2004. "*Babban Riga* Production and Marketing in Zaria, Nigeria." *African Economic History* 32: 103–22.

Renne, Elisha. 2015. "The Changing Contexts of Chinese-Nigerian Textile Production and Trade, 1900–2015." *Textile: Cloth and Culture* 13, no. 3: 211–31.

Renne, Elisha. 2018. *Veils, Turbans, and Islamic Reform in Northern Nigeria*. Bloomington: Indiana University Press.

Renne, Elisha. 2019. "United Nigerian Textiles Limited and Chinese-Nigeria Textile Manufacturing Collaboration in Kaduna, Nigeria." *Africa* 89, no. 4: 696–717.

Schneider, Jane, and Annette Weiner. 1986. "Cloth and the Organization of Human Experience." *Current Anthropology* 27: 178–84.

Shea, Philip J. 1975. "The Development of an Export-Oriented Dyed Cloth Industry in

Kano Emirate in the Nineteenth Century." PhD dissertation, University of Wisconsin, Madison.

Shea, Philip J. 2006. "Big Is Sometimes Best: The Sokoto Caliphate and Economic Advantages of Size in the Textile Industry." *African Economic History* 34: 5–21.

Singleton, John. 1991. *Lancashire on the Scrapheap: The Cotton Industry, 1945–1970*. Oxford: Oxford University Press.

Sofaer, Joanna. 2008. *Material Identities*. London: Blackwell Publishing.

Staudinger, Paul. 1990 [1899]. *In the Heart of the Hausa States*, 2 vols., trans. J. Moody. Athens: Ohio University Press.

Tabuchi, Hiroko. 2015. "Chinese Textile Mills Are Now Hiring in Places Where Cotton Was King." *New York Times* (August 2), https://www.nytimes.com/.

Taylor, Ian 2007. "China's Relations with Nigeria." *The Round Table: The Commonwealth Journal of International Affairs* 96, no. 392: 631–45.

Ulrich, Laurel. 2001. *The Age of Homespun*. New York: Alfred A. Knopf.

United Nations. 1968. "The Textile Industry in the West African Sub-Region." *Economic Bulletin for Africa* 7: 103–25.

Vogelsang-Eastwood, Gillian. 2010. *Embroidery from the Arab World*. Leiden: Primavera Press.

Weiner, Annette, and Jane Schneider, eds. 1989. *Cloth and Human Experience*. Washington DC: Smithsonian Institution Press.

Williams, Mike, with D. A. Farnie. 1992. *Cotton Mills in Greater Manchester*. Preston, UK: Carnegie Publishing.

World Trade Organization. 2015. "Textiles: Agreement, Textiles Monitoring Body." https://www.wto.org/english/tratop_e/texti_e/texintro_e.htm.

CHAPTER 1

The Social Context of Precolonial Northern Nigerian Handwoven Textiles

ELISHA RENNE

Kakan sa ta yanke saƙa
—Hausa saying
Grandmother cut the finished cloth from her loom

The well-known Hausa saying, *Kakan sa ta yanke saƙa*, literally refers to a grandmother completing the weaving of a cloth. It also implies the good fortune of her grandchildren who will benefit from her resulting wealth when she sells it on the next market day. While this saying is now applied to any situation in which one is likely to see financial gain, many younger people no longer understand its reference to cloth and handloom weaving. In many communities in northern Nigeria, women weaving on vertical broad looms is a thing of the past.[1]

Similarly, many of the extensive number of words that referred to various aspects of textile production during the nineteenth and early twentieth century have been forgotten as well. The cloth known as *hamakuku*, a cloth with a thin line of silk, was described by Heinrich Barth (1857, 1:510), who saw it in Kano market in 1851. Eighty years later, a cloth called *hamakuku* was defined by Bargery as "a native-made cloth, black warp threads and blue weft." He added in parentheses, however, that it was "not now made" (1993 [1934], 442). Indeed, many of the cloth terms included in Bargery's *Hausa-English and English-Hausa Dictionary*, first published in 1934, are unknown to many presently living in northern Nigeria. Yet some handwoven cloths—such as black and white "guinea fowl" (*saƙi*) cloth and very narrow handwoven cotton strips called *turkudi*, which are sewn together to produce the cloth

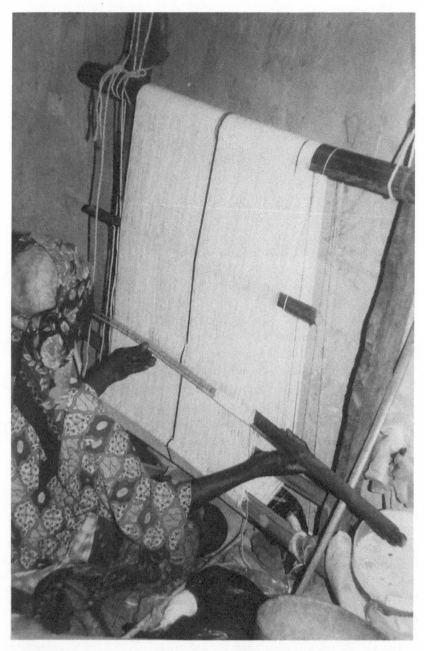

Fig. 1.1. Hausa woman weaving on vertical single-heddle loom in Zaria City, January 1995. (Photograph by E. P. Renne.)

which is subsequently dyed with indigo to make blue-black turbans (*rawani baki*), both mentioned by Barth and Bargery—continue to be known in the twenty-first century (see introduction). Their persistence underscores the importance of cloth in northern Nigerian social life, even as the vast system of nineteenth-century textile production is greatly reduced.

Distinctive aesthetic and moral evaluations were associated with the various social uses of cotton, silk, and indigo-dyed textiles and dress in the nineteenth-century Sokoto Caliphate. These evaluations were supported by the material qualities and types of cloths produced, which were distinguished by different names as well as by the distinctive types and gradations of indigo dyeing. Indeed, aesthetic distinctions applied to cloth were sometimes related to the moral evaluation of men and women, as when specific terms applied to cloth or clothing are also applied to people. Thus the word *baraka* not only refers to the "coming undone of a seam of a cloth or garment" but also to "the first evidence of a blemish in a person's character" (Bargery 1993 [1934], 82) or to a "breach of trust" (Newman 2007, 28). There are numerous examples of such associations made between people and cloth, which—as well as the many names for cloth—suggest the pervasiveness of textiles in people's think-ing in northern Nigerian social life at that time.[2]

This chapter begins with a consideration of the many definitions for cloth and clothing found in Bargery's dictionary. As the anthropologist Franz Boas (1911) noted during his research on Baffin Island, Canada, in the early 1880s, the extensive Inuit vocabulary for ice and snow reflected their exten-sive engagement with these materials.[3] One could make a similar argument for the Hausa-speaking people of northern Nigeria as there are more than a hundred words defined by Bargery relating to cloth and clothing that were locally made or imported. The chapter continues with a discussion of the connections between words that both describe particular types of cloth and refer to a moral evaluation of people as well as aesthetic assessments of cloth. Finally, the use of cloth as tribute to the sultan of Sokoto by representatives of the emirates under his jurisdiction and as gifts by European travelers and long-distance Hausa traders will also be considered. The many different types of cloth and robes used during the period of the Sokoto Caliphate suggest the various ways that an aesthetics of cloth and clothing reflected not only the judgment of individuals' character but the connections between cloth and socioeconomic standing as well.

TEXTILES, PRODUCTION, AND TRADE DURING THE
NINETEENTH-CENTURY SOKOTO CALIPHATE

The 1804 jihād that led to the establishment of the nineteenth-century Sokoto Caliphate in 1808 encompassed much of the area of northern Nigeria (Last 1967). The Caliphate was headed by the Islamic scholar Shehu dan Fodio, who wrote extensively on reforms he prescribed for the proper observance of Islam. These reforms reflected his extensive knowledge of the Qur'ān, hadith, and the opinions of distinguished Islamic scholars and what he considered to be appropriate Islamic dress and inappropriate royal garments. Nonetheless, his son, Muhammad Bello, realized the importance of socioeconomic development and unity as well as communal worship and Islamic education (Bello 1983; Last 1966). The tremendous growth of the nineteenth-century textile industry in northern Nigeria, which resulted in the production of handwoven textiles used for turbans, robes, and wrappers within the Caliphate, was made possible through his administrative efforts. Bello sought to foster unity among people with different backgrounds and occupations. "One way of achieving co-operation was to leave the communities under rulers loyal to Sokoto and to improve conditions so that trade and agriculture could prosper," as Murray Last (1966, 57–58) observed. Textile production was particularly important for Bello's development of commerce in Sokoto: "Textile industries were located in separate quarters of the city; one produced white cotton cloth (*fari*) and the other, manned by Nupe, produced blue checked cloth (*saki*)" (Bello 1983, 102). In addition, plantations were established for the growing of cotton and indigo necessary for textile production expansion, which was made possible through the security that the garrison towns (*ribats*) provided (Bello 1983; Chafe 1990; Lovejoy 1978; Philips 1992). For Bello, this security was enhanced further through the social cohesion that community worship fostered. By attending to community well-being—both materially and spiritually—Bello hoped to promote Caliphate unity and avoid the destructive violence of the past.

Textile production and trade in the nineteenth-century Sokoto Caliphate supported this cohesion, not only by providing work for weavers and dyers but also for cotton farmers, embroiderers, tailors, and cloth beaters. Their combined efforts contributed to the production of a finely discernible range of textiles and robes that were in demand throughout West Africa (Kriger 2006, 86; Shea 1975). The expansion of production in many areas of the Caliphate—of plain white (*fari*), red and white (*barage*), and blue-black and

SOKOTO CALIPHATE, c. 1880

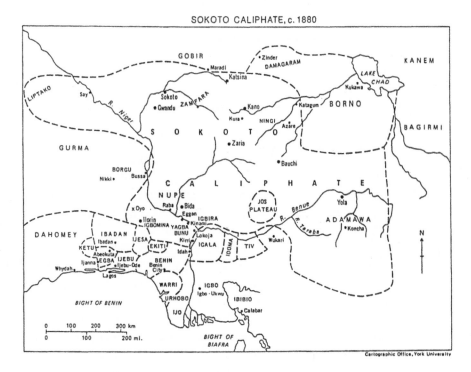

Map 1.1. Map of the Sokoto Caliphate ca. 1880 (Kriger 1990, 40; map by the Cartographic Office, York University). (Courtesy of Colleen Kriger.)

white (*saki*) cotton strips as well as handwoven strips made with imported magenta silk (*alharini*) or local wild silk (*tsamiya*)[4]—made the expression of socioeconomic and political distinction possible (Perani and Wolff 1992, 1999). The expansion of trade networks did so as well.

During the nineteenth century, increasing imports of European industrially woven textiles reached northern Nigeria via trans-Saharan trade routes and through long-distance trade associated with important textile markets in southern Nigeria. As will be discussed in chapter 2, much of the European-manufactured cloth brought by trans-Saharan caravans consisted of unbleached and bleached white cotton cloth (Johnson 1976; Lydon 2009). However, increasing quantities of silk, velvet, and cotton print textiles came north overland via Lagos and up the Niger River by boat to be sold in the large trading towns of Onitsha and Egga. On their way to Egga, Richard and John Lander met the king of Zagozhi Island, who was wearing a mélange of imported and locally handwoven textiles:

The "King of the Dark Water" . . . was dressed in a full bornouse, or Arab cloak, of inferior blue cloth, underneath which was a variegated tobe made of figured satin, country cloth and crimson silk damask, all patched together, he likewise wore a cap of red cloth, Haussa trowsers, and sandals of coloured leather. . . . The king was also accompanied by six of his wives . . . dressed in neat country caps [cloths] edged with red silk (*alharini*). (Lander and Lander 1965 [1854], 187)

At Egga, also in October 1830, they observed considerable quantities of imported cloth: "The Portuguese cloth [worn by many inhabitants] which were observed here on our arrival is brought up the river from a place called *Cuttumcurrafee* [Koton Karfe], which has a celebrated market for Nouffie [Nupe] cloths (Lander and Lander 1965 [1854], 209).

In the 1850s, Reverend Samuel Crowther also described Egga as a major center for the trade in textiles from the confluence area, which included Nupe, Kabba, and Bunu cloths as well as imported textiles from the coast:

[Nupe traders] pursue as their chief business buying and selling with little profits. Among them the women are the most active; they not only deal in cloths of native manufacture, but also in such European goods as they can purchase from traders from the coast. The men, many of whom are weavers as well as traders, deal mostly in tobes, shirts, trousers, country cloths and other garments used by men; whereas the women are mostly engaged in country cloth, caps for both sexes, beads, etc. (Crowther and Taylor [1968] 1859, cited in Johnson 1973, 354)

Yet as may be seen from the list of textiles acquired by members of the 1841 Niger Expedition who visited Egga in the intervening decade, a range of handwoven cloths—from inexpensive open lace-work cotton cloths to expensive wide-width cloths made with indigo-dyed and magenta *alharini* silk thread—were for sale. This demand for locally handwoven and indigo-dyed cloths reflected the continuing prestige associated with finely woven, indigo-dyed textiles. Alternately, low-quality imported print textiles and poorly woven handwoven cloths were disparagingly called *julajula*, which was defined by Bargery (1993 [1934], 551) as: "Originally, any poorly woven cloth. Later, it was applied to all European-made cloth as opposed to native-made. Now it is mainly applied to poorly-woven native cloth and to cheap, thin European-made cloth." While bright, imported cotton print textiles were attractive to buyers, they did not supplant the costly shiny blue-black indigo-dyed *kore* robes and *ɗan* Kura turbans made in the Kano Emirate or the *saki* robes made by Nupe weavers in Kulfo, Raba, Egga (Perani and Wolff 1999, 138) and Sokoto (Kriger 2006, 87). As Bargery (1993 [1934], 64) put it in his example of the use of the word, *baƙi* (very dark blue, [black]): "*Ya naɗa baƙin rawani ja-wur kamar wuta*, he has put on a 'black' turban which glistens like a hot fire," underscoring the powerful attractiveness of *ɗan* Kura turbans and of those who wore them.[5]

Cloth Terms Defined by Bargery

Some of the cloth terms defined in the Bargery dictionary suggest the history of textile production and trade during the period of the Sokoto Caliphate. For example, *bunu* is defined as "A woman's black-and-blue cloth (originally made in Ilorin) called by some *gwado* because woven in the same way" (Bargery 1993 [1934], 131).[6] Presumably, the "same way" refers to these cloths being woven on vertical looms by women. While it is possible that the cloth was made in or purchased from Ilorin—the capital of the Emirate of Ilorin under the Sokoto Caliphate during the nineteenth century—the women weavers of many such wide-width cloths originally came from the area known as Bunu.[7] Indeed, one of the cloths listed in the 1841 textile collection from Egga is referenced as "Abunu" (Johnson 1973, 357; Kriger 1990, 46),[8] from the Bunu area, immediately across the Niger River from Egga.

It is interesting to note that another cloth defined by Bargery (1993 [1934], 97) is called *bawan bunu* (literally, "the slave of Bunu"); it is described as "A striped black-and-blue cloth." Such cloths may have been woven by Bunu women, who were indeed sold as slaves to Nupe rulers during the nineteenth century. As one elderly man, Chief Tolufa Moses, from Aiyetoro-Kiri in northern Bunu, interviewed in 1988 explained:

> This practice [of sending slaves to Nupe overlords] was not easy to stop for us, because at that time [the Nupe] devised a method of paying our chiefs every month on the basis of their success in persuading villagers to contribute people. (Renne 1995, 159)

However, according to him, "It came to a time when we could not get people to be taken away to Bida . . . [then] they said that we should begin to pay money as well as our locally woven cloth" (Renne 1995, 210 note 21).[9]

This situation underscores the fact that during this period, the Sokoto

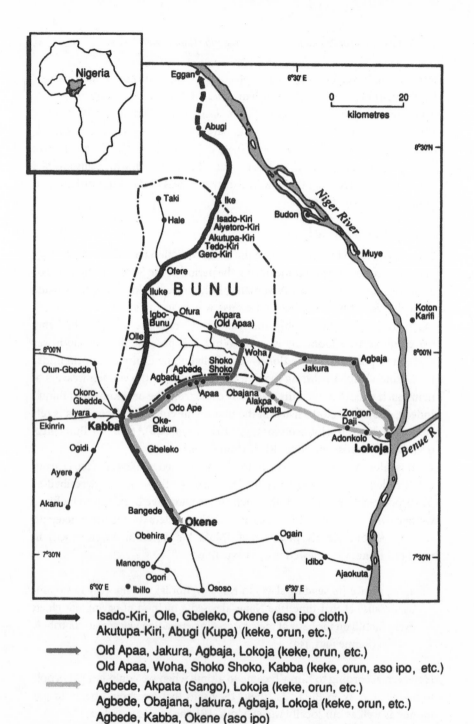

Map 1.2. Map of Bunu District indicating market routes used by Bunu weavers. (Renne 1995, 140.)

Caliphate maintained ascendancy through the Kingdom of Gwandu over the Nupe Kingdom (Smith 1960, 77), while the Nupe oversaw the northeastern Yoruba area to the south. Nadel (1942, 297) suggests that women slaves from northeastern Yorubaland brought their knowledge of handweaving on the vertical loom with them:

> This technique of weaving is said to be comparatively new, and not tradition-ally Nupe, and may indeed have come to Nupe from Yoruba in the times of the Yoruba wars, through the medium of Yoruba wives and slaves of the Nupe nobility. For women's weaving is restricted to the womenfolk of the upper classes of Nupe society.

This explanation has been proposed by others (Perani 1977). Thus, along with Bunu cloths that were given to Nupe rulers as tribute, Bunu-style wide-width handwoven cloths that were woven by women in Bida could have been taken by traders to cloth markets in Kano and Zaria, where they were known by the name *bunu*.[10] Furthermore, Bunu women slaves themselves could be sent to Sokoto, Kano, and Zaria by their Nupe owners, where they practiced the handweaving of *bunu* cloths that came to be known as *bawan bunu*. These women could have also taught Hausa-Fulani women to weave wide-width cloths. Indeed, Richard Lander, who visited Zaria in 1830, was introduced by the emir's eldest son to his wives: "They were fifty in number, and on my entrance were industriously employed in preparing cotton and thread, and weaving it into cloth (Lander 1830, 2:143).[11]

Sections of Sokoto are populated by people who came from Nupe (Clapperton 1829), while the Emir of Kano encouraged Nupe weavers to come to produce handwoven cloth and robes for the court (Kriger 2006, 88). As Shea (1975, 57) notes, "The heavily embroidered *saki* gowns of the Nupe have long been expensive and highly prized items throughout Hausaland, and many Nupe weavers immigrated into Kano in the nineteenth century to produce this and other high-quality cloths for which they were famous." Similarly, people of Nupe descent moved to Kura as well as to Zaria, where they are also living in the old walled section of Zaria.[12]

Visualizing Cloth

Along with providing a sense of the historical origins of particular cloths present in nineteenth-century northern Nigeria, cloth terms defined in the Bargery dictionary provide visual descriptions of some of the different named cloths that were being woven. These descriptions suggest some common qualities among these cloths as well as characteristics that distinguished them. Some named cloths incorporated colors such as the cloth, *bukunasi* ("a black and red cloth of native make") or *kashi da kashi* ("a native-made coloured cloth"). Other cloths combined two different types of handwoven cloths; the cloth known as *giwar basa* was made "with wide, uneven strips of alternate *saki* and white" (Bargery 1993 [1934], 393). Another cloth, *targi*, was a black cloth with a strip of *saki* cloth at the top edge. Some named cloths referred to specific textures; the *kazuwa* cloth was woven with thick and thin weft threads while *bato* was "a native made cloth with long plaited fringe. The cloth is worn in double thickness, folded so that the fringe is at one side only" (Bargery 1993 [1934], 94).

Several named handwoven cloths consisted of broad blue and blue-black warp stripes such as *agogi* and *manja*. Others are dyed a deep blue-black color such as the cloth known as *dan gwarabjawa* ("a black cloth of the *bunu* variety"; Bargery 1993 [1934], 219), *falfalwa* ("a native-made cloth dyed with indigo"; Bargery 1993 [1934], 295), or the cloth known as *nati* (Bargery 1993 [1934], 817). Indeed, the abundance of cloths that are described as black, blue-black, or blue suggest the variety as well as the preference for indigo-dyed cloth during the nineteenth century.

WEARING BLACK CLOTH: THE IMPORTANCE AND BEAUTY OF INDIGO

As with hand-spinning and handweaving, indigo dyeing was pervasive in nineteenth-century northern Nigeria, and there are many words defined by Bargery that are related to indigo and indigo dyeing (known as *baba* and *rini* respectively; Bargery 1993 [1934], 49, 858). Expert indigo dyeing contributed to the significant attraction of textiles produced in Kano and Zaria. As Philip Shea (1975, 74) has noted, innovations in indigo dye-pit (*karofi*) construction and mordant preparation in major indigo-dyeing centers such as Kura, Dal, and Makarfi in the emirates of Kano and Zaria also enabled increased production of a range of textiles that could be exported to various markets. The importance of indigo dyeing, as with indigo-dyed textiles themselves, is reflected in the many terms associated with this process. In some cases, these terms reflected techniques and materials associated with indigo dyeing. Thus, the verb *bantauri* refers to the technique of beating two or three lots of indigo into a garment (Bargery 1993 [1934], 1009). When excessive indigo is applied to a robe or gown, this practice is referred to as *jigilib* or *domoso* (Bargery 1993 [1934], 500, 266). A consequence of wearing cloth or garments with such an excessive "richness" (*domoso*) is noted by Bargery (1993 [1934], 266) in an explanatory sentence: "*ya yi domoso cikin kore*—his body is well stained, coloured, with indigo from a 'black' gown [*kore*] worn next to his skin." In order to make such black *kore* robes, an indigo paste known as *shuni* was beaten into indigo-dyed materials.[13]

The *turkudi* cloth consists "of twelve [very narrow] strips of material sewn together (each strip is 8 cubits in length), dyed indigo, rendered glossy, folded and wrapped in paper (Bargery 1993 [1934], 1063).[14] These handwoven cloths, woven with finely handspun cotton and then saturated with indigo *shuni* paste, were a specialty of the town of Kura, southwest of Kano. Worn as turbans, these *dan* Kura cloths (as they were called) were expensive and produced an indigo blue cast to the faces of their wearers (Murphy 1964, 1260). Indigo was also directly used by women's hair "as a form of adornment" (*yafiya*; Bargery 1993 [1934], 1099). This aspect of indigo—that it not only enhanced the beauty of robes and turbans, which were made a shining deep blue-black color, but also of the person wearing such clothing or who were tinged by indigo itself—is related to the prestige of being able to afford such expensive things.

Not surprisingly, the desire to appear wealthy and attractive led some to engage in various forms of deception, either to color undyed robes with indigo or to impart bluish color to their skin. Thus the term *shunin batta* is defined as "Rubbing indigo on the body to impart a bluish tinge to a gown," or as "Sprinkling a mixture of indigo and sand on to a white garment to make believe one has been wearing it next to an indigo-dyed one" (Bargery 1993 [1934], 945). The term *ban shuni* refers to similar (or identical) processes:

> 1. Wearing an indigo-dyed gown outside a white one so that the latter may become tinged blue. 2, Rubbing indigo on the body that the gown worn may be tinged blue. (=shunin batta) 3. Sprinkling indigo on a sleeping mat and wearing a gown at night for same purpose as 1 and 2. 4. Sprinkling mixture of indigo and sand on a white gown and beating it with similar intent. (Bargery 1993 [1934], 78)

At times, indigo dyers experienced problems with dye pits, as when "New indigo dye which, though apparently all right, will not dye well" (*makaho da dara*) or when "indigo dye . . . has 'gone wrong'" (*dasusu*) (Bargery 1993 [1934], 752, 237). Consequently, dyers might be forced to cut corners, as the term *zandam* suggests: "a deceitful practice of dyers, soaking a cloth in a prepared solution to enable it to be dyed with the use of very little indigo" (Bargery 1993 [1934], 1126).[15]

Yet not everyone aspired to the wealth and political power associated with wearing blue-black and white checked *saki* robes, shiny black *kore* robes, and *dan* Kura turbans. Other members of the Sokoto Caliphate, including its leader, Shehu dan Fodio, preferred to dress simply, wearing white robes and turbans. Indeed, "*saki* cloth became associated with caliphate officials and title holders, lending a very special aura of power, position, and prestige" (Kriger 2006, 85). But *saki* also became "a vernacular term connoting intrigue and untrustworthiness: *Wurin nan da sak'i* means 'There is a stranger present here' or 'There is someone here we don't quite trust' " (Kriger 2006, 86). This distrust suggests why some preferred white robes, which would be worn until they were irredeemably soiled and had to be indigo-dyed (Bargery 1993 [1934]). Such moral distinctions and preferences are reflected in the multiple meanings of several cloth terms.

CLOTH AND CHARACTER: TEXTILES TERMS AND SOCIAL MEANINGS

Hausa-Fulani men's social identity during the nineteenth-century Sokoto Caliphate was associated with large robes (*babban riga*) and turbans (*rawani*), while women wore a variety of wrappers, shoulder cloths, and head coverings. Many of these garments were made with handwoven cotton cloth, some constructed with narrow cloth strips and others with two or three wide-width pieces. While many handwoven cloths were woven with white and indigo-dyed threads in a range of patterns, most were plain white, for as Picton and Mack (1979, 103) have noted, "it should not be forgotten that probably the greater volume of cloth produced in West Africa is plain white." These white cloth strips could be sold and then sewn into the requisite garments and possibly dyed indigo-blue. However, by mid-century, the availability of imported manufactured textiles grew with increased steamboat traffic up the Niger and continuing trans-Saharan caravan trade. Imported colored and print cotton textiles gradually came to be worn by women, while white cotton robes for men, some of which were embroidered, came to be made with plain white imported industrially woven cotton yardage.

This appreciation of textiles should not be surprising considering their close relationship with the human body. Finely woven cotton cloth, beaten with indigo *shuni* paste to produce a metallic sheen, enhanced the appearance of a person (Shea 1975). It could also hide deformities or imperfections that the wearer would rather not reveal (Schneider and Weiner 1986). An indigo-dyed robe that has become dim ("*riga ta dushe*," the gown has lost its sheen) may also be related to the idea that one's star has dimmed: "*tauraronsa ye dushe*," he is out of favor (Bargery 1993 [1934], 284). Thus, when Paul Staudinger (1990 [1889], 1:239) and his porters visited Kano City in 1885, the porters "quickly had their clothes dyed blue once more" by the Galadima at *karofi* indigo dye pits there. This intersection of particular qualities of textiles and people was frequently reflected in reference to appearance. The term *gunta* refers to a short man or woman (*guntun mutuum; guntuwar mace*), short robe (*guntuwar riga*), or short piece of cloth left over from sewing a wrapper (*guntun zane*). This short, leftover piece is also related to the term *guntun gatari*, which is defined as "a destitute man" (Bargery 1993 [1934], 441). Similarly, the term *bi tsatso* is defined as "Repairing a worn cloth by joining sides to the middle by enclosing a worn part of a pleat (*hadin bakin tsumma*)" and "a cloth so repaired," but also that "wearing such a cloth indicates the direst poverty" (*bi tsatso matukar waya*; Bargery 1993 [1934], 114). Alternately, the word *kakisa*, used to define a plump woman (who is presumably well-off), is the same word that is used for "A big, heavy well-made gown" (Bargery 1993 [1934], 534).

Cloth as Metaphor in Northern Nigeria

Given the many words associated with cloth during the nineteenth century in northern Nigeria, it should not be surprising to find many metaphorical connections that relate people's social or political status, their physical appearance, or their moral character to aspects of cloth. As has been mentioned, several well-known nineteenth-century garments associated with one's particular social and political status were worn during the period of the Sokoto Caliphate handwoven textiles.

Thus, throughout the Caliphate, white garments were worn by Islamic scholars, and glossy blue-black turbans (*bakin rawani*) and large indigo-dyed embroidered robes, *babban riga* or *rigan giwa*, were worn by Caliphate emirs and members of their courts. These garments, many of which were made in different parts of the Caliphate, visibly expressed its unity in terms of textile manufacture and trade but also delineated the particular ranking of officials within it (Candotti 2010; Kriger 1988, 2006; Last 1967; Shea 1975). Furthermore, the material qualities of cloth used in its making, its color, texture, appearance, hand, and odor, contributed to its association with particular moral or aesthetic states (Bayly 1986; Schneider and Weiner 1986). For example, regarding color, within the Sokoto Caliphate, Shehu dan Fodio, citing Ahmad al-Zarrūqin's commentary on *al-Waghlisiyya*, wrote, "It is desirable for a scholar, as well as a pupil, to adorn himself particularly with white clothes" (dan Fodio 1978, 92), while the shiny blue-black *dan* Kura turbans and *kore* robes associated with kings and courtiers were distinguished by "the smell of the dyed cloth but more particularly from the beauty of its metallic sheen" (Flegel 1985 [1885], 7).

The "white robe," *rigar fari,* worn by Caliphate leaders and scholars, often consisted of "strips of native woven white material" (Bargery 1993 [1934], 305), but it could also be made "of any white material" (i.e., imported industrially woven unbleached cotton cloth known as *akoko* or *alawayyo*.) This connection between white robes and Islamic scholarship is reflected in the expression, *mai farin kai*, an educated person or Islamic scholar (*malami*; Bargery 1993 [1934], 306). Similarly, their wearing of white turbans (*harsa*: "a white muslin used only as a turban; Bargery 1993 [1934], 455) reflected this association of white garments with Islamic knowledge. Alternately, the blue-black *dan* Kura turbans were worn by royal members and officials of the emirate courts (Perani and Wolff 1992), which distinguished them from ordinary free-born citizens, from members of the working class (*talakawa*), and from slaves (*bawa*). While glossy blue-black *kore* robes were also worn by court officials,[16] robes made with narrow strips of the finely checked blue-black and white cloth ("pepper and salt") known as *saki* were solely associated with emirate aristocrats. Some of the finest *saki* robes were produced in the Nupe Kingdom, where white and indigo-dyed finely spun cotton enabled weavers to produce narrow strips with high thread counts and hence high cloth density.

A range of *saki* cloths of different qualities and styles were produced within the Caliphate, which could indicate the ethnic background, affluence, and political status to viewers of those wearing these cloths. Bargery (1993 [1934], 67, 394, 998) cites three different styles of *saki* cloth wrappers: *bakurde* ("a cloth of native make, blue and black strips joined to *saki*"), *gindin dakwalwa* ("a native cloth made mainly grey and blue, pepper and salt cloth with a few white stripes let in"), and *targi* ("a black cloth with a top of *saki*, both of double thickness"). Such cloths could be marketed internally, with finely woven *saki* cloth robes marketed in Kano, Zaria, and Bida, while other robes and wrappers were exported to markets elsewhere in West Africa such as Timbuktu (Barth 1857, 1:511). The fineness of the highest quality *saki* cloth contrasted with cloth that was poorly woven with irregular selvages (*kunnen bera*; literally, the ears of a rat) or with "carelessly made thread" (*burcici*; Bargery 1993 [1934], 133). The word *burcici* refers to a "rough appearance of weaving," resulting from the use of such thread and is also used to refer to "the unkemptness, disheveled state, of woman's head," or to the roughness of a person's skin.

As was the case with the deceptive uses of indigo, cloth could also be used as a means of duplicity. Thus, the cloth "used to cover a bride when she is being taken to the bridegroom's home," known as *algargi*, could also be worn to imitate "the appearance of a young woman by an old one" (Bargery 1993 [1934], 20). Women could also wear a wrapper that, while apparently made from costly *sanyan* silk, was actually "a mixture of cotton and silk passed off as wholly silk" (Bargery 1993 [1934], 573). Aside from asserting youth or wealth, the ways in which cloths were worn could also communicate a message. The phrase *leɓan uwar miji* refers to a wife's allowing the top corner of her cloth "to hang down outside, originally a sign that she held her mother-in-law in contempt, and was illustrating the length of her lower lip" (Bargery 1993 [1934], 725).

The literal appearance of a cloth could also be related to the literal appearance of a person. For example, the white *fari* cloth known as *kemo*, was described as "cloth dishonestly woven very narrow," which was also used to refer to people who were slightly built (Bargery 1993 [1934], 596; see also Abraham 1962, 514). Similarly, the term *ɗaukar dungu*, meaning "A piece of cotton material etc which is just four yards long and therefore shorter than that called *zane* [a woman's wrapper]" and hence insufficient, is related to the word *dungu*, "an empty promise" (Bargery 1993 [1934], 278). While the word *kece*, defined as "tear a piece off cloth" or "tear, rend cloth," is related to the phrase *"ya kece raini,"* he did just what he pleased (Bargery 1993 [1934], 595) and has a clearly negative association with human behavior, the word *madeba* (or *madebi*), is more ambiguous. It refers to "a strip of material sewn to the top right-hand corner of a woman's cloth to enable her to know the right and wrong side in the dark" (Bargery 1993 [1934], 739). A woman getting up early before sunrise might benefit from the placement of a cloth strip although it might also facilitate an illicit affair carried out under cover of darkness.

Cloth Names and Trade

Several cloths mentioned in the Bargery dictionary refer to cloths made in specific places associated with the Sokoto Caliphate, such as the cloth *bagaladime*, a black and white cloth from Kano (Bargery 1993 [1934], 57). As has been discussed regarding the cloths known as *bunu* and *bawan bunu*, some cloths originally were woven in northeastern Yoruba, across the Niger River south of the Nupe Kingdom. Another cloth from this area, known as *arigidi*, defined as "A black and white cloth of Yoruba make," is also mentioned by Bargery (1993 [1934], 36). While *arigidi* cloth was woven on vertical looms during the first half of the twentieth century by Bunu Yoruba women, it was probably also woven in the late nineteenth century. Unlike wide-width *bunu* cloths previously discussed,[17] *arigidi* cloth was only woven for sale in local markets:

> [This cloth] was woven not for Bunu consumption but strictly for sale at the large Igbo market at Onitsha. This cloth consisted of two very narrow, loosely woven, handspun cotton strips [white with fine blue warp stripes] and was said to be used by Igbo tapsters and fishermen as loincloths, as towels, and as chair slings. Bunu women would carry it to local markets at Odogi and Kabba, or cloth traders from Kabba would come to Bunu villages to buy arigidi cloth. (Renne 1995, 136)

While these *arigidi* cloths were likely sold in the late nineteenth century, one cloth trader from Kabba recounted his experience selling *arigidi* cloth beginning in the early 1930s:

> I started buying arigidi cloth [in Bunu villages] after the Omi Mimo [Holy Water] movement. When I first bought it, I paid one shilling for two pieces. I also used to buy arigidi in Odogi market [between Okene and Kabba] for two shillings when it was good. When I had collected it, I would enter a motor going to Lokoja (for five shillings) and then take a ferry to Onitsha. At Onitsha, I would sell the cloth to an Igbo trader. . . . I used to do this every three months. (Renne 1995, 136)

While this trade in *arigidi* cloth was described for the early twentieth century, it is likely that it had been part of the earlier trade in Bunu cloth to Onitsha during the nineteenth century and traveled to northern markets with other traders. As described by Hodder and Ukwu (1969, 234), Onitsha became a major market after the establishment of European trading stations on the Niger River. In 1857, the British steamships the *Dayspring* and the *George* landed at Onitsha with European traders and missionaries. As Bishop Crowther (1857, cited by Hodder and Ukwu [1969, 235]) described the scene:

> It was market day and the canoes had brought men belonging to the neighbouring tribes to Onitsha to exchange their products for European wares which the black traders sell either on their own account or that of the factors they represent. . . . The traveller is everywhere struck with the diversity of the races.

The expanding market led colonial officials to construct permanent market stalls in an area just to the south in 1928. It is also possible, however, that *arigidi* cloths, as well as wide-width cloths woven by women in Bunu, were taken to the Onitsha market in the nineteenth century, where they were bought by Hausa traders for sale in the north.

CLOTH AS TRIBUTE, CLOTHS FOR OPENING RELATIONS

In the Merina kingdom of central Madagascar, "cloth was one of the primary material goods that flowed from subjects to sovereigns and from sovereign to subjects" (Fee 2002, 65). Gifts of cloth were also used by the Merina Prime Minister Rainilaiarivony in nineteenth century Madagascar to establish relations with Europeans, who were in turn "rivaling each other to supply the finest satin and velvet confections to Merina monarchs" (Fee 2002, 66). During the nineteenth century in the Sokoto Caliphate, tribute in the form of robes and handwoven cloth was also practiced. For example, robes were also used as gifts to encourage consideration of a request made to a Caliphate official. Last (1967, 196) notes that when the Vizier at Sokoto received "an in-coming letter [it] was often accompanied by some gowns or cloths, occasionally a slave or a horse or a parcel of kola-nuts."

Nigerian Political Leaders: Gifts Given to and Received from the Sultan and Emirs

The practice of gift giving, particularly the tradition of distributing robes by Muslim political leaders to members of their constituencies, contributed to a particular form of governance (Heathcote 1972; Kriger 1988; Renne 2004). For example, in the seventeenth century, the king of Kano, Sarkin Mohamma Nazaki, was said to have distributed a thousand robes to workers who extended the Kano City walls (Palmer 1908, 83). Similarly, Last mentions the nineteenth-century Sokoto Caliphate practice of both receiving robes as revenue and distributing them as gifts during Ramadan and with administrative appointments:

> Presents were the form that much of the revenue which Sokoto received from the emirates took. [For example], the Zaria payment referred to was 20 slaves, 70 gowns, of which 20 were fine Nupe gowns. (Last 1967, 105, 105 note 59)

> Another letter, just before his appointment [Emir Muhammad Sambo of Zaria], carries compliments and a present of four black tobes. (Last 1967, 169)

This practice was also witnessed by Heinrich Barth (1857, 3:95), when traveling to Sokoto in March 1853:

> We here separated from most of our companions, the governor of Kátsena, as well as the people from Kanó and Záriya, who were carrying tribute to the Sultan of Sókoto. . . . The Kanáwa and Zozáwa, or Zegézegé [those from Kano and Zaria], of whom the latter carried 2,000,000 shells, 500 tobes [robes], and 30 horses, as tribute, were too much afraid of their property to accompany us.

These robes were in turn distributed by Sokoto officials to those doing work for the Caliphate, as in the construction of walls and also when confirming political appointments.

The official, intragovernmental uses of cloth as gifts was paralleled by European travelers who sought to establish good relations with the sultan of Sokoto, emirs, and court officials, as well as village chiefs. Referring to these things as "objects as envoys" (Kreamer and Fee 2002), *gaisuwa*, literally greetings, were often accompanied by gifts of cloth. There are numerous examples of Europeans traveling in northern Nigeria who brought textiles with them to give as gifts. For example, Richard Lander in 1830 wrote that he "visited the king [of Zaria] this morning, taking with me four yards of blue, and the same quantity of scarlet damask; four yards of blue and scarlet silk; . . . a scarlet cap, six yards of white muslin, and a blank drawing book." He also travelled to Cowro where he met the town chief:

Its chief, a noble looking Houssa, behaved with the most studied civility towards his guests. He was neatly clad in a white tobe, trousers, and cap. . . . In return for the chief's kindness, and the excellent provisions he supplied us with, I made him a present of an old piece of carpeting, a scarlet cap, white turban, and gilt chain. (Lander 1830, 136)

Barth, traveling through northern Nigeria twenty-three years later, observed the necessity of gift exchange. When he visited Katsina in March 1853, he distributed his gifts to the Emir of Katsina, which consisted of "a very fine blue bernus, a kaftan of fine red cloth, a small pocket pistol, two muslin turbans, a red cap, two loaves of sugar, and some smaller articles" (Barth 1857, 3:184). He also attended the market to purchase cloth and clothing for later giving when he traveled eastward to Timbuktu:

I made considerable purchases in this place, amounting altogether to 1,308,000 shells, employing the greatest part of my cash in providing myself with the cotton and silk manufactures of Kano and Nupe, in order to pave my way by means of these [p. 85] favorite articles, through the countries on the middle course of the Niger, where nothing is esteemed more highly than these native manufactures. . . .

I bought here altogether 75 *turkedis* or women-cloths, which form the usual standard article in Timbuktu, and from which narrow shirts for males are made; 35 black tobes of Kano manufacture; 20 ditto of Nupe manufacture; 20 silk of different descriptions; 232 black shawls [veils] for covering the face, as the best presents for the Tawarek. I also brought here, besides, four very good cloth bernuses from some Tawak traders lately arrived from their country. (Barth 1857, 3:84–85)

Apparently, Barth thought carefully about the appropriateness of the gifts he gave. When he arrived in Wurno, where the sultan of Sokoto was then residing in late March 1853, he had misgivings about the gifts he planned on giving to the sultan:

Thinking that what I had selected might not prove sufficient to answer fully his expectation, in the morning, when I arose, I still added a few things more, so that my present consisted of the following articles: a pair of pistols, richly ornamented with silver, in velvet holsters; a rich bernus (Arab cloak with hood) of red satin, lined with yellow satin; a bernus of yellow cloth; a bernus of brown cloth; a red cloth kaftan embroidered with gold; a pair of red cloth trowsers; a Stambuli carpet; three loaves of sugar; three turbans and a red cap;

two pairs of razors; half a dozen large looking-glasses; cloves, and benzoin. (Barth 1857, 3:106–7)

The sultan in his turn gave Barth 100,000 kurdi "to defray the expenses of my household."

Another nineteenth-century European traveler, Paul Staudinger, visited Gwandu, Zaria, and Kano to establish trading relations with Caliphate political leaders. At Gwandu, the capital of the Emirate of Gwandu (which had authority over the Nupe Kingdom), he lamented the confusion caused by his predecessor, who had left gifts for the sultan of Gwandu with the Nupe king that apparently were never delivered: "In doing so he quite disregarded the fact that presents are the only passport in these countries" (Staudinger 1990 [1889], 1:308). He later had a dispute with the sultan about four yards of silk and gold brocade that resulted in his having to buy back a piece of brocade he had given to someone else. "This episode should give an idea of how very careful the traveler has to be in his choice of presents in these countries," Staudinger (1990 [1889], 1:309) noted. This sentiment was also expressed by a British colonial military official, A. F. Mockler-Ferryman (1892, 299): "to some it is sufficient to give a packet of needles or a few yards of cheap cotton stuff, while to others (such as the Mahommedan emirs) handsome presents of English and Oriental goods are necessary."

European travelers were not the only ones who needed to give thought to appropriate gifts during their travels. Long-distance traders such as Kano-born Madugu Mohamman Mai Gashin Baki, who regularly traveled in northern Nigeria, distributed gifts as he went (Flegel 1985 [1885]). Handwoven embroidered robes were also given to chiefs by Hausa caravan leaders traveling west as part of the kola trade:

> These varied in price and quality, and the caravan leader was responsible before leaving the Hausa cities, for the purchase of enough gowns of the right kind to use as gaisuwa . . . kola caravan leaders viewed gifts of robes to the rulers of towns through which they travelled as a voluntary "symbol of respect and appreciation to the ruler and an offering which pledged their good faith in the market exchange with local people." (Lovejoy 1980, 108–9)

The range of distinctive sizes and styles of robes—made with diverse materials, simply or elaborately embroidered and finished—made such refined gift giving possible. While the documentary evidence of such travelers does not include the names of the particular robes or cloths given, the more than one hundred names of cloth provided by Bargery suggests the range of possible textile distinctions.

CONCLUSION

The plethora of terms relating to cloth, indigo, cotton, and clothing defined by G. P. Bargery were collected from different parts of northern Nigeria. Some cloths have different names in different areas, which is sometimes indicated and which may account for the many names in the dictionary. These names and their variations, however, suggest the intimate connections between the myriad handwoven cloths that were produced and traded within the Sokoto Caliphate and their owners. In addition to cloths produced in nineteenth-century northern Nigeria, other textiles manufactured in India and Europe were brought to northern Nigeria, mainly by trans-Saharan traders and also by long-distance traders who traveled between Kano, market towns in the confluence area of central Nigeria, and Lagos. As they became incorporated into local circuits of use, they too received names that distinguished them from other cloths.

European travelers such as Clapperton, the Lander brothers, Barth, and Staudinger brought various types of cloth and garments as gifts, which piqued demand for new types of cloth—silk satin, gold-embroidered brocades, damask, and cotton prints. By midcentury, European traders traveled up the Niger River and established trading stations that were visited by Nupe, Hausa, and Bornu traders, among others. Some imported manufactured cloths were of low quality—as Mockler-Ferryman suggested—and some of these cloths received Hausa names, such as *julajula*, "applied to poorly-woven native cloth and to cheap, thin European-made cloth" (Bargery 1993 [1934], 551), *dan ganaso*, "a cheap cotton material of European make" (Bargery 1993 [1934], 217), and *cakiri*, "an imported cloth of European manufacture" (Bargery 1993 [1934], 147; see chapter 2). Yet other types of European cloths were admired for their quality, were in demand, and also received names. For example, the cloth known as "*lele,*" a white calico (=*alawayyo, zawati*), also could be "applied to anything which is especially good" (*Na lele na atijo;* Bargery 1993 [1934], 725–26).[18] Well-woven white cotton calico (or muslin), heavy with sizing, was used for plain and embroidered robes. Printed cotton cloths with bright and fast colors were also admired and were known as *abada*, "a European trade-cloth, so called because, although of many colours and shades, these are fast and do not fade" (= *atamfa*; Bargery 1993 [1934], 1).

With the advent of British colonial rule in Nigeria, many more European cotton print textiles, mainly British and Dutch, became available in Nigerian markets by the early twentieth century. Yet even then and certainly during the period of the Sokoto Caliphate, two colors of cloth prevailed: plain white and blue-black indigo. These colors might be combined in handwoven cloth strips (such as those used to make *saki* robes) or in wide-width cloth panels (such as types of black and white striped *bunu* cloths). Other colored materials were sometimes present—magenta-colored *alharini* silk and tan *sanyan* silk—but overall the colors white and blue-black prevailed. This situation may be explained by the aesthetic preferences and associations with these cloths. As has been discussed, the wearing of white garments was associated with Islamic scholarship and the moral virtues of Islam, while the blue-black sheen imparted to robes and turbans worn by emirate court members and wealthy traders expressed an aesthetic that conflated beauty and wealth. Yet while white garments continued to be favored by Islamic leaders and scholars as well as for embroidered kaftan and robes, the demand for heavy and heavily dyed blue-black robes and turbans diminished during the twentieth century. Shea (1975, 85) observed this declining demand when he noted that "Even if other information were not sufficient to demonstrate this fact, the thousands and thousands of abandoned dye pits in the Kano countryside are ample testimony to the decline of the industry in Kano." The many indigo-dyed garments were replaced by lighter-weight colored solid or printed cotton cloths.

Jane Schneider (1978), in her essay on peacocks and penguins, has discussed the persistence in the production and demand for black dyed cloth in Britain and central Europe in the face of multicolored cloth imports from India as well as cloth produced in Italy. Black cloth continued to be worn by clerics, at funerals, and at as a way of asserting a local cultural identity and of supporting local production. This dynamic also played a part in the widespread demand for blue-black indigo dyed cloth and its continuing role in the configuration of beauty and wealth in northern Nigeria. A blue cast on the skin and on white robes as well as *shuni* indigo paste used directly on women's hair reflected these ideas, yet they began to change as people no longer wanted textiles that faded or left a colored residue on bodies or clothes. It is interesting that one of the terms for an esteemed imported white cotton cloth, *lele*, was also associated with something valued from the past, while the term for well-made, imported colored cotton print cloths, *abada*, referred to their fastness, which distinguished them from older indigo-dyed cloth. Yet despite this shift in textile preference, an aesthetic that related beauty and wealth also continued, as will be discussed in the following chapter.

NOTES

1. When I first came to Zaria in 1994, there were a few older women who were still handweaving cloth on vertical looms but none of the younger women in their households did so.

2. George Percy Bargery began work on the dictionary after he accepted a post with the Colonial Education Service in 1912. (He had acquired his fluency in Hausa during his earlier stay in northern Nigeria, from approximately 1900 to 1911, as a Church Missionary Society minister.) According to the dictionary's preface, Bargery explained that "most of the work was done in the cities of Kano and Katsina with short visits to Daura, Gumel, Hadejia, and the French territory north of Nigeria, including Gobir," while others from Sokoto and Zaria also assisted him. But he specifically named Malam Mamudu of Kano for his extensive assistance (Bargery 1993 [1934], viii). After returning to England in 1930, he taught Hausa at the School of Oceanic and African Studies at the University of London. There he also worked on finalizing the first edition of his dictionary, which was published in 1934 by the government of Nigeria. Bargery later returned to Kano in 1953, where he worked on translating the Bible into Hausa (Parsons 1967).

3. The argument based on research conducted by Boas was initially disputed but has later been accepted (Robson 2013).

4. These textile terms are all defined by Bargery 1993 [1934]: *alharini* (p. 21), *barage* (p. 81), *fari* (p. 305), and *saki* (p. 887).

5. According to Nadel (1942, 128), in the Nupe capital of Bida, only men from the royal family were allowed to wear *dan* Kura turbans.

6. The cloth, *gwado*, is defined as "A cloth of native make (usually white with stripes of blue)" (Bargery 1993 [1934], 419).

7. Indeed, Frobenius (1913, 412) noted the importance of Bunu as a source of handwoven cloth.

8. This cloth was sold for 3,500 cowries (the second most expensive cloth) and consisted of two strips, 18½" wide and 5'5" long (Johnson 1973, 357).

9. Perani (1977, 135 note 10) was told that "A plain, dark blue cloth, called *Bunu* was woven by Nupe women in the early 20th century. Personal communication with Mallam Tiffin, *Sarkin Kudu*, Bida, June 1973."

10. Another cloth, *dan* Yaraf, is defined as "A woman's large, long-fringed cloth (of the bunu variety) of specially good quality" (Bargery 1993 [1934], 229).

11. It is possible that some of these women were servants.

12. In Kano City, people of Nupe descent are found in Madungurum, Bakin Ruwa, and Tudun Nufawa wards. They are also found in Kura and Zaria (Shea 1975, 95 note 3).

13. Bargery (1993 [1934], 945) defines *shuni* as a "Prepared indigo extracted from the plant baba and sold in cones or lumps. It is beaten into a dyed cloth to give it a darker hue."

14. *Turkudi* is also defined as "2. Woven strips sufficient for the above cloth. 3. Cotton thread made ready for weaving into the above" (Bargery 1993 [1934], 1063).

15. The term *burbure*, which is defined by Bargery (1993 [1934], 133) as: "1. Sprinkling indigo on the hair by women, 2. Sprinkling indigo on cloth (instead of rubbing it on) prior to beating it in, and so not getting such good result," suggests the sometimes deceptive measures taken to reduce the cost of these efforts.

16. See Renne 2018, 29. In the photograph, emirs and chiefs are seen waiting for audience with His Excellency Frederick Lugard, in Kano [in 1914?]. One chief seated on the far right is wearing a shiny black *kore* robe, while the chief seated to his immediate left is wearing a glossy black *ḍan* Kura turban.

17. Some of these wide-width cloths were used as marriage cloths by Bunu women (Renne 1995).

18. The phrase *na lele, na atijo* may be pidgin English for "it is very good, it is from past times"; *atijo* is a Yoruba word meaning "the past, past times."

REFERENCES

Abraham, R. C. 1962. *Dictionary of the Hausa Language*. London: University of London Press.

Bargery, G. P. 1993 [1934]. *A Hausa-English and English-Hausa Dictionary*, 2nd ed. Zaria: Ahmadu Bello University Press.

Barth, Heinrich. 1857. *Travels and Discoveries in North and Central Africa*, vols. 1–3. New York: Harper & Brothers.

Bayly, C. A. 1986. "The Origins of Swadeshi (Home Industry): Cloth and Indian Society, 1700–1930." In *The Social Life of Things*, edited by A. Appadurai, 285–321. Cambridge: Cambridge University Press.

Bello, Omar. 1983. "The Political Thought of Muhammad Bello (c. 1781–1837) as Revealed in his Arabic Writings More Especially *Al-Ghayth al-Wabi fi Strat Al-Imam Al-'Adl*." PhD dissertation, University of London.

Boas, Franz. 1911. "Introduction." In *Handbook of American Indian Languages*, Part 1. Smithsonian Institution, Bureau of American Ethnology, *Bulletin* 40, edited by B. Franz, 1–84. Washington DC: Government Printing Office.

Candotti, Marisa. 2010. "The Hausa Textile Industry: Origins and Development in the Precolonial Period." In *Being and Becoming Hausa: Interdisciplinary Perspectives*, edited by A. Haour and B. Rossi, 187–211. Leiden: Brill.

Chafe, Kabiru. 1990. The Transformation of Socio-Political Policies of the Leaders of the Sokoto Caliphate." In *States and Societies in the Sokoto Caliphate*, edited by A. Kani et al., 31–62. Sokoto: Usman Danfodiyo University.

Clapperton, Hugh. 1829. *Journal of the Second Expedition into the Interior of Africa, from the Bight of Benin to Soccatoo. To Which Is Added, the Journal of Richard Lander from Kano to the Sea-Coast.* London: John Murray.

Crowther, Samuel, and J. C. Taylor. 1968 [1859]. *The Gospel on the Banks of the Niger: Journals and Notices of the Native Missionaries Accompanying the Niger Expedition, 1857–1859.* London: Dawsons.

dan Fodio, Uthman. 1978. *Bayan Wujub al-Hijra 'ala 'l-Ibad.* Edited and translated by F. H. El Masri. Khartoum and Oxford: Khartoum University Press and Oxford University Press.

Fee, Sarah. 2002. "Cloth in Motion: Madagascar's Textiles Through History." In *Objects as Envoys*, edited by C. Mullen Kreamer and S. Fee, 33–93. Washington DC: Smithsonian Institution Press.

Flegel, E. R. 1985 [1885] *The Biography of Madugu Mohamman Mai Gashin Baki.* Translated by M. Duffill. Los Angeles: Crossroads Press.

Frobenius, Leo. 1913. *The Voice of Africa*, 2 vols. London: Benjamin Blom.

Heathcote, David. 1972. "Hausa Embroidered Dress." *African Arts* 5, no. 2: 12–19, 82, 84.

Hodder, B. W., and U. I. Ukwu. 1969. *Markets in West Africa: Studies of Market and Trade Among the Yoruba and Ibo.* Ibadan: Ibadan University Press.

Johnson, Marion. 1973. "Cloth on the Banks of the Niger." *Journal of the Historical Society of Nigeria* 6: 353–63.

Johnson, Marion. 1976. "Calico Caravans: The Tripoli-Kano Trade after 1880." *Journal of African History* 17: 95–117.

Kreamer, C. Mullen, and S. Fee, eds. 2002. *Objects as Envoys.* Washington DC: Smithsonian Institution Press.

Kriger, Colleen. 1988. "Robes of the Sokoto Caliphate." *African Arts* 21, no. 3: 52–57, 78–79, 85.

Kriger, Colleen. 1990. "Textile Production in the Lower Niger Basin: New Evidence from the 1841 Niger Expedition Collection." *Textile History* 21, no. 1: 31–56.

Kriger, Colleen. 2006. *Cloth in West African History.* Lanham, MD: AltaMira Press.

Lander, Richard. 1830. *Records of Captain Clapperton's Last Expedition to Africa*, 2 vols. London: H. Colburn and R. Bentley.

Lander, Richard, and John Lander. 1965 [1854]. *Journal of an Expedition to Explore the Course and Termination of the Niger: With a Narrative of a Voyage Down that River to its Termination*, 2 vols. New York: Harper & Brothers.

Last, Murray. 1966. "An Aspect of the Caliph Muhammad Bello's Social Policy." *Kano Studies* 1: 56–59.

Last, Murray. 1967. *The Sokoto Caliphate.* London: Longman.

Lovejoy, Paul. 1978. "Plantations in the Economy of the Sokoto Caliphate." *Journal of African History* 19, no. 3: 341–68.

Lovejoy, Paul. 1980. *Caravans of Kola: The Hausa Kola Trade 1700–1900.* Zaria: Ahmadu Bello University Press.

Lydon, Ghislaine. 2009. *On Trans-Saharan Trails: Islamic Law, Trade Networks, and*

Cross-Cultural Exchange in Nineteenth-Century West Africa. Cambridge: Cambridge University Press.

Mockler-Ferryman, A. F. 1892. *Up the Niger*. London: G. Philip & Son.

Murphy, Robert. 1964. "Social Distance and the Veil." *American Anthropologist* 66, no. 6: 1257–74.

Nadel, S. F. 1942. *A Black Byzantium: The Kingdom of Nupe in Nigeria*. London: Oxford University Press.

Newman, Paul. 2007. *A Hausa-English Dictionary*. New Haven, CT: Yale University Press.

Palmer, H. S. 1908. "Kano Chronicles." *The Journal of the Royal Anthropological Institute of Great Britain and Ireland* 38: 58–98.

Parsons, F. W. 1967. "Obituary: George Percy Bargery." *Bulletin of the School of Oriental and African Studies* 30, no. 2: 488–94.

Perani, Judith. 1977. "Nupe Crafts: The Dynamics of Change in 19th and 20th Century Weaving and Brassworking." PhD dissertation, Indiana University, Bloomington.

Perani, J., and Norma Wolff. 1992. "Embroidered Gown and Equestrian Ensembles of the Kano Aristocracy." *African Arts* 25, no. 3: 70–81, 102–4.

Perani, J., and. N. Wolff. 1999. *Cloth, Dress and Art Patronage in Africa*. Oxford: Berg.

Philips, J. E. 1992. "Ribats in the Sokoto Caliphate: Selected Studies 1804–1903." PhD dissertation, University of California, Los Angeles.

Picton, John, and John Mack. 1979. *African Textiles*. London: British Museum.

Renne, Elisha. 1995. *Cloth That Does Not Die: The Meaning of Cloth in Bunu Social Life*. Seattle: University of Washington Press.

Renne, Elisha. 2004. "*Babban Riga* Production and Marketing in Zaria, Nigeria." *African Economic History* 32: 103–22.

Renne, Elisha. 2018. *Veils, Turbans, and Islamic Reform in Northern Nigeria*. Bloomington: Indiana University Press.

Robson, David. 2013. "There Really Are 50 Eskimo Words for 'Snow.'" *Washington Post*, January 14. www.washingtonpost.com, accessed December 13, 2017.

Schneider, Jane. 1978. "Penguins and Peacocks." *American Ethnologist* 5: 413–47.

Schneider, Jane, and Annette Weiner. 1986. "Cloth and the Organization of Human Experience." *Current Anthropology* 27, no. 2: 178–84.

Shea, Philip J. 1975. "The Development of an Export-Oriented Dyed Cloth Industry in Kano Emirate in the Nineteenth Century." PhD dissertation, University of Wisconsin, Madison.

Smith, M. G. 1960. *Government in Zazzau, 1800–1950*. London: Oxford University Press.

Staudinger, Paul. 1990 [1899]. *In the Heart of the Hausa States*, 2 vols. Translated by J. Moody. Athens: Ohio University Press.

CHAPTER 2

Textile Manufacturing, Printing, and Trade during Colonial Rule

ELISHA RENNE

Then they gave her lovely cloths, her marriage cloths and slippers and covered her head and face with cloth.
—*Baba of Karo* (Smith 1954, 247)

This chapter focuses on a particular type of textile imported to northern Nigeria: cotton prints from England and the Netherlands. While these prints were only a fraction of cotton manufactured textiles shipped from Tripoli to Kano in the nineteenth century, they formed the basis for demand for printed cotton textiles, both imported and locally manufactured. By the early twentieth century, printed cotton textiles were imported via Lagos and distributed by a range of traders, some from Kano, Zaria, and Ilorin, others from Ibadan and Lagos. Some were independent traders, while others were associated with expatriate trading firms such as United African Company (UAC), Paterson Zochonis Ltd., and A. Brunnschweiler & Co. (Bauer 1954; Pedler 1974). This chapter considers examples of these early manufactured cloths, which were available and attractive to the northern Nigerian consumers. British- and Dutch-manufactured textile samples from museum collections underscore the range of images and colors used in their manufacture as well as their relationship to earlier patterned textiles from India and Indonesia (Kroese 1976; Picton 1992, 1995).[1] Some of these samples included special company trademarks, which also contributed to their appeal (Pedler 1974). This discussion is followed by the memories of cotton print textiles recounted by older residents of Zaria, Kaduna, and Kano. Their recollections of the names of these textiles, when they were worn, and who wore them suggest that while there were no official sumptuary rules regulating the wearing of particular print textiles, the keen evaluation of their qualities coincided with an evaluation of the social standing of those wearing them. As was the case regarding the proliferation of cloth names and textile terminology that reflected the importance of textiles in nineteenth-century northern Nigerian socioeconomic life, memories of particular printed textiles in the first half of the twentieth century underscore the intimacy of people and things and clarify, historically, how such textiles were valued and assessed. The growing popularity of these industrially manufactured textiles also suggests the increased importance of the mechanization of cloth production, which, as Orwell has noted in the British context, contributed to the decline of hand-spinning and of handwoven cloth production.

EUROPEAN PRINTED COTTON TEXTILE TRADE IN WEST AFRICA

Several researchers have discussed the introduction of manufactured cotton print textiles from Europe to West Africa (Gott and Loughran 2017; Nielsen 1979; Pedler 1974; Picton 1995, 2017). These textiles were the result of European efforts to supersede the popularity of Indian chintz textiles, which, through hand-blocked and painted patterns using combinations of mordants and dyes that did not fade, were popular among West African consumers (Picton 1995, 25), as well as in England and North America (Peck 2013, 108) and in France (Gottman 2014). Thus, in the 1880s, William Watson collected numerous examples of Indian dyed, printed, and woven cotton textiles as examples for British manufacturers to reproduce (Anonymous 2014; Paterson Zochonis Collection; Watson, "Textile Collection"). Through the use of improved dyes for screen printing techniques on one side of the bleached cotton cloth, the market for English-manufactured prints in West Africa expanded. In addition to these cotton prints (or super prints as they are sometimes called), the development of engraved-roller printing machines for applying a resin-resist led to the manufacture of so-called wax prints. While the resin sometimes produced cracking and bubbling effects, these inadvertent designs added another dimension to the printed designs, a dimension that was attractive to West African buyers (Picton 1995, 26). These wax prints were marketed mainly along the West African coast to port cities such as Accra (Ghana) and Whydah (Benin). Following the establishment of Nigeria under British colonial rule in 1903, several trading firms with offices in Manchester and Liverpool became involved in selling wax print and super print textiles in this country (Gertzel 1959; Hopkins 1973; Kirby 1975; Pedler 1974). Large trading firms such as Paterson Zochonis Ltd. commissioned textile prints according to their specifications, which included company trademarks, from British textile manufacturers. These cloths would then be shipped from the company headquarters in Manchester to branch offices in Accra, Lagos, Ibadan, and Zaria. As Bauer (1954, 52), writing in the 1950s, noted:

> There are a few manufacturers' representatives in West Africa. They do not themselves carry stocks, and orders placed with them are executed by the overseas principals as direct shipments to the importers. . . . The large European import houses are vertically integrated; that is, besides importing they also operate wholesale and retail establishments. But not all their imports reach the consumer through subsequent stages of their own organization.

Indeed, there was a range of sources for printed textile import purchases, from European import houses (both wholesale and retail), from independent Lebanese traders, or from Nigerian market stalls or traveling petty traders (in Ekiti, such cloth traders were referred to as *osomaalo*; Peel 1983). Furthermore, purchases could range in size, depending on the needs of the customer:

> A successful African trader may buy in one transaction four or five pieces of cotton cloth of 10 to 12 yd. each for his or her own future use. . . . On the other hand, the purchaser of a single cotton print of 6–12 yd. often cuts it up into pieces of 2 yd. with a view to resale. (Bauer 1954, 53–54)

Such decisions depended on the intended market and wherewithal of its patrons.

TEXTILE TRADING NETWORKS IN KANO AND ZARIA

In southern Nigeria, cotton print textiles reached consumers through markets in Lagos, Ibadan, and Onitsha. However, cloths were also taken up the Niger River by steamer to trading towns such as Lokoja and Egga, as was described by the British trader John Whitford (1877, 200):

> In 1865–6 white men commenced to trade, and then stores were erected and became settled institutions. . . . There are three British firms now trading,

besides well-to-do Sierra Leone and Lagos merchants, and, by judicious presents to those in authority residing about them, protection is freely accorded.

Whitford traveled to the Niger confluence area in 1865 and described how the trade in a range of British and Indian textiles was carried out from on board his steamer at Egga:

> We constructed a barrier of empty oil puncheons as a counter, behind which was our wholesale and retail shop. We broke off the iron hoops and cut open well-packed bales of Manchester goods, and exposed Madras kerchiefs of glowing red and yellow colours, Turkey-red chintz and twills, red blankets, and a variety of eye-pleasing patterned cottons too numerous to mention. (Whitford 1877, 239)

The presence of "a variety of eye-pleasing patterned cotton too numerous to mention" explains why many women sought to obtain and wear such cloths.

Despite the presence of northern Nigerian traders from Kano at the confluence trading towns of Egga and Lokoja, much of the European-manufactured cloth that reached markets in Kano and Zaria in the late nineteenth and early twentieth centuries came via trans-Saharan trade routes. According to Johnson (1976, 100):

> In 1897, the consul-general [of Tripoli] compiled a list of merchandise sent from Tripoli by caravan; the total value amounted to £54,766 of which just over half was British cotton manufacture; Austrian cloth accounted for a further £2,210, and silks from France and Germany for another £560. In addition, there was £6,716 work of waste silk [magenta; *alharini*] from Italy and France. . . . By the consul's reckoning, some 84 per cent of the goods sent from Tripoli were destined for Kano.

This situation continued through the first decade of the twentieth century. Photographs taken by British colonial officials, such as George Gibbs and Stanhope White (1967) show men wearing mainly robes, kaftan, and pants made with white manufactured cotton materials, probably obtained via the trans-Saharan trade routes.

With the establishment of British colonial rule of northern Nigeria in 1903 and the development of a national postal system, however, traders in Kano began to utilize the postal system to obtain textile samples and to ship

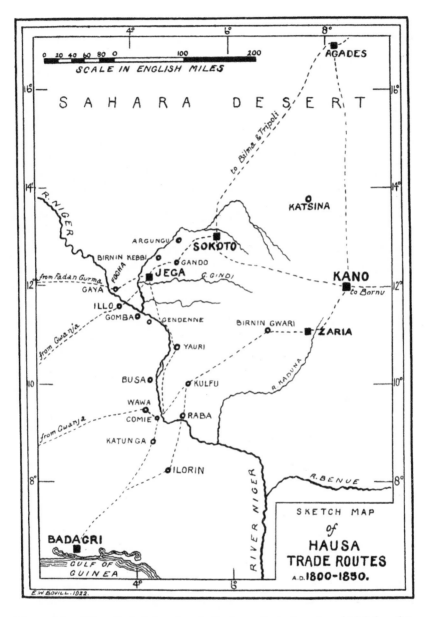

Map 2.1. Map of Kano-Zaria-Sokoto-Jega, indicating earlier trade routes, which led north to Agades and onto Tripoli and south to Ilorin and Badagri, 1800–1850. (Bovill 1922, opposite page 50.)

orders by 1907 (Johnson 1976, 114). Furthermore, with the opening of the railway route between Kano and Lagos in 1914, the shift toward obtaining British-manufactured textiles via the southern Nigerian ports contributed to a significant reduction in trans-Saharan trade. This situation, along with the increased security of Lagos-Kano trade routes by road, contributed to increasing amounts of printed cotton textiles reaching Kano and Zaria from the south. The greater availability of imported wax print textiles from Manchester and the Netherlands was mentioned by Zaria City women, who referred to these cloths as 'yar Onitsha, referring to the southeastern Nigerian town of Onitsha, from where Igbo traders who traveled to Kano had brought them.[2]

Kano traders such as Alhassan Dantata, who had traded in kola nuts from Gonja (in Ghana), which he then sold in Kano, began to branch out, buying items such as European textiles (DanAsabe 2000, 55). After he settled in Kano in 1918, he maintained agents in southern trading cities; his brother, Alhaji Bala, maintained the Dantata Lagos office. Furthermore, "His wife, Hajiya Umma Zaria . . . was his chief agent for trading with other women." In Kano, she worked through older women she hired as agents who were able to visit married women in their homes to learn of their textile requests (DanAsabe 2000, 58).

These trade routes between Kano, Zaria, Ilorin, and Lagos were also plied by Yoruba traders, some of whom settled in Kano in the 1930s and in Zaria in the 1940s. In Kano, they took up numerous occupations: Western-educated Yoruba took up positions in the colonial administration and in trading firm businesses, while others worked as traders, photographers, and truck drivers (Olaniyi 2008). In Zaria, some settled in Zaria City and became involved in the textile trade in the main market there. Alhaji Mohammed Bashir came to Zaria shortly after World War II (*bayan yakin Hitila*) and set up a stall in the Zaria City market, which he provisioned with many types of cloth: wax prints (*atamfa*, also known as *abada*), lace (*leshi*), and damask (*shadda*). Once settled in Zaria City, the textiles he sold were purchased mainly from Kano.[3] Other family members came to the Zaria City market to sell textiles, some of which were obtained from European trading firms (such as Paterson Zochonis), mainly *akoko* (plain baft) cloth.[4] Later, textiles were purchased from Nigerian agents for the United Nigerian Textiles Ltd. and Arewa Textiles mills, which had opened in Kaduna in the mid-1960s. According to another member of this family, Hausa men who were agents for Kaduna Textiles Limited also sold cloth to them for sale in Zaria City market. Initially they were selling mainly plain unbleached cotton baft (*akoko*), although they also sold handwoven narrow-strip cloth (*sakakke*), head ties (*gyale*), and cotton prints (*atamfa*).

PRINTED COTTON TEXTILES: WAX AND SUPER PRINTS

While textile prints were available in the early twentieth century, they became more widely available in northern Nigerian markets in the 1940s, when more cloths were brought from Lagos, Ibadan, Ilorin, and Onitsha to Kano, Kaduna, and Zaria by Hausa, Yoruba, and Igbo traders. As will be seen, these cloths were evaluated by their visual and material qualities: clarity of fast colors, attractive designs, sheen, and soft hand. Wax (actually resin) prints cloths produced with duplex-engraved metal rollers were distinguished by their clear designs on both sides of the cloth. Fancy or super prints were produced with engraved metal rollers and at times with rotary screen prints, with a design that was only clear on one side of the cloth. These printed cotton textiles were also distinguished by the presence of trademarks, associated with particular textile marketing firms.

UK Textile Manufacturers and Trading Firms in Colonial Kano, Kaduna, and Zaria

A distinctive trademark (known as a *lamba* or *tambari* in Hausa[5] or "chop marks" by the British) was (and continues to be) a defining feature of cotton print *atamfa* cloths; such trademarks were associated with the different manufacturers of cotton wax print textiles. Pedler (1974) noted the importance of trademarks in attracting buyers. Similarly, some Kano area handweavers identified their cloth with particular woven marks in order to assure customers of the quality of their purchases (Shea 1975, 143):

> Two strips of cloth which may seem identical to the inexperienced viewer can vary considerably in price, one costing several times as much another of equal size. Each weaver puts his "signature" at the end of the roll of cloth by weaving a tiny pattern in faint colors so he can later recognize his own work and prevent dealers from switching the cloth with other[s] of lower quality.

Following the implementation of British colonial rule in Nigeria, European textile manufacturers relied on the registration of company trademarks.

Once the requirements of the 1907 Trade Marks Ordinance had been met, notices had to be published in the *Nigerian Gazette* as well as filed in the Registry of Trade Marks office in Lagos. Thereafter the use of specific trademarks was limited to the registering manufacturer (or to companies that had obtained permission to use the trademark on their cloths).

The earliest recorded trademarks tended to be registered by major trading firms in Nigeria. Some of these early registered trademark motifs were then used within subsequent, more elaborately designed marks. For example, the United Africa Company (UAC, formed in 1929 from the amalgamation of the African and Eastern Trade Corporation and the Niger Company) took up the trademark of the manilla and arrow originally registered by the African and Eastern Trade Corporation (Pedler 1974, 224). This motif—along with the acronym UAC and the letter Y (sometimes inscribed with the words "Ars Jus Pax")—was often incorporated into newer designs, thus maintaining customer recognition while keeping up with the latest fashions.

The unauthorized use of trademarks by rival local firms could lead to prosecution and remedial actions, such as the case cited by Pedler (1974, 223):

> Shortly after the end of the war in 1918, a merchant who imported textiles for sale at Kano made a close copy of Ollivant's horse-and-rider mark, and had it stamped on his cloth. Ollivant lodged an objection and the offender was obliged to remove the pirated mark. He did this by cutting a circular hole in the cloth, which was offered for sale in that condition. It sold like wildfire. The circular hole provided some positive identification of a unique variety, and for some years that importer continued to place his cloth on sale with a circular hole, and his lines were best sellers in the Kano market.[6]

The importance of even "a circular hole" in distinguishing particular textiles and encouraging sales suggests why so many textile trademarks were registered by trading firms in Nigeria, despite the considerable expense involved.

Trademarks Registration by Firms in Nigeria

Aside from the trademarks themselves, registration applications published in the *Nigerian Gazette* also provide some information on the backgrounds of trading firms involved in textile sales in the country. While the majority of these firms were British-based or British-owned, other European manufacturing and trading companies were represented.[7] In addition, several

Nigerian-run trading firms registered textile trademarks in the 1940s, including Messrs. Tekumo Onalaja & Co. of Lagos (in 1945) and the London & Kano Trading Company, also headquartered in Lagos (in 1931). Texts were often incorporated into these trademarks in several ways. The simplest way was the use of company acronyms, such as AGL (for A. G. Leventis), UAC (United Africa Company), SOAC (Société Commerciale de l'Ouest Africain), LKTC (London & Kano Trading Company), and DWS (David Whitehead & Sons), as trademarks. Other trademarks utilize a single word, such as *Maidoki* (horseman; G. B. Ollivant) and *Damo* (iguana; UAC) along with these visual images.

The use of trademarks on textiles in Nigeria, then, operated on several different levels, some of which were intentionally promoted by foreign textile manufacturers and local and foreign textile traders. A popular and well-regarded trademark was a valuable commodity that could enhance cloth sales. At this level, textile trademarks established and reinforced customer recognition, confidence, and "name-brand" loyalty. At another level, a textile bearing a trademark associated with prestigious foreign firms such as Gottschalck or the United African Company could be "read" as representing the economic acumen and social status of its wearer. Even in the twenty-first century, when textile trademarks have diminished in size and elaborateness, either being printed along the selvage or on an adhesive label, these trademarks continue to be displayed and noticed. A wax print cloth outfit with a Vlisco "V" printed on the selvage will be viewed as expensive and its wearer will be assessed accordingly (see chapter 8).

In the context of colonial West Africa, there is another aspect of the use of these textile trademarks. While Arabic script had been written in the northern Sahel areas for several centuries (and evidence suggests that such script was also incorporated into textile designs used on tailored gowns [Perani and Wolff 1999, 141]), the use of texts in Roman script came to be viewed as a symbol of modernity. This modernity, or so-called "enlightenment" (Peel 1978), was associated with Western education and literacy, often in English and sometimes in Yoruba and Hausa. Wearing textiles with trademarks—themselves associated with modern, manufactured imported cloth (Renne 1995)—that had texts associated with Western sources of knowledge identified wearers as sophisticated and literate arbiters of new fashion tastes.

The main European manufacturing firms selling textiles in Nigeria included the United Africa Company (UAC) (and its subsidiaries G. B.

Ollivant and G. Gottschalck), A. G. Leventis, Paterson Zochonis, Société Commerciale de l'Ouest Africain (SCOA), J. T. Chanrai and K. Chelleram, all based in Manchester, while John Holt was based in Liverpool.[8] All had distinctive trademarks, some of which included Hausa words and sayings to attract buyers. It was mainly the textile traders, however, who were familiar with these trademarks. Two such marks were mentioned by Zaria City traders: the ship trademark used by G. Gottschalck and Co. and the young woman's head (*"yarinya"*). Older women in Zaria often did not know many names of particular *atamfa* patterns and rarely knew the company associated with an *atamfa* cloth's trademark. This situation reflected the social setting of Kano and Zaria in the 1940s, when Hausa women mainly obtained their printed cotton cloths from their fathers and husbands. Yet as the popularity of the circular cut trademarks suggests, they could "read" these marks and associate them with a particular cloth's value.

SOCIAL DYNAMICS AND TEXTILE DESIGN PREFERENCES IN ZARIA AND KANO MARKETS

West African consumers had local aesthetic preferences, so French and British manufacturers attempted to document and then satisfy them with printed cotton textiles made for specific markets (Steiner 1989). For the older women living in Zaria interviewed about *atamfa* during the colonial era, however, it should be remembered that as young unmarried women they neither had the means to purchase *atamfa* cloth nor the autonomy as married women to purchase cloths directly from the market because they were secluded within their husbands' compounds. Cloths were purchased for them, either by their fathers or husbands, at Zaria City market, Sabon Gari market in Zaria, and at times from markets in Kaduna and Kano. As Hajiya Zaineb recalled, "My husband used to buy wrappers in Zaria because at that time, women didn't go to the market. But the *atamfa* materials came either from Lagos or Kano before coming to Zaria."[9]

Yet there were other ways that secluded Hausa women could select *atamfa* textiles they preferred. Several women mentioned that Yoruba women, members of cloth trading families living in Zaria who could freely move in the market, would come to their compounds with cloths for secluded women to purchase: "Yoruba women would come with cloth and they would also cut hair."[10]

ATAMFA CLOTH MEMORIES

Most of the women interviewed were young girls when they received their first *atamfa* cotton printed textiles. Hajiya Zaineb, who was born around 1940 in Zaria City, the old walled section of the larger town of Zaria (Smith 1954), received her first cloth when she was twelve years old, during the reign of the Emir Sarkin Zazzau, Ja'afaru dan Isyaku (1936–1959). She wore this cloth, along with members of her group of young unmarried girls, for Sallah celebrations following the Muslim holiday of 'Id-el-Kabir. They came out to watch the Hawan Daushe procession—with elaborately dressed horsemen and horses on parade through the City (Renne 2013)—wearing identical *atamfa* cloth, which, as she remembered, was known as *'yar* Douala.[11] According to Hajiya Zaineb, "it had a design with mangoes and lemons—in green and yellow." Later, she was given another *atamfa* cloth to wear for the Sallah holiday, which was called *'yar* Onitsha (literally, daughter of Onitsha), which people believed came from the large Igbo trading town of Onitsha to the southeast (Bastian 1998).

Several women mentioned *'yar* Onitsha cloth, which as another woman, Hajiya Habiba, explained, "came from the Igbo side. It looks like Hollandais [Dutch wax prints] and was the most expensive and highest quality *atamfa....* One that I owned had designs with flowers, another had a design depicting houses."[12] *'yar* Onitsha cloth was mentioned by several older women who saw it as the most beautiful and prestigious of the *atamfa* cloths.

Other women mentioned the name Wax, referring to English wax prints with different designs. They also remembered receiving wax *atamfa* cloths as young girls for Sallah celebrations. One woman, Maryam, wore *atamfa* cloths, one with a *bishiya* (tree) pattern, another with a pattern known as *mai gwangwala* (the long leaf-less stem of a raffia palm frond; Bargery (1993 [1934], 424), for Sallah, which were bought for her at the Zaria City market. Her neighbor, Hajiya Rakiya, also wore an *atamfa* cloth with a flower design for Sallah as a young girl, which she referred to as *atamfa Ghana*. These cloths were associated by some women with the early cotton print textiles that traders had initially brought from Ghana via Lagos (Picton 1995).[13] Such cloths were then brought north by traders to the large cloth market in Kano, where Zaria traders traveled to purchase them to sell in Zaria City market.

Atamfa cloths were worn (or received) for two other significant life events: marriage and childbirth. Hajiya Rakiya also remembered receiving an *atamfa* cloth when she married as part of her *kayan aure* (literally, marriage load), the cloths carried with her during the marriage procession to her husband's house as was described by Baba of Karo in the chapter's epigraph. The cloth was decorated with depictions of birds, which she referred to as *tsuntsu da kudi*, birds and money, because imported *atamfa* cloths such as 'yar Onitsha and Wax were considered to be very expensive.[14] Rakiya's elderly neighbor, Rabi, remembered one particular *atamfa* cloth that she was given when she married; it was called *mai karta*, which referred to the depiction of playing cards as its main motif. It was an expensive cloth purchased in Zaria City market from Yoruba traders there, who had probably obtained it from markets in Kano and brought it and others like it to Zaria.

Living in Kano expanded women's access to a wider range of textile prints. Malama Hajera mentioned cotton prints described by women in Zaria and Kaduna—*mai tsuntsu da kudi* ("birds and money") and *mai fankeke* ("owner of a silver-colored bicycle"). But she also mentioned several cotton prints with images of political figures (the Nigerien president Hamani Diori and the Emir Bayero of Kano) and the famous Nigerienne singer Fati Sangara, cloths which are referred to as commemorative textiles (Spencer 1982). She described all these cloths as Hollandais wax prints that were purchased by her father and husband in Kantin Kwari market in Kano. Her husband put one of these cloths, *mai fankeke*, in her wedding box; she wore others during Sallah. While these wrappers had writing and trademarks printed on them, she couldn't remember them. But she did remember that women liked to wear these wrappers "because people will see them and know you have money. And they will last long and don't fade."[15]

Aside from preferences for wax print textiles with particular patterns and colors that were both bright and fast, women were also aware of the hand of a cloth. For plain white baft material, it needed to have a "heavy" hand, stiff and soft, but not limp. Women admired the softness—as well as substance—of 'yar Onitsha (Dutch) and Wax (English) cotton prints. But another characteristic of English Wax cotton print cloth that distinguished it from all other *atamfa* cloth was its odor. One woman described it as "a chemical odor," while another said it smelled like perfume (*turare*). Even after washing it, this attractive odor remained and was one of the defining features of so-called wax cloths from Britain.[16]

Because of the bright, clear fast colors, designs, hand, odor, and, for some, distinctive trademarks of 'yar Onitsha and Wax *atamfa* cloths, women preferred to wear them. As one woman explained, "People [seeing you] will know the value of the wrapper by the trademark and the pattern—the color is clearer—will be slightly different and people who know wrappers will see the difference.... Because these cloths are more beautiful than other wrappers, it makes people value you."[17]

Another aspect of the evaluation of *'yar* Onitsha cloth was its association with emirs and their families. "At that time [when I married, probably around 1945], only the royal people and their children, and judges (*alkalai*) wore *'yar* Onitsha cloth. For my dowry, I had a good *atamfa* wax cloth but not a *'yar* Onitsha cloth." Later, when she married, she was given a *'yar* Onitsha cloth called *mai ɗawisu*, which had a pattern depicting a peacock (*ɗawisu*).[18]

This connection between aesthetic beauty and wealth or social value was also noted by Hajiya Habiba, who explained:

> I liked wearing the *'yar* Onitsha cloth, *mai ɗawisu*—when you washed it, it would look good and people seeing you wearing it will respect you. Since I was young, I used to wear these types of wrappers [*'yar* Onitsha and Wax], especially during Sallah, weddings, and naming ceremonies (*biki*). When you wear these cloths, people will know that you come from a wealthy family—or a royal family—or a family with Western education.[19]

One aspect of wax print cloths suggests the prestige of women who wore them in another way. When attending the naming ceremony for the Walin Zazzau's daughter in Zaria City in the early 1950s, Hajiya Zaineb wore a cloth, printed with large green and red flowers, called *Raka ta gidan lawiya*, "escort her to the lawyer's house." Rather than use the term *gidan alkali*, the name for the traditional Hausa judge's house, by using the term, *lawiya* (or *lauya*, lawyer), its wearers (and namers) displayed their knowledgeable modernity by using an English word.

Alternately, other less costly *atamfa* cloths—other than the type worn by Hajiya—were mentioned by women. These included *azabari karya* (an imported cotton cloth with a flower design), *fago* (an imported cotton cloth with blue and white bands), *tsamiya* (an imported cotton cloth with tan and white stripes), and *cakiri* (a cloth with small blue and white bands, "an imported cloth of European manufacture" (Bargery 1993 [1934], 147). These cloths were associated with village women and with the poor, hence more affluent urban women were loath to wear them. This reluctance was evident in one interview with an older woman in Zaria City. I read her a list of names of *atamfa* cloths that we had been told about, asking her to tell me the cloths she had owned. When I came to the *atamfa* called *cakiri*,[20] she loudly

Fig 2.1. Young woman wearing cotton cloth print with peacock (*mai dawisu*) pattern, Zaria City. (Photograph of photograph by E. P. Renne.)

disagreed that she had ever owned such a cloth, while other women sitting nearby and listening hooted in agreement.

ADIRE COTTONS PRINTS MADE IN KANO AND ZARIA

The first *atamfa* cloth I remember was *adire*.
—Mallama Maryam, Zaria City, November 10, 2017

Several women in Zaria City mentioned cloths known as *adire* when asked about what *atamfa* wrappers they had owned. While the name *adire* derives from the indigo-dyed cloth produced by Yoruba specialists in southwestern Nigeria (Barbour 1970; Stanfield 1971), these women are referring to a type of patterned cloth made initially with handwoven white cotton cloth (*sakakke*) and later with imported white cotton cloth (*akoko* or *alawayyo*) manufactured in the UK and locally resist-dyed with indigo. Initially, *adire* cloths were brought to Zaria and Kano by Yoruba women traders, who later began making *adire* cloths in these northern Nigerian towns. Eventually, Hausa women began making *adire* cloths themselves, as Hajiya Lamidi explained:

At that time, if you wanted a beautiful *adire* wrapper you will get plain cloth, tie it, and then take it to the indigo dye pits (*rimi*) to be dyed. This cloth pattern was called *mai dawisu* (peacock). You can use seed cotton to tie it and make your [resist] pattern. You can do the tying yourself or get someone who knows how to do it. [Some] used white handwoven cloth to do the dyeing. . . . For my dowry, I had good *atamfa*. But any girl, if she married and didn't have the dyed *sakakke* one [*adire*], she was not a respectable girl.[21]

Hajiya Lamidi was married in the early 1950s during the reign of Emir Sanusi I of Kano, when men were still handweaving and dyeing cloth in indigo dye pits in Zaria City.

Another woman in Zaria City also mentioned wearing an *adire* cloth when she married, probably in the late 1950s:

I wore *adire* during my marriage, for my own my father had to go to the *rimi* [indigo dye pit] dyers to make a beautiful *adire*, just for me for my marriage things (*kayan aure*). It was in the area behind the market [*bayan kasuwa*] in Zaria City where they were dyeing cloth with indigo then. . . . *Adire* came in little patterns but most of them looked like little, little flowers. They used white calico (*alawayyo*) cloth to do *adire*. At that time *adire* was the popular cloth, not for rich people, not for the poor people—but the in-between ones. It was popular during the time of Emir Ja'afaru [during the 1950s]. . . . And people liked it because it had many colors—they used kola nut (*goro*) and potash (*kunya kanwa*) to make the blue color different. It was a popular wrapper among the middle class and Western-educated (*'yan boko*).[22]

Thus, for parents or husbands who could not afford to buy expensive imported cotton wax or super print cloths for their daughters or wives,[23] the production of *adire* cloths enabled them to dress fashionably. "That's why when you wear *adire*, they don't look down on you but they don't look up to you either," Hajiya Zaineb explained.

In Kano, locally made *adire* followed a similar but distinctive trajectory. While Yoruba women brought *adire* cloths to sell and later some Hausa women also began tying cloth for dyeing at the *karofii* dye pits in Kano, another means of *adire* cloth production came to take the place of previously fashionable indigo-dyed *sakakke* cloths that were produced in Kura, Gwarzo, and many other towns and villages in the Kano area. Beginning in the 1950s, northern Nigerian production of *adire* cloth was centered in Kano City and represented a major change in indigo-dyed cloth production and marketing (Shea 1975, 148–49). By the early 1970s, when Shea was conducting research on the history of indigo dyeing in Kano, *adire* cloth production was being mass-produced:

> The most successful dealers in *adire* cloth today are individuals (some of them dyers) who own sewing machines for stitching the resist patterns on the cloth and have a lot of money to invest in factory produced cloth. They oversee the dyeing and beating of the cloth and take it to "Kantin Kwari" [see chapter 6], a newly developed marketing center just outside Kano City's walls on one of the major motor roads, where the cloth can be sold quickly in medium sized lots to the petty traders who travel by truck from market to market throughout the state. If business is good, the city entrepreneurs can sell all the cloth in a single day and then re-invest their capital and profit in producing more *adire*. Thus, the development of *adire*, while giving employment to many dyers in the city and to those rural dyers and beaters who have chosen to move into the city or who travel there for seasonal work, has side-stepped the traditional organization of dyeing as well as the traditional institutions for marketing the dyed cloth. (Shea 1975, 248–49)

As is often the case with fashion trends, as more women in the 1970s could afford to purchase locally manufactured (in Kano and Kaduna) and imported cotton textile prints (from the Netherlands and the UK), these textiles took the place of *adire* cloth as northern Nigerian women's fashionable attire.

The Popularity of the Peacock Pattern

There are several ways to explain why the peacock pattern was favored by northern Nigerians who purchased cloth depicting this bird. The peacock (*dawisu*) probably came to Nigeria through connections associated with the hajj,[24] as one of the names for peacock, *tsuntsun Maka* (bird of Mecca), suggests. Indeed, its early appearance in the Middle East is evoked in the description of King Solomon in the Old Testament: "For the king had a fleet of ships of Tarshish at sea with the fleet of Hiram. Once every three years the fleet of ships of Tarshish used to come bringing gold, silver, ivory, apes, and peacocks" (1 Kings 10:22). It is also possible that peacocks were brought from India through British colonial connections. Seen in the palaces of various emirs in northern Nigeria, the male species of these birds—the peacock—and its extravagant display of the tail feathers came to be associated with royal prestige and pageantry. This association as well as their unusual attractiveness contributed to their depiction in both wax and super print textiles as well as in locally made *adire* cloths in Zaria, as Hajiya Lamidi mentioned. By tying individual cotton seeds in a fan-like pattern and then dyeing the cloth with indigo, the beautiful "eyes" of the peacock tail feathers were suggested. Several older women also distinctly remembered having received cotton textile prints with a peacock (*dawisu*) pattern, perhaps because of their encounters with these birds on the emir's palace grounds.[25] Indeed, the emir's palace in Zaria is home to several peacocks, which, even if they are not regularly seen, may still be heard some distance away. Thus, peacock-patterned cloths were seen as associated with royalty and as markers of wealth and beauty, the aesthetic qualities these women sought to impress upon those viewing the wearers of these cloths.

ATAMFA CONTINUITIES AND CONTRADICTIONS

At the end of the nineteenth and the beginning of the twentieth centuries, the preponderance of goods shipped by caravan via trans-Saharan trade routes from Tripoli went to Kano. As Johnson (1976, 100) observed, the majority of these goods consisted of plain white cloth: "The British consul in Tripoli estimated in 1891 that Manchester cottons (chiefly grey T-cloths, white long-cloths and a few prints) formed 70 per cent of the total" of the goods carried by trans-Saharan caravans to Kano. Even with the growing trade in cotton prints by the early nineteenth century in Lagos and by the mid-nineteenth century in Lokoja, only a small percentage of such cloths reached Kano and Zaria, as is evidenced by photographs, mainly of men, taken by colonial officials. Most women continued to wear a range of handwoven textiles in the first decades of the twentieth century. Only women from royal families were able to afford the relatively expensive imported wax cotton prints. Yet women and their families aspired to wearing such wax prints, which were generally known by the names of the places from which they came. Thus, 'yar Onitsha wax prints, which were later referred to as Hollandais, were believed to have been brought to Kano and Zaria from Onitsha and originally from the Netherlands, while wax prints referred to as "English Wax" were believed to have originated in the UK. Both were expensive and only accessible to women from wealthy families. Because of their high price as well as their clear colors, softness, hand, and distinguishing trademarks, these cloths were seen as enhancing both the beauty and the social value of their wearers. The aesthetics of wax print textiles, then, was to some degree related to price; what was expensive was beautiful. Not surprisingly, as Simmel (1971) has noted, fashion tastes set by the elite influence the aspirations of those without titles or substantial resources. As wax print and super print textiles became increasingly available in northern Nigeria, more women aspired to wear them.

Yet despite their value, women interviewed in Zaria, Kaduna, and Kano tended not to keep these cloths but rather to give them out as they became worn or outdated. It is possible that many of these cloths were not kept as a result of cultural conventions associated with *zakat* (donations to the poor). There were some cloths that did have names—*mai tabarma* (mat), *mai dawisu* (peacock), and *tsuntsu da kudi* (birds and money)—which were mentioned by several women. Yet the extensive association of cloths with proverbs and inventive names was not as common as discussed by researchers working in Ghana and Côte d'Ivoire (Bickford 1994; Domowitz 1992). Nor could older women remember the company names of particular trademarks associated with these cloths, which suggests that a certain level of literacy contributed to a familiarity with these distinctions. As has been mentioned, Shea (1975, 148) noted that some handweavers marked the end of their cloth rolls with a small, woven pattern to identify their origin.

Similarly, Higgins and Tweedale (1996, 218) discuss the use by some British manufacturers of line headings—"stripes of coloured yarn, cord, or thread which were woven at the end of cotton piece goods." These distinguishing lines had the advantage of being woven into cloth, which hence could not be altered. Furthermore, line headings were more easily "read" by customers not familiar with trademark images and written phrases. Indeed, "Some merchants believed that such was the importance of headings in certain markets that grey cotton cloth could not be sold without them" (Higgins and Tweedale 1996, 219). By the time cotton print textiles were being marketed in northern Nigeria, however, trademarks were uniformly used to identify the manufacturers of these cloths and eventually they became important signs of value for northern Nigerian women.

If trademarks were not initially meaningful to northern Nigerian women, they clearly were valuable for manufacturers. It is likely that distinctive trademarks were more important for traders and company agents as guarantees of the quality of cotton prints. And since these older women usually did not purchase cloths themselves, they would have been less discerning of the significance of different trademarks. This discernment would come later, when women were free to enter shops to make their own cotton print textile purchases and trademarks became even more important. Thus trademarks, such as the Paterson Zochonis sandal, which came to be incorporated into some of the company's print textile designs, enhanced the overall pattern and reminded buyers of the cloth's quality and authenticity.

Yet as will be seen in later chapters, the registration of specific cloth patterns and trademarks, which was done to verify the authenticity of a cotton print textile associated with a particular manufacturer, was no guarantee that a pattern or trademark might not be used by other manufacturers. Earlier registered textile patterns might be slightly changed by artists in Kaduna textile mills—a practice referred to as making a "counter copy"—in order to evade copyright restrictions. And in the twenty-first century, the use of identical patterns as well as the copying of trademarks is practiced by some Chinese textile firms. For example, one can find a six-yard packet of patterned print cloth marked with the Vlisco "V" trademark in a textile shop in Zaria selling for 5,000 *naira* whereas the authentic Vlisco cloth with the same trademark will sell for 35,000 *naira* for six yards (see chapter 8).[26] Rather than relying on trademarks, color, hand, or scent alone, people also determine the authenticity of wax and super print cloths by price.

CONCLUSION

By the end of the colonial era, the manufacture of cotton textiles had begun at the Kano Citizens Trading Company and at the Kaduna Textiles Limited mills (in 1952 and 1957, respectively). While neither of these mills initially produced cotton print cloths, the growing popularity of wax and super print cotton textiles led to an expansion of their production, with several mills in Kaduna and Kano producing cotton prints in the following decade. These mills enabled Nigerian traders and dealers in Kano, Kaduna, and Zaria to make a range of brightly colored printed cotton materials available to local customers. Although British and Dutch wax prints (A. Brunnschweiler & Co. and Vlisco Hollandais) continued to attract buyers from the political and economic elite, Nigerian wax and super print textiles became more widely available for purchase by urban and rural women alike. The handwoven *sakakke* and hand-dyed *adire* cloths, which had been an essential part of Hausa women's marriage things in the 1940s and 1950s, were replaced with textiles woven and dyed with machines. The increasing reliance on industrially produced textiles and thread, reflected in the growth of plain (*akoko*) and printed (*at-amfa*) textile manufacturing in Kaduna and Kano, are discussed in subsequent chapters.

NOTES

1. The origins of resist-dyed textile prints are associated with Indian cotton prints and Javanese wax-resist batik cloths (see Kroese 1976; Picton 1995; and Gott and Loughran 2017), although there is some disagreement about the precise trajectory of these connections.

2. See Onyemelukwe (1974, 54–55) for a discussion of Igbo trade networks between the Niger River commercial center of Onitsha and the city of Kano in northern Nigeria. While Onyemelukwe focuses on food commodities, it is likely that Igbo traders traveling north by road brought *'yar* Onitsha (literally, "daughter of Onitsha") imported English and Dutch cloth, which had been sold to them when European vessels stopped at Onitsha.

3. Alhaji Mohammed Bashir, interview with E. Renne, June 3, 2011, June 4, 2011, Zaria City.

4. One of the trademarks that he remembered was called Yarinya, which depicted the head of a young woman.

5. The seal on official emirate documents was known as a *tambari*; trademarks were also referred to as *tambari kamfani*, literally "company seal."

6. A similar suit was filed in 1938 against "a Syrian trader" who attempted to sell

cloth with a textile design registered by the Lagos firm G. Gottschalck and Company (*West African Pilot*, March 4, 1938, p. 1).

7. For example, the French company Société Commerciale de l'Ouest Africain (of Paris and London; SOAC) filed for several trademarks, as did the Dutch firm N.V. Handelmaatschappij; the Dutch firm was eventually recognized by the name of Vlisco.

8. Also, Saul Raccah was an important trader of European textiles during the colonial era in Kano (Albasu 1995, 112–13).

9. Hajiya Zaineb Abdulkadir, interview with E. Renne, November 16, 2017, Zaria City.

10. Hajiya Lamidi, interview with E. Renne, November 16, 2017, Zaria City.

11. 'yar Doula literally means "daughter of Doula (Cameroun)" and could refer to people's understanding of the source of this cloth.

12. Hajiya Habiba, interview with E. Renne, Kaduna, November 13, 2017.

13. Indeed, the Yoruba name for cotton print textiles, *ankara*, probably derives from traders' pronunciation of Accra, the Ghanaian capital and center of coastal trade, from which cloths were taken to Lagos (Renne 2017).

14. Hajiya Rakiya, interview with E. Renne, November 13, 2017, Zaria City. Similarly, Shea (1975, 95) noted the association of cloth with money in the phrase "'*saki da kudi*', or 'black woven cloth with money'—because the red thread (*alharini*) [used to weave alternating strips] was so expensive."

15. Malama Hajera, interview with E. Renne, November 21, 2017, Kano.

16. The German explorer Paul Staudinger (1990 [1899], 238), observed, on seeing a civet cat for sale on the road to Zaria in November 1885, that these animals were kept in order to obtain civet musk from their glands, which "is a scent favoured for perfuming the clothes of the Hausa." The association of particular odors with the value of cloth may also be seen in the case of expensive indigo-dyed blue-black ɗan Kura turbans and *kore* robes, which were associated with emirs and courtiers who were distinguished by "the smell of the dyed cloth but more particularly from the beauty of its metallic sheen" (Flegel 1985 [1885], 7).

17. Hajiya Zaineb, interview with E. Renne, November 16, 2017, Zaria City.

18. Hajiya Lamidi, interview with E. Renne, November 16, 2017, Zaria City.

19. Hajiya Habiba, interview with E. Renne, November 13, 2017, Kaduna.

20. Bargery (1993 [1934]) defines *cakiri* as "imported European cloth." But he also defines it as "a name given [by Hausa speakers] to Yorubas as offensive," possibly because of their association with selling such an inferior type of textile.

21. Hajiya Lamidi, interview with E. Renne, November 16, 2017, Zaria City.

22. According to Salihu Maiwada, one of "the indigo-resist patterns that was used was called *jaki ya sha wuta* (literally, 'the donkey drinks fire'), as it resembled the immunization mark made on donkeys for the treatment of certain illnesses."

23 · Hajiya Zaineb noted that "*Atamfa* at that time was expensive—around 30 shillings. Only those who had money could afford *atamfa*, many people could not afford it" (interview with E. Renne, November 26, 2017, Zaria City).

24. M. Last, personal communication.

25. While not as common as trademarks depicting the turkey (three turkeys constituted the trademark for cotton piece goods sold through its Lagos office by the Compagnie Française de l'Afrique Occidentale, registered on October 29, 1959 [*Nigerian Gazette Extraordinary* 1960, 1324]), the peacock was registered as a trademark used by J.T. Chanrai & Company (Nigeria) Limited in November 1959 for articles of clothing sold through their Lagos office (*Nigerian Gazette Extraordinary* 1960, 1329).

26. Interview with E. Renne, November 25, 2017, Tudun Wada, Zaria.

REFERENCES

Albasu, S. A. 1995. *The Lebanese in Kano: An Immigrant Community in a Hausa Society in the Colonial and Post-Colonial Periods*. Kano: KABS Print Services.

Anonymous. 2014. "An 'Industrial Museum': John Forbes Watson's Indian Textile Collection." New York: Metropolitan Museum of Art, August 12, 2013–January 20, 2014, https://www.metmuseum.org/exhibitions/listings/2013/indian-textiles.

Barbour, Jane. 1970. "Nigerian *Adire* Cloths." *Baessler-Archiv, Neue Folge*, band XVIII.

Bargery, G. P. 1993 [1934]. *A Hausa-English and English-Hausa Dictionary*, 2nd ed. Zaria: Ahmadu Bello University Press.

Bastian, Misty. 1998. "Fires, Tricksters and Poisoned Medicines: Popular Cultures of Rumor in Onitsha, Nigeria and its Markets." *Etnofoor* 11, no. 2: 111–32.

Bauer, P. T. 1954. *West African Trade*. Cambridge: Cambridge University Press.

Bickford, Kathleen. 1994. "The A.B.C's of Cloth and Politics in Cote d'Ivoire." *Africa Today* 41, no. 2: 5–24.

Bovill, E. W. 1922. "Jega Market." *Journal of the Royal African Society* 22, no. 85: 50–60.

DanAsabe, Abdulkarim. 2000. "Biography of Select Kano Merchants, 1853–1955." *FAIS: Journal of Humanities* 1, no. 2: 45–60.

Domowitz, S. 1992. "Wearing Proverbs: Anyi Names for Printed Factory Cloth." *African Arts* 25, no. 3: 82–87, 104.

Flegel, E. R. 1985 [1885]. *The Biography of Madugu Mohamman Mai Gashin Baki*. Translated by M. Duffill. Los Angeles: Crossroads Press.

Gertzel, Cherry. 1959. "John Holt: A British Merchant in West Africa in the Era of Imperialism." PhD dissertation, University of Oxford, UK.

Gott, Suzanne, and Kristyne Loughran. 2017. "Introducing African Print Fashion." In *African-Print Fashion Now! A Story of Taste, Globalization, and Style*, edited by S. Gott, T. Loughran, B. Quick, and L. Rabine, 23–49. Los Angeles: Fowler Museum.

Gottman, Felicia. 2014. *Global Trade, Smuggling, and the Making of Economic Liberalism: Asian Textiles in France 1680–1760*. Basingstoke, Hampshire: Palgrave Macmillan.

Higgins, D. M., and Geoffrey Tweedale. 1996. "The Trade Marks Question and the Lancashire Cotton Textile Industry, 1870–1914." *Textile History* 27, no. 2: 207–28.

Hopkins, A. G. 1973. *An Economic History of West Africa*. New York: Columbia University Press.

Johnson, Marion. 1976. "Calico Caravans: The Tripoli-Kano Trade After 1880." *Journal of African History* 17: 95–117.

Kirby, Peter. 1975. "Manufacturing in Colonial Africa." In *Colonialism in Africa 1870–1960*, vol. 4, edited by P. Duignan and L. Gann, 470–520. Cambridge: Cambridge University Press.

Kroese, W. T. 1976. *The Origin of the Wax Block Print on the Coast of West Africa*. Hengelo: NV Uitegeverij Smit van 1876.

Nielsen, Ruth. 1979. "The History and Development of Wax-Printed Textiles Intended for West Africa and Zaire." In *The Fabrics of Culture*, edited by J. Cordwell and R. Schwartz, 467–98. Mouton: The Hague.

Nigerian Gazette Extraordinary. 1960. *Nigerian Gazette Extraordinary*. Lagos: Government Printer.

Olaniyi, Rasheed. 2008. *Diaspora Is Not Like Home: A Social and Economic History of Yoruba in Kano, 1912–1999*. Germany: Lincom Europa.

Onyemelukwe, J. 1974. "Some Factors in the Growth of West African Market Towns: The Example of Pre-Civil War Onitsha, Nigeria." *Urban Studies* 11, no. 4: 7–59.

Paterson Zochonis Collection, Museum of Science and Industry. 2012. Manchester, UK.

Peck, Amelia. 2013. "'India Chints" and 'China Taffaty': East India Company Textiles for the North American Market." In *Interwoven Globe: The Worldwide Textile Trade, 1500–1800*, edited by A. Peck, 104–19. New York: Metropolitan Museum of Art.

Pedler, Frederick. 1974. *The Lion and the Unicorn in Africa: A History of the Origins of the United Africa Company 1787–1931*. London: Heinemann Educational.

Peel, J. D. Y. 1978. "*Olaju*: A Yoruba Concept of Development." *Journal of Development Studies* 14, no. 2: 139–65.

Peel, J. D. Y. 1983. *Ijeshas and the Nigerians*. Cambridge: Cambridge University Press.

Perani, J., and N. Wolff. 1999. *Cloth, Dress, and Art Patronage in Nigeria*. Oxford: Berg.

Picton, John. 1992. "Tradition, Technology, and Lurex: Some Comments on Textile History and Design in West Africa." In *History, Design, and Craft, in West African Strip-Woven Cloth*, 13–52. Washington DC: Smithsonian Institution.

Picton, John, ed. 1995. *The Art of African Textiles: Technology, Tradition and Lurex*. London: Lund Humphries Publishers.

Picton, John. 2017. "Preface." In *African-Print Fashion Now! A Story of Taste, Globalization, and Style*, edited by T. Loughran, S. Gott, B. Quick, and L. Rabine, 18–21. Los Angeles: Fowler Museum.

Renne, Elisha. 1995. *Cloth That Does Not Die: The Meaning of Cloth in Bunu Social Life*. Seattle: University of Washington Press.

Renne, Elisha. 2013. "The Motorcycle Sallah Durbars of Zaria, 2012." *Anthropology Today* 29, no. 4: 12–16.

Renne, Elisha. 2017. "*Ankara* Fashions in Nigeria." In *African-Print Fashion Now! A Story of Taste, Globalization, and Style*, edited by T. Loughran, S. Gott, B. Quick, and L. Rabine, 162–75. Los Angeles: Fowler Museum.

Shea, Philip. 1975. "The Development of an Export-Oriented Dyed Cloth Industry in

Kano Emirate in the Nineteenth Century." PhD dissertation, University of Wisconsin, Madison.

Simmel, Georg. 1971. "Fashion." In *Georg Simmel: On Individuality and Social Forms*, edited by D. Levine, 294–323. Chicago: University of Chicago Press.

Smith, Mary F. 1954. *Baba of Karo*. New Haven, CT: Yale University Press.

Spencer, Anne M. 1982. *In Praise of Heroes: Contemporary African Commemorative Cloth*. Newark, NJ: The Newark Museum.

Stanfield, Nancy. 1971. *Adirẹ Cloth in Nigeria; The Preparation and Dyeing of Indigo Patterned Cloths among the Yoruba*. Ibadan: Institute of African Studies.

Staudinger, Paul. 1990 [1899]. *In the Heart of the Hausa States*, 2 vols. Translated by J. Moody. Athens, OH: Ohio University Press (originally published as *Im Herzen der Hausaländer* (Berlin: A. Landsberger, 1889).

Steiner, Christopher. 1985. "Another Image of Africa: Toward an Ethnohistory of European Cloth Marketed in West Africa, 1873–1960." *Ethnohistory* 32, no. 2: 91–110.

Watson, John Forbes. "Textile Collection, 2nd series." New York: Cooper-Hewitt Museum.

West African Pilot. 1938. *West African Pilot*, March 4, 1.

White, Stanhope. 1967. *Dan Bana: The Memoirs of a Nigerian Official*. New York: J. H. Heineman.

Whitford, John. 1877. *Trading Life in West and Central Africa*. Liverpool: The "Porcupine" Office.

CHAPTER 3

Declining Supply and Continued Demand for Handwoven Textiles, Kano State

SALIHU MAIWADA

In the past, handwoven textile production was a thriving business in towns such as Gwarzo, Minjibir, and neighboring villages in the area surrounding the metropolis of Kano. Indeed, handweaving was widely practiced throughout Hausaland including the area currently known as Kano State during the seventeenth century on through the first half of the twentieth century (Ferguson 1973; Lamb and Holmes 1980; Picton and Mack 1979). Even after 1960, during the early independence era, there were many handweavers—both men and women—in Kano State and elsewhere in northern Nigeria. Yet by the late 1970s, when Lamb and Holmes (1980) conducted extensive research on handweaving, they found that handweaving was on the decline in the region. The reasons for this decline, which has continued in the twenty-first century, will be discussed. Nonetheless, while the aesthetic preference for lighter-weight manufactured textiles has reduced the demand for handwoven cloth (*sakar hannu*) made with handspun or industrial-spun cotton thread, the social context of handwoven textile use as traditional dress has supported continued demand by affluent Fulani consumers for wide-width handwoven cloth from weavers in the Gwarzo area and for warp-striped, handwoven textiles by Hausa royal customers from weavers around Minjibir. This demand thus reflects the role that cloth plays in asserting an ethnic and social identity. In the Gwarzo area, however, older men weavers noted that while there continues to be demand for the wide handwoven textiles known as *mudukare* cloth favored by Fulani customers, they are finding it increasingly difficult to find young men interested in pursuing handweaving careers. Even while

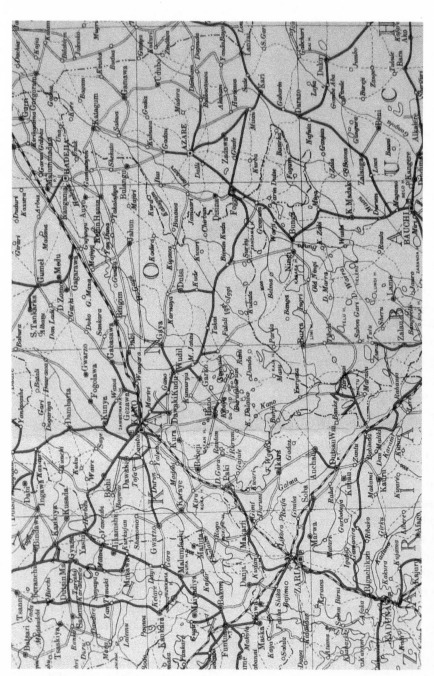

Map 3.1. Map indicating Kano State towns of Gwarzo, Kura, and Wudil as well as the road linking Kano-Zaria-Kaduna. Road Map of Nigeria, drawn, printed, and published by Federal Survey Department, Lagos, Nigeria, 1955. (Courtesy of the University of Michigan Library, Stephen S. Clark Map Library.)

handweaving may be a profitable occupation, the slow pace of handweaving is unattractive to younger men who prefer a fashionable faster pace. Yet in villages around Minjibir, young men along with their elders continue to weave warp-striped and checked *saki* cloth that is used to make traditional Hausa-style robes worn by traditional rulers—emirs and chiefs—during ceremonial functions. In this case, the slow pace of handweaving is ameliorated by an ethnic pride that Hausa handweavers feel, which is associated with their role in perpetuating Hausa tradition.

The chapter begins with a discussion of handweaving in the Gwarzo area and continues with an examination of the types of equipment used and the different types of handwoven textiles that have been produced. Interviews with weavers and traders of these handwoven textiles provide a deeper understanding of obstacles to handwoven cloth production and trade. Since much of this cloth is used by Fulani men and women for traditional dress, the use of Gwarzo wide-width textiles in Fulani fashions is then discussed. Handweaving in the Minjibir area northwest of Kano is then examined, with weavers interviewed there describing the types of wide-width handwoven cloths they produce and sell mainly to traditional rulers and participants in horse-and-rider processions following Eid-el-Fitr and Eid-el-Kabir (known as Sallah in northern Nigeria). Their assessment of the prospects for continued handweaving in the Minjibir area suggests the importance of an aesthetics of ethnicity, not only in supporting the demand for handwoven textiles by a particular group of customers but also for the self-identity of handweavers. The chapter concludes with a consideration of this difference and its impact on the future prospects of handweaving in Gwarzo, Minjibir, and surrounding villages in Kano State in the twenty-first century.[1]

HANDWEAVING IN THE GWARZO LOCAL GOVERNMENT AREA, KANO STATE

Handweaving has long been practiced in Gwarzo, the headquarters of the Gwarzo Local Government Area. Weaving is also done in other villages in the Gwarzo LGA including Ruga, Zango, Tsohon Garu, and Sabon Garin Kayyu. Alhaji Usman Kayyu is the head weaver of Sabon Garin Kayyu village. He was born in 1956 in Sabon Garin Kayyu and attended primary school there. He was fifty-eight years old at the time of our first interview in 2014 and actively continues to weave. He was taught to weave by his father, the late Alhaji

Mika, in Kayyu. He first learned to weave the cloth *farin mudukare* and later was taught to weave the finely checked blue-black and white *saki* cloth when he was seventeen years old. When he began weaving in the early 1960s, there were many weavers in the town, and even children who went to school were encouraged to learn to weave.

Even twenty years later, both young and old were handweaving in the Kayyu area (Sani 1990). At that time, the majority of the weavers were young; their ages ranged from eighteen to thirty-five years. In a 1988 interview, a weaver named Sule reported that children were not learning in school, and when they finished they were not getting government jobs. Sule added that instead of allowing the craft to die, villagers attempted to encourage their children to learn to weave since they could earn a living by weaving cloth for Fulani consumers (Sani 1990).

Handwoven Cloth Produced in Twenty-First- Century Kayyu

Alhaji Usman Kayyu described the various types of handwoven cloth woven in Kayyu today. One of the cloths he described is called *mudukare* and that is the kind of cloth he weaves most. This name may refer to the type of cloth woven by the Kare people of Yobe State (Lamb and Holmes 1980, 107). Perani and Wolff (1999, 160) describe this cloth:

> The most successful of the Hausa broad loom cloths innovated during the colonial period—*gwado* and *mudukare*—draw upon the aesthetics of strip-woven caliphate cloth, both cloths have a plain ground color and narrow warp-face stripes. New to these cloths is the addition of weft-float patterns, a feature shared with women's cloth but not caliphate cloth.

"There is a large concentration of *mudukare* weavers in the Wudil area [just east of Kano] . . . all producing a type of cloth called *bale* which was intended expressly for the migrant Fulani." Since Wudil is close to Kano, it is likely that handweavers to the west of Kano in the Kayyu area were also weaving *mudukare* cloth at that time. In the Gwarzo area, *mudukare* cloth is woven on looms that are approximately twenty-four inches wide.

This increased width enabled weavers to produce cloth more quickly and efficiently, particularly as weavers could use industrially spun thread in its operation. As Perani and Wolff (1999, 160) have observed, "the younger generation of weavers, responding to changing economic opportunities, became increasingly interested in weaving cloth to be sold for everyday domestic

Fig. 3.1. Malam Iliyasu Muhammad, weaving on wide-width loom (*masakin mudukare*), Sabon Garin Ƙayyu, November 11, 2017. (Photograph by AbdurRahman S. Maiwada.)

use. . . . They were not as affected by the aesthetic restrictions that imposed constraints on the older generation of weavers" associated with very narrow handwoven strip-weaving.

As has been noted, *mudukare* cloth is woven for rural Fulani patrons:

> Broad loom *mudukare* cloth is based on an older strip cloth called *bale*, made of handspun yarn with very thin black, red and blue stripes set against a solid ground color. *Mudukare*, like other broad loom cloths, is now made with commercial yarn. *Mudukare* weavers, concentrated in the countryside around Kano and Wudil (a town east of Kano) directed their production to Hausa traders who carried the cloth to pastoral Fulani peoples in Niger and northern Cameroon. . . . The centers of *mudukare* production tended to specialize in weaving different varieties. (Perani and Wolff 1999, 161)

The chief characteristic of *mudukare* cloth woven in Kayyu is the presence of wide warp stripes of black, blue, or red, with colored weft. *Bale*, another type of *mudukare* cloth, is named after the narrow warp-striped cloth, *bale*, mentioned above. It is woven with four evenly spaced black and white warp stripes with a black-colored weft. Other types of *mudukare* cloth woven by weavers in Kayyu include *fari* (white cloth) and *ja* (red cloth), while some cloths combine white and blue, black, or red warp threads. According to one weaver:

> The different names of cloth—*zane* [or *zani*] *mai biro, zane mai sukari* (sugar cube), *zane mai hakorin fara* (locust tooth) were old types of cloth woven by our great grandfathers who created these names. We only heard of their history and we do not know why these names were given to these cloths. *Zane mai sukari* was woven of black and white threads which we are not weaving now.

One well-known *mudukare* cloth, known as *ilajo*, is completely white without any stripes on it, while threads of various colors are used to produce inlaid designs. There are two named *ilajo* cloth—*ilajo mai tuta* and *ilajo mai ciko*—which refer to the nature of the decoration on them. Several wool or polyester threads of various colors of about two inches are used as supplementary weft threads to produce the desired laid-in design. The *mai ciko* pattern refers to the circular hand-embroidered pattern known as *ciko*, which is a type of young boy's hairstyle. Much like the shaved patterns of hair on a boy's head, the *mai ciko* pattern is distributed on the face of the cloth.

The *ilajo mai ciko* cloth is special as it is used by young Fulani women. It is worn during wedding ceremonies and naming ceremonies, particularly after birth of a first-born child, when a young Fulani woman returns to her husband's house. Traditionally, Fulani people and even Hausa people request that their daughters return to their parents' houses during their first pregnancy, where they will give birth. When the daughters are going back to the husbands' houses, they are usually accompanied by many gifts and garments made with *ilajo* cloths of different designs, which are worn at that time.

Other cloths woven in Kayyu include two types of wrapper, *bakin zane* (black wrapper) and *farin zane* (white wrapper), and two types of narrow bands, *saki dan damara* (black woven band) and *fari dan damara* (white woven band). Black and white wrappers are plain weave cloths without any stripes and are worn by women. The woven bands are long strips that are about twenty-four inches long and about three inches wide, which are tied around the waist like belts. They are also plain without any stripes. All these cloths are now produced with industrially spun thread, which is considered preferable for weaving because of its fineness, evenness, and strength. Even though handspun cotton thread might be preferred by some, it is no longer readily available.

USES OF GWARZO HANDWOVEN TEXTILES

While Hausa patrons may use handwoven wide-width cotton cloth woven in the Gwarzo district for garments, blankets, bedspreads, and curtains, these cloths are mainly used by Fulani men and women. *Mudukare* cloth is in much demand by Fulani consumers for making garments such as *yarshara* (smocks), *bunjuma* (a wide smock), and *kwakwata* (a robe-like garment; Maiwada 2013). *Zugu* and *sawaye* cloths are used for women's wrappers and blouses. Both men's and women's garments are usually embroidered with colored woolen threads. It is interesting to note that the majority of cloths handwoven by weavers in Kayyu reflect the continuing demand by Fulani for traditional types of dress.

The styles and sizes of traditional Fulani men's dress are based on the age and status of the wearer. For instance, the *gambari* shirt is sleeveless, has a circular neck opening without a pocket, and is short, with a straight or slightly flared bottom edge. This shirt is worn by young Fulani men and boys during their everyday activities or when they accompany their cows out for grazing.

Middle-aged and elderly men also wear *gambari* shirts made of *mudukare* material as casual wear. The wide *bunjuma* smock is another style. Like the *gambari* shirt, it is sleeveless, has a circular neck opening, has side pockets, and is short with a flared bottom edge. There is another style of *bunjuma* smock with long sleeves that is worn by middle-aged and elderly men. *Kwak-wata* is another form of Fulani men's dress with wide sleeves, often lined with cloth of a contrasting color, a flared bottom edge, with a circular neck opening with a short vertical slit at the front and two vertical pocket openings in the gown's front. This style of garment is for wealthy Fulani men and political leaders (Maiwada 2013).

The *mudukare* cloth used to make most of these Fulani garments is unique and functions to reinforce a particular ethnic identity. Aesthetically, Fulani men and women consider this dress to be beautiful; the best garments are made from various types of *mudukare* cloth. Clothing made from *mudukare* cloth is so distinctive that wherever it is seen, it is identified with the Fulani people of northern Nigeria. It portrays the strong connection between this type of cloth and style of dress that enables individual Fulani men and women to express an attractive individual as well as collective identity.

Despite the importance of garments made from handwoven *mudukare* and related handwoven cloths, changes in their production as well as the social status of western-educated Fulani has affected their use. Some Fulani young men now wear smocks and shirts tailored in the traditional style but made with industrially woven cloth. The style of garments has also been adapted to suit modern tastes. For example, most of the Fulani men I interviewed in 2006 said that they changed their dress because they wanted to appear modest. According to one man, the "*gambari* smock is too short for his liking and the body is unnecessarily exposed." He confirmed that genuine *mudukare* garments have become quite scarce but added that if he could get a smock that would cover his body more properly, he would wear it.

Marketing Handwoven Cloths

Nonetheless, there *is* a market for *mudukare* and other cloths handwoven in Kayyu and other Gwarzo villages. In the past, handwoven cloth was sold in open markets such as Kurmi market in Kano, and it is still being sold there today as well as in village markets, such as Rimin Gado and Minjibir markets, on their market days. Handwoven cloths are usually taken to these markets for sale either by traders or the weavers themselves (Smith 1962). Presently, some active weavers with substantial amounts of money for travel also work as long-distance traders to places outside of Kano State to sell handwoven cloths from Gwarzo. Alhaji Usman Ƙayyu, as the leading weaver and trader in Sabon Garin Ƙayyu, is engaged in this type of trade. He goes to these village markets to buy handwoven cloths from both weavers and traders. After returning from village markets, he engages the services of tailors in Sabon Garin Ƙayyu who will sew Fulani garments for him, which he will take to places for sale. Whenever he is traveling and wherever he is going, Alhaji Usman travels by commercial transport. He has a permanent rented room in Minna where he stays whenever he goes there, but in other places he is put up by friends for as long as he is there.

Thus, as the head weaver in Sabon Garin Ƙayyu, he works as a dealer who supplies handwoven cloth to places such as Minna, Lapai, and Zungeru (in Niger State), Lokoja (in Kogi State), and Birnin Kebbi (in Kebbi State). Apart from his own handwoven cloths, Alhaji Usman collects handwoven cloths from his colleagues and sells their cloths for them when he is traveling out of Kano State. When he goes to these towns, he distributes the cloths as well as sewn garments to retailers and waits for ten to fourteen days after collecting his money before he returns to Ƙayyu. In a telephone interview,[2] Alhaji Usman described Lapai market as the largest of all the markets he attends. He added that Lapai market is where he makes the biggest sales and that he can make as much as N200,000 (approximately US$700) per visit. This market operates once a week, on Tuesdays only. Zungeru market operates on Wednesdays, also once a week, while Minna market, which is the main market in the capital of Niger State, operates daily. *Mudukare* cloth is in high demand whenever he travels to these markets, and he sells more *mudukare* cloth than any other types of handwoven textiles.

Cotton Spinning, Indigo Dyeing, Saki Weaving, and Cotton Growing in the Gwarzo Area

Presently, Alhaji Usman does all his weaving under trees in front of his house with his colleagues. Although greatly reduced, the handweaving of *mudukare* and related cloths for sale to Fulani patrons continues in the Gwarzo area. Yet certain aspects of *mudukare* weaving have changed in recent years. As has been mentioned, the hand-spinning of cotton has essentially ended in Gwarzo. While it was commonplace for young girls to practice hand-spinning in many villages in northern Nigeria, young women and girls, particularly those attending primary school, no longer have learned to spin cotton. Some of the older women who hand spun as young girls have stopped hand spinning, while others have died, so there is no longer a source of handspun cotton in the Gwarzo area. The demand for handspun cotton has also been affected by the availability of industrially spun thread, which is stronger and has fewer irregularities. Thus, handweavers prefer to weave with it rather than with handspun thread. Also, the cloth woven with industrially spun thread is lighter and is preferred by consumers.

Indigo dyeing was also widely practiced in Kano State, and the Gwarzo area was known for its indigo dyeing (Shea 1975). According to Alhaji Usman Ƙayyu, indigo dyeing is no longer being done in Gwarzo.[3] As is the case with hand spinning, indigo dyeing has stopped in Gwarzo because all the dyers have died and no one has replaced them. Consequently, many dye pits that were located in Gwarzo and surrounding villages have disappeared. According to Alhaji Usman Ƙayyu, all the dye pits were covered up more than thirty years ago and the leveled area is now being used as the Eid prayer ground in Ƙayyu.

One thing leads to another, for once indigo dyeing had stopped it led to the discontinuation of *saƙi* weaving in Gwarzo as well.[4] *Saƙi* was one of the handwoven cloths produced in Gwarzo, even before *mudukare* wide-width looms were introduced to the area (Kriger 2006; see chapter 1). Sometimes referred to as "guinea fowl cloth" (Barth 1857, 1:512–13), this cloth consists of a finely checked pattern using indigo-dyed threads of blue, black, and, at times, undyed white cotton. When the women who handspun cotton thread and the men who dyed it had died, these sources for thread for traditional *saƙi* cloth disappeared and *saƙi* weaving ended in Gwarzo. When asked where people are now getting *saƙi* cloth, Alhaji Usman Ƙayyu said that it comes from Minjibir town, in Kano State. As will be seen, weavers in Minjibir (more specifically, the village of Gidan Gabas) are still weaving *saƙi*, as some indigo-dyeing activity is continuing there. Dyers, however, are using industrially spun cotton thread and weavers use it on wide-width *mudukare* looms. In order to obtain *saƙi* cloths for Fulani customers, "Traders from Minjibir bring *saƙi* to Rimin Gado market and that is where we get it on market day," Alhaji Usman explained.

Yet even though women no longer spin cotton in the Gwarzo area and handweavers use industrially spun cotton in their work, farmers are still growing cotton in Gwarzo and surrounding villages. As one is driving from Kano to Gwarzo, cotton farms are a common sight, particularly as one is approaching Gwarzo town through Rimin Gado. Alhaji Usman's second occupation is farming and, like any wealthy man in the rural area, Alhaji

.Usman is a great farmer.[5] As a farmer, he hires laborers to work for him on his farms. When I asked Alhaji Usman Kayyu why farmers still grow cotton when hand-spinning has stopped, he said that cotton agents come to the area to purchase cotton from them in order to supply textile mills in Kaduna.[6]

EFFORTS TO REORGANIZE HANDWEAVING IN GWARZO AND MINJIBIR

The Kar Kari Trading Cooperative

In 1959, weavers in Gwarzo discussed the possibility of forming an organization to modernize the equipment they were using for handweaving and to promote their craft. According to Sani (1990), they decided to form a cooperative society and were successful. The association was formed on April 14, 1981, and was registered in Kano on April 22, 1982, with the name the Kar Kari Trading Cooperative. It was started with ten members, who later approached the government's Ministry of Trade, Industry and Commerce to provide floor looms with fly-shuttles for weavers in Gwarzo. Ministry officials agreed and the Indian High Commission to Nigeria facilitated the planning and establishment of the weaving workshop. In 1985, production began for this joint venture between the Ministry of Trade, Industry, and Commerce and the Gwarzo Local Government (Sani 1990). The textiles produced by cooperative members on these floor looms were good and were patronized by government and the general public alike.

The handloom workshop was located in Gwarzo town and there were certain rules involved. For example, only traditional handweavers who could weave well were allowed to work in the workshop. All the cloths woven were the property of the government since the state government was providing the raw materials while the Gwarzo Local Government was paying workers' salaries. The workshop was managed by a management team with the honorable commissioner for commerce as the overseer.[7] Mismanagement and inefficiency, however, brought about the collapse of the cooperative, and floor loom weaving was discontinued in 2000 (Sani 1990). It may be that the top-heavy administrative aspect of this workshop discouraged weavers from participating or simply that they preferred the flexibility of weaving on *mudukare* looms and maintaining their own production schedules.

Since that time, the weavers in Gwarzo have not formed any other organizations, although Alhaji Usman has promised to do so in the future. While handweaving continues in Gwarzo and surrounding villages, it is not on the large floor looms introduced by the government but rather on the older *masakin mudukare* looms that had previously been used in Gwarzo.

The Kano Textile Training Center in Minjibir

Another workshop using large floor looms had been established earlier in Minjibir town when the Kano Native Authority instituted the Kano Textile Training Center in the late 1940s. Following World War II, British colonial officials sought to find employment in textile training centers for soldiers returning from overseas service. Four centers were started in Nigeria, one in Oyo and another in Ado-Ekiti in 1947 (Renne 1997) and then two others in the Kano and Sokoto States in 1949. While Perani and Wolff (1999, 159) believe that the Hausa wide-width *mudukare* handlooms derived from the introduction of these wide floor looms in the training centers, Alhaji Sa'idu Adhama of Kano argues that when the British colonial officials came to the Kano area, they found Minjibir men weaving different types of handwoven cloth on both narrow-strip *turkudi* looms and also on wide-width *mudukare* looms.[8] While the Kano textile training center at Minjibir subsequently closed, the continuing strength of the handweavers' organization in Minjibir was evident from the construction of "a new dyeing center [which] was formed by the weavers themselves who claimed that the dyers were taking up too much of the profits." These pits were used to dye thread for handweaving, which did not require the expertise of cloth dyeing (Shea 1975, 14–15). Consequently, handweavers in Minjibir produce a range of warp-striped cloths with indigo-dyed thread.

HANDWEAVING IN MINJIBIR LOCAL GOVERNMENT AREA

Thus the situation for handweaving in Minjibir, the headquarters of Minjibir Local Government, differs from that of Gwarzo. Minjibir is northeast of Kano in the area known as the Kano Closed Settlement Zone and historically is known as an important weaving town (Shea 1975). In the past, Minjibir weavers mainly used narrow-strip looms, although they currently use *mudukare* looms to weave. The town's proximity to Kano City has enabled weavers to sell their handwoven cloth at markets within Kano and to interact with customers for special orders. In the past, according to Alhaji Sabo Minjibir, "Almost every household was involved in handweaving activities in Minjibir."[9] Minjibir and surrounding villages are renowned for particular types of wide-strip handwoven white cloth, known as *bullam*, as well as for the blue-black cloth known as *bunu* (see chapter 1) and for the black-white *saki* cloth (as has been discussed).[10] Indeed, while *saki* cloth is no longer woven in the Gwarzo area, Minjibir weavers continue to produce it for use by traditional rulers in Kano State and elsewhere in Nigeria.

When Ashiru Abdullahi visited the Minjibir Local Government Area in February 2018,[11] he was told that the Kano Textile Training Center in Minjibir had been closed for many years. He noted, however, that handwoven cloth continues to be produced in the area although weavers are found not in the district headquarters, Minjibir town, but in Gidan Gabas, which is one of the surrounding villages. He observed that there are more handweavers in Gidan Gabas than in Kayyu and that they weave more varieties of cloth, rather than weaving solely *mudukare* cloth as is done in Kayyu. Furthermore, the cloths woven in Gidan Gabas represent older styles of cloths woven for Hausa consumers although all are woven with factory-spun thread. Malam Muhammadu Haladu, one of the weavers interviewed, said that these cloths include *bunu, farin Hausa, gwado, ɗan barasoso, ɓarage, banbarashi,* and *bakin fara.*[12] These cloths are briefly described as follows:

1. *Bunu* cloth is woven on a wide-width loom using indigo-dyed thread. The warp of this wide-width cloth is clearly divided into two equal lengthwise parts. The right-hand part has six warp stripes of different widths[13] and each of the stripes has fine stripes within. All the stripes are of a lighter blue-black color, which alternate with the wider blue-black warp stripes.
2. *Farin Hausa* cloths are made with plain white narrow handwoven strips. Emirs and chiefs are the main patrons of this type of cloth. When they buy it, they will have it dyed with indigo and will use it to sew their royal garments.
3. *Gwado* is woven with blue-black warp thread, interspersed with alternating wide warp stripes of blue-black and white. Like *farin Hausa* cloth, it is mainly used for garments worn by traditional rulers, the emirs and chiefs.
4. *Dan barasoso* is woven with blue-black indigo-dyed warp threads with narrow warp stripes.
5. *Baraje* is made with indigo-dyed blue-black and white warp stripes.
6. *Bakin fara* (locust's mouth) is made with indigo-dyed warp thread with blue and blue-black weft bands at the top and bottom edges.

7. *Banbarashi* cloth comes in different colors with metallic threads used to decorate the two selvages. The main color may be deep brown, combined red and white stripes by the two edges, which are embellished with shiny metallic (fancy) threads added as decoration. This cloth is mainly used for *rawani* (turban) by emirs and chiefs as well as other traditional title holders in most emirates of Kano State.

These cloths, along with the finely checked *saki* cloths, historically have been associated with the political power and prestige of emirate rulers. Hence they are presently used by emirs and chiefs as well as other traditional title holders on special occasions such as for horse-riding processions known as Hawan Daushe during Sallah. For example, during the Hawan Daushe procession in July 2016, the emir of Kano, Alhaji Muhammadu Sanusi II, paid a Sallah visit to his mother, wearing a robe made of alternating handwoven warp-striped cloth strips, in purple and violet, tan and beige, and all tan, with leno weave and supplement warp patterning. While I do not know if the handwoven cloth strips used in making this robe came from Minjibir, it exemplifies the continuing demand by Kano traditional rulers for handwoven textiles worn on such occasions.

Aside from the greater number of different types of cloth being woven in Gidan Gabas, in the Minjibir Local Government Area, it is interesting to note that unlike the situation in Sabon Garin Ƙayyu, young men are actively taking part in handweaving. Ashiru Abdullahi noticed several younger men weaving along with older weavers, thus assuring the continuity of handweaving in the Minjibir area, unlike the situation in the Gwarzo area. Why this is the case is considered in the following section.

DISCUSSION

In September 2014, I questioned one older handweaver, Alhaji Al Hassan Ƙofa, about the future prospects of handweaving in Gwarzo.

Q: Do you think that in fifty years' time, this business will be operating?
A: Really, it is difficult to reach fifty years with this business—it will have stopped.
Q: Why?
A: Because no one is learning the business now; most of our traditional businesses are being abandoned.

Q: Why?

A: Because now, things they are modern. Things people cared for before, we have abandoned our tradition that we inherited.

Furthermore, the *mudukare* cloths being woven in Gwarzo are not worn by local residents. Rather, they are sold in markets to the south—in Niger State and in the confluence area—where there are large Fulani *bororo* cattle-rearing populations who use *mudukare* handwoven textiles. Also, younger Fulani men I interviewed in 2006 were less likely to wear traditional *mudukare* smocks and trousers, which suggests that such handwoven textiles are likely to be replaced by industrially woven cloth, which is less expensive and may be sewn in styles associated with a Fulani ethnic identity.

Thus there are several reasons for the decline in the production of handwoven textiles in the Gwarzo area, which reflect both demand and supply. One reason is that handwoven cloth was not competitively priced compared with industrially woven cloth, as Fulani young men explained to me. A second related reason has to do with cloth preferences. Industrially woven cloth is lightweight, washes and dries quickly, and is available in a wide range of colors and patterns. A third reason is the supply of handwoven cloth reflects the question of production. In the Gwarzo area, the number of weavers is drastically lower because most of them are elderly and some have died, while young men are not ready to take up weaving as their occupation. In an interview with Alhaji Usman Ƙayyu in Sabon Garin Ƙayyu, he said that the youths, especially those who attended schools with Western education, are not ready to do handweaving, but rather prefer government jobs. They do not have the patience to do handweaving; they prefer to do something that will fetch them quick money.[14]

The situation regarding handweaving differs in the Minjibir area. Young men, along with their elders, are continuing to weave a range of different, named cloths that had been woven mainly on narrow-strip looms for several centuries. While now using *mudukare* looms to produce wide-width textiles that replicate the patterns of older cloths, the continued practice of handweaving may be explained by cultural factors, particularly ethnicity and prestige. The types of warp-striped, checked *saki*, and white handwoven cloth that continues to be woven by Hausa weavers in Gidan Gabas is associated with a Hausa ethnic identity and with a proud emirate past. Perhaps the fact that the products of their looms are being used by high-ranking Hausa emirs and chiefs conveys a certain prestige that compensates for the slowness of their work. Indeed, Minjibir weavers may see themselves as part of a historical process that supports the continuing importance of traditional rulers in Hausa society, with their heavy robes and handwoven turbans worn during religious festivities and turbaning ceremonies. Hausa handweavers in Gwarzo have no such connection to their Fulani cattle-rearing customers.

Marion Johnson (1978) has hypothesized that craft work such as handweaving will continue as long as the cloths being woven are in demand, perhaps because of their beauty or because they are seen as symbols of ethnic identity and reflect pride in a time-honored past. This explanation is surely the case for weavers in the Minjibir area, part of the Kano Closed Settlement Zone, who see themselves as part of the long history of the great city of Kano. The situation in the Gwarzo area, however, contradicts Johnson's hypothesis. As Alhaji Usman has noted, there is considerable demand for *mudukare* cloths by Fulani consumers who are willing to pay a high price to acquire them, yet younger men in the Gwarzo area are not interested in handweaving despite the financial incentives. For them, the practice of handweaving might be considered an aesthetically unattractive form of work. Its slowness and repetitiveness contrast with the prestige of white-collar government jobs and the relative quickness of the Internet, which links workers with the global community. Not surprisingly, the youth, especially those who had Western education, preferred government jobs. Yet young men in Minjibir, some of whom surely have had Western education, are handweaving cloth for Hausa consumers, which suggests that ethnic identity on the part of both weavers and consumers should be incorporated into the Johnson hypothesis. Indeed, younger Fulani men who have settled in urban communities have themselves stopped wearing traditional dress, preferring to wear Hausa styles of clothing made with industrially woven materials (Maiwada 2013, 390). And while there is also demand for Fulani dress as costume, both in theatrical and dance performances as well as in photography studios (Maiwada 2013), industrially manufactured white cloth embroidered with pattern in brightly colored wool may serve these purposes equally well. Thus, as Alhaji Al Hassan Kofa said, handweaving will probably not continue in Gwarzo. Yet it is likely to continue in Minjibir.

CONCLUSION

The handweaving of strip-woven cloths has been practiced for centuries in most parts of northern Nigeria. Since the beginning of the twenty-first century, however, it has suffered a serious decline, although there were signs of its demise by the late 1970s. This situation reflects that fact that many master weavers have died and that young men are not interested in taking their place, particularly those living in urban areas who have Western education. Yet despite the decline in many parts of the north, in areas such as Minjibir, both young and old men are handweaving cloth for Hausa consumers. Thus there is every hope that the craft will survive in the next fifty years in Kano State and perhaps in other parts of northern Nigeria. Indeed, Alhaji Sa'idu Dattijo Adhama noted that the federal government is planning to budget substantial funds to revive traditional crafts, most especially traditional handweaving.[15] With the example of the village of Gidan Gabas, in the Minjibir Local Government Area where young men are taking up handweaving, there is every hope that more young men and perhaps young women will be encouraged by this revival, which, along with the continued patronage of Kano traditional rulers, will ensure the survival of handweaving in northern Nigeria.

NOTES

1. For background histories of Gwarzo and Minjibir, see Gwarzo 1999 and Smith 1997.

2. Alhaji Usman Kayyu, interview with Salihu Maiwada, February 11, 2018.

3. Alhaji Usman Kayyu, interview with Salihu Maiwada, November 2017, Sabon Garin Kayyu.

4. Malam Alhasan Kofa, interview with Salihu Maiwada, January 2018, Sabon Garin Kayyu.

5. When asked what his children are doing since they are not weavers, he said they attend schools to obtain a Western education. Two of them have just completed Federal College of Education. They are also doing farming, he added.

6. During a visit to the United Nigerian Textiles Ltd. mill in November 2017, I learned that the company needs raw cotton supplies for its operation.

7. Several local government officials were part of the management team. They included the managing director, director of small scale industry, chief industrial officer, accountant, industrial officer, and officer in charge of the Nigerian weaving industry, chief designer, salesman and advertisement officer (Sani 1990).

8. Alhaji Sa'idu Dattijo Adhama, interview with E. Renne and A. DanAsabe, February 6, 2018, Kano.

9. Abdulkarim DanAsabe, October 10, 2018, Kano.

10. *Bullam* is defined as "a white gown of very narrow strips of native weaving" (Bargery 1993 [1934], 128). Presumably, the names of the gown and of the handwoven cloth strips are the same. *Bunu* and *saki* cloths are also defined in the Bargery dictionary.

11. Ashiru Abdullahi is a postgraduate student of textile design at the Department of Industrial Design, Ahmadu Bello University–Zaria.

12. Malam Muhammadu Haladu, interview with Ashiru Abdullahi, February 11, 2018, Gidan Gabas.

13. Of the six stripes, two are about 4 cm wide while four are narrower, about 2 cm wide.

14. Alhaji Usman Ƙayyu, interviews with S. Maiwada, November 2017, Sabon Garin Ƙayyu.

15. Alhaji Sa'idu Dattijo Adhama, interview with S. Maiwada, February 6, 2018, Kano.

REFERENCES

Bargery, G. P. 1993 [1934]. *A Hausa-English and English-Hausa Dictionary*, 2nd ed. Zaria: Ahmadu Bello University Press.

Barth, Heinrich. 1857. *Travels and Discoveries in North and Central Africa*, vols. 1–3. New York: Harper.

Ferguson, Douglas. 1973. "Nineteenth Century Hausaland Being a Description by Imam Imoru of the Land, Economy, and Society of His People." PhD dissertation, University of California, Los Angeles.

Gwarzo, Ibrahim Bala. 1999. *Mazan Kwarai: Tarihin Samuwar Kasar Gwarzo*. Private publication.

Johnson, Marion. 1978. "Technology, Competition, and African Crafts." In *The Imperial Impact*, edited by C. Dewey and A. Hopkins, 259–69. London: Athlone Press.

Kriger, Colleen. 2006. *Cloth in West African History*. Lanham, MD: AltaMira Press.

Lamb, Venice, and Judith Holmes. 1980. *Nigerian Textiles*. Hertingfordbury: Roxford Books.

Maiwada, Salihu. 2013. "The Assessment of Fulani Society and Traditional Dress in Northern Nigeria." *Journal of International Academic Research for Multidisciplinary* 1, no. 8: 97–108.

Perani, Judith, and Norma Wolff. 1999. *Cloth, Dress, and Art Patronage in Nigeria*. Oxford: Berg.

Picton, John, and John Mack. 1979. *African Textiles*. London: British Museum.

Renne, Elisha. 1997. "'Traditional Modernity' and the Economics of Handwoven Cloth Production in Southwestern Nigeria." *Economic Development and Cultural Change* 45, no. 4: 773–92.

Sani, Binta. 1990. "A Nigerian Small-Scale Weaving Industry: The Gwarzo Experience." Master's thesis, Ahmadu Bello University, Zaria.

Shea, Philip J. 1975. "The Development of an Export-Oriented Dyed Cloth Industry in Kano Emirate in the Nineteenth Century." PhD dissertation, University of Wisconsin–Madison.

Smith, M. G. 1962. "Exchange and Marketing Among the Hausa." In *Markets in Africa*, edited by P. Bohannon and G. Dalton, 299–334. Evanston, IL: Northwestern University Press.

Smith, M. G. 1997. *Government in Kano 1350–1950*. Boulder, CO: Westview Press.

CHAPTER 4

Kaduna Textile Industry, Trade, and the Coming of Chinese Textiles

MOHAMMADU YAHAYA WAZIRI,

SALIHU MAIWADA, AND ELISHA RENNE

Kaduna Textiles Ltd (KTL), the first large textile mill to be built in Kaduna, in northern Nigeria, was opened on November 22, 1957 (David Whitehead & Sons 1973; Onyeiwu 1997, 238). Within its first year of operation, approximately eight million meters of baft material (unbleached plain weave cotton cloth known as *akoko*) woven with Nigerian-grown cotton had been produced.[1] Although not initially the first choice for siting the mill,[2] Kaduna, the capital of the Northern Protectorate, had the advantage of being situated along the Kaduna River, with access to locally grown cotton and rail service. The opening of this mill was a significant event as it represented the combined efforts of Northern Nigerian political leaders, officials from the Ministry of Trade and Industry and the Northern Regional Development Corporation, the management of the British textile manufacturing firm David Whitehead & Sons, and British colonial administrators. Its production of unbleached, bleached, and printed cotton textiles was appreciated by northern Nigerian women as it enabled them to dress fashionably without going to the expense of buying imported textiles described in chapter 2.

In the following years several other large textile mills were built, which included Nortex (with support from the Sudanese businessman E. A. Senoussi) in 1962, United Nigerian Textiles Ltd. (UNTL, with support from the Hong Kong–based Cha Group) in 1964, Arewa Textiles (with support from Japanese textile manufacturers) in 1965, and Finetex (which took over operations the Nortex plant in 1993 under a Chinese majority shareholder), among others (Andrae and Beckman 1999). Yet by 2005 Kaduna Textiles Ltd., Nortex/Finetex, and Arewa Textiles had all closed; UNTL closed in 2007. In 2010, it was reported that, country-wide, approximately 175 Nigerian textile mills had stopped production since the 1990s; by early 2010, only 24 remained in operation (Abubakar 2010). Rather than reviving the textile industry in Kaduna, the Structural Adjustment Program introduced in 1986 and implemented in 1987, which was formulated by the International Monetary Fund (IMF) and carried out by the Nigerian government, contributed to the industry's demise (Olukoshi 1993).[3] This program, which included currency devaluation and restrictions on federal spending in exchange for the continuation of IMF loans, was intended to promote local production, but it was inappropriate for the situation of nascent industrialization in Nigeria, where neither updated shuttle-less looms nor spare parts were manufactured locally. The causes of the textile industry's decline are complex, however, with a range of local and global political and economic factors contributing to the situation in Kaduna. Technological changes in the textile industry, neoliberal reforms and changing trade agreements, uneasy labor-management relations, obsolete equipment, inadequate infrastructure for providing electricity and water, reduced cotton production and increased textile imports—mainly from China (Minchin 2013)—as well as an influx of secondhand clothing from the West (Hansen 2000), have all contributed to the industry's demise. Furthermore, frequent shifts in political leadership during the independence era undermined support for the development of this industry. Yet it was the strength of local political leadership at the end of the colonial period and during the early independence period that led to the commencement of the textile industry in Kaduna in the first place, which suggests that such political vision might again be mustered to revitalize textile manufacturing in northern Nigeria.

This chapter examines the establishment and growth of textile manufacturing in Kaduna as well as the reasons for its decline. We begin with the plans for the opening of KTL in 1955, which was part of the transition from British colonial rule to Nigerian independence that was officially recognized in 1960. The main textile mills in Kaduna began operations during this decade. Following the end of the Nigerian Civil War (1967–1970) and the expansion of oil extraction—the "oil boom years"—textile manufacturing continued to expand. But with a fall in oil prices, the economic constraints of the early 1980s, and the 1986 introduction of the IMF-sponsored Structural Adjustment Program, textile manufacturing in Kaduna faltered during the 1990s.

This situation was exacerbated by the smuggling of Chinese cotton print and damask textiles into Kano's Kantin Kwari market, the largest textile market in northern Nigeria, and subsequently into Kaduna. The logistics of traders' considerable efforts to smuggle Chinese textiles from Cotonou, Benin, through Niger, and then into Kano are presented in detail. (Such shipments later continued to be smuggled to avoid customs duties, as will be discussed in chapter 6.) By 2007, all four of the largest mills had closed. On December 3, 2010, with the implementation of the Textile Revival Fund, one textile mill in Kaduna, United Nigeria Textiles Plc, reopened (Ahmadu-Suka 2011a; Mudashir 2010). However, the continuing irregular supply of electricity in Kaduna, changes in Nigerian government policies on textile imports, and increased Nigerian-Chinese trade and collaborative development projects had contradictory consequences for textile industry revival plans. We conclude the chapter with an assessment of the prospects of cotton textile manufacturing in Kaduna in the face of global economic forces and infrastructural problems that continue to work against these possibilities.

THE BEGINNINGS OF THE TEXTILE INDUSTRY IN KADUNA

The political context of the Kaduna Textiles Ltd. mill's opening in the final years of colonial rule in Nigeria reflected a major shift in British manufacturers' and colonial officials' views on manufacturing in the country. Outside of the Kano Citizens Trading Company (KCTC) mill established by the Kano Citizens Trading Company in Kano in 1949, which began production in 1952 (discussed in chapter 5), there had been no large modern textile mills set up in northern Nigeria, reflecting the British colonial policy of extracting raw materials from its colony for textile manufacturing in the UK. These textiles were then sold by the agents of British trading firms in Nigeria (Johnson 1974). In the 1950s, however, British manufacturers began to see the advantages of manufacturing closer to the source of raw materials—cotton—and customers—Nigerian consumers. Also shipping and rail services to Kaduna made the transport of equipment and building materials feasible.

Thus in 1954 the chairman of David Whitehead & Sons, Mr. J. C. Whittaker, established the David Whitehead & Sons Overseas Liaison Office to pursue these goals.[4] Yet the earlier antimanufacturing policy advocated by Sir Frederick Lugard, the governor-general of Nigeria between 1914 and 1919 (Johnson 1974, 182–84), had consequences for building and running a large textile mill; Nigerian officials and workers had no experience or training in the operation of such an enterprise.[5] Consequently, Northern Nigerian officials sought to partner with a textile manufacturing firm that could provide textile technology and expertise. Sir Ahmadu Bello, who was the premier of the Northern Regional government, was a major force behind industrial development in northern Nigeria (Paden 1986, 265). He became interested in the British manufacturing firm David Whitehead & Sons, possibly as a consequence of a visit to southern Rhodesia (now Zimbabwe), where he had seen the mill the company had built there, its first in Africa.[6]

In March 1955, the Northern Regional government invited David Whitehead & Sons officials to establish a textile mill in Kaduna, in collaboration with the Northern Regional Marketing Board (NRMB) and the Northern Regional Development Corporation (NRDC). Officials at David Whitehead & Sons also saw the advantages of siting a mill in Kaduna. In April 1955, Ahmadu Bello and officials from the NRDC, the NRMB, and David Whitehead & Sons met in the UK to discuss the details of becoming partners in a textile manufacturing plant in northern Nigeria. An agreement was subsequently negotiated to provide construction plans and equipment and to train a staff, and the agreement was signed in Rawtenstall on September 7, 1955, with Ahmadu Bello, Alhaji Aliyu, Turakin Zazzau (the minister of trade and industry, later director of the NRDC), other NRMB and NRDC board members, and officials of David Whitehead & Sons in attendance. The mill site was selected by the British firm Taylor Woodrow (West Africa) Ltd; Fred Fuller, as David Whitehead & Sons production manager, was instrumental in keeping the site preparation and mill construction on schedule. On November 22, 1957 the mill was opened amidst much fanfare, which was reported widely in the international press.

Kaduna Textile Mill's Early Operations

The mill began producing unbleached baft (*akoko*) of the sort that had earlier been manufactured in Manchester for the Nigerian market. Gordon Hartley, a former employee of David Whitehead & Sons and commercial manager of KTL, described the experimental process whereby the right combination of weave and starch led to the desired result:

> I remember various samples coming through from Kaduna which we had bound up at Higher Mill into a pretty folder which I could trail around Whitworth Street [in Manchester]. The first sample got me no further than UAC.

The grey cloth buyer there, Steve Goulding, almost laughed at what I showed him. It did, indeed, resemble a limp piece of rag. He showed me what he wanted—a fabric heavily filled with starch and calendered so that it almost shone. We sent the sample to Kaduna and eventually we had a product which I could confidently take around Manchester and Liverpool. (Hartley 2012)

Mill management and workers successfully produced increasing quantities of quality unbleached cotton cloth, which was attractive to agents from major textile firms operating in Nigeria and to discerning Nigerian customers (Pedler 1974).

Along with producing a desirable textile for the Nigerian market, it was also important that textile trading firms such as UAC, A. Brunnschweiler & Co. (known as ABC), and Paterson Zochonis bought Kaduna Textile Limited products and allowed it to use their company trademarks ("chop marks") on the textiles that were sold to these firms (see chapter 2). Nigerian traders who in turn bought this cloth wanted to see such marks, which increased their sales. According to Hartley:

The important thing was to get the customers—representative of trading firms—to give us their best 'chop marks'. The chop mark was a device stamped onto the top of each folded bolt of cloth along with the merchant's name: an eagle, a castle or some similar device which the Nigerian customer had come to recognize as a mark of reliable quality. This mark would wash out (along with the calendered finish we had striven so hard to replicate) but without this chop mark the premium price would not be reached. Fortunately, all the customers gave us their best chop marks. (Hartley 2012)

Gradually, the distribution of Kaduna Textiles Ltd. products shifted from trading firms in the United Kingdom to sales through their Nigerian offices, although the control of distribution remained in European hands. After Nigerian independence in 1960, however, KTL officials increasingly sought to sell bales to independent Nigerian traders who had their own distribution networks. KTL sales to Nigerian traders increased as production gathered pace and new products, such as bleached starched shirting, were developed. The production of bleached baft cotton cloth (known as *zauwati*) led to the production of a line of printed textiles under the Kaduna Textiles Ltd. name. An agreement with Northern Nigerian Textiles Mill in 1974 made this possible. This mill's owner, Mr. Ibrahim Yusuf Gardee, had decided to donate his majority shares (79 percent of the mill) to Ja'amatu Nasril Islam (JNI)—an umbrella organization for Islamic groups in northern Nigeria—when he left Nigeria. Because Abubakar Gumi, the director of JNI, did not want to be responsible for running a textile operation, he made a special arrangement with KTL; the company would take over the operation of Northern Nigerian Textiles Mill, with Gumi becoming member of the KTL board of directors (Loimeier 1997, 144). While printing was not carried out on the KTL mill site, the Northern Nigerian Textiles Mill (NNTM) provided color print facilities for Kaduna Textiles woven cotton cloth (Maiwada and Renne 2013). Its products included super print and wax print yardage as well as mattress and pillow cover materials, using rollers and flatbed screens for the former and engraved copper roller prints for the latter.

Cotton swatches from cotton print textiles produced by the NNTM and marketed by KTL were kept in books documenting customers' names and order dates. One popular pattern called batik was produced in October 1997 in three color combinations—blue/black/red/white, turquoise blue/black/red/white, and green/black/red/white, all with tan cracking on a central motif. Cloths with flower motifs were also popular. One swatch sample included in sales for May 2001 depicted a flower and leaves in orange, brown, black, and white. Indeed, color combinations often included red, orange, blue, and yellow along with black and white, as customers for KTL printed textiles preferred cloths with geometric and floral patterns in clear, bright colors within a certain color range.

THE EXPANSION OF THE KADUNA TEXTILE INDUSTRY IN THE 1970S

Aside from Kaduna Textiles Limited and the Northern Nigerian Textiles Mill, other textile firms, such as Arewa Textiles, UNTL, Norspin, and Nortex (later re-established as Finetex), encouraged by the success of KTL, began production in the following decade.

Arewa Textiles

Arewa Textiles, which consisted of a consortium of ten Japanese cotton spinning companies, began production in 1964. While the mill initially produced plain and bleached cotton cloth, it later opened a section for the production of wax and printed cotton textiles as well as army khaki cloth (on special order). According to Muhammed Buhari, who worked at Arewa Textiles from 1990 to 2005:

> In 1960, the Sardauna [Ahmadu Bello] went to Japan and the Japanese backers came to Nigeria to set up the company. The major shareholders were Japanese—the Overseas Spinning Investment Company, others were the Nigerian Fed Govt. After 1992, they packed up to Japan, then the management became Nigerian. The management of the company was experienced but not well educated—they had come through the ranks.[7]

Some workers did get special overseas training, as one Arewa Textiles worker who was transferred to the printing department in September 1972 explained:

> By May 1973 I was sent to Japan for further training for one year, yes, before I came back to printing. They were training me in maintenance, to maintain the machine. . . . I worked with Kasuna Sinko, they deal with printing, because if you are in maintenance you must know about printing. . . . I was there for almost 4 months before I left there for Kansaki Iron Works, that one is in Wakaiyama City. . . . Because when they send you to Japan you have to go to the training school, you have to go to language school to teach you the language.[8]

When Gideon Oloruntobi returned to the Arewa Textile mill, he was assigned to printing maintenance where he worked until 2004, when Arewa Textiles closed. With his training and experience, he was able to describe in detail the machines, which were mainly from Japan, and processes involved in printing at this mill.

> We have a roller printing machine—from Japan. Then we have the washing machine—that was also from Japan. Also, we have steaming machines . . . a hot stenter and J-box for scalding and bleaching. Before we can print we have to make the cloth white. . . . After bleaching we send it to drying machine, then we send it to another stentor again. . . . Shrinkage will take place during the scalding so after scalding, we dry it and . . . send it to another stentor to get the required width we want. So many ingredients are part of preparation for printing, there are so many things involved.

Despite the extensive knowledge and expertise of Arewa Textiles workers, there were problems that affected its production, as Muhammed Buhari noted. "There were serious problems even at the beginning in 1990 when I started. The major problem was obsolete equipment. This equipment had not been replaced in 35 years, since the company started in 1965. Power generation was the second problem, after obsolete equipment." [9] While there has been recent talk of renovating the Arewa Textiles mill (even after the fire there in 2015), the mill remains closed as of December 2017.

United Nigeria Textiles Ltd.

The United Nigerian Textiles Limited (UNTL) mill—the largest in northern Nigeria and the first overseas operation for the newly established Hong Kong–based Cha Group, headed by Mr. Cha Chi Ming—was opened in Kaduna in 1964. UNTL represented a partnership between the Cha Group and the Northern Nigerian Regional Development Corporation (Renne 2019). In the following years, the Cha Group established several other mills in northern Nigeria, which included the vertically integrated textile mill Funtua Textiles Ltd. (in Funtua, Katsina State, in 1978), in association with the Nigerian government, and Zamfara Textiles (in Gusau, Zamfara State, in 1966). Both Chinese and Nigerian managers and workers were involved in these mills, which by 1980 provided plain and printed cotton textiles both to the Nigerian market as well as to other markets in West Africa (Axelsson 2012, 41). In 1980, the company acquired equipment from the spinning mill Norspin, which facilitated the opening of its spinning mill, United Spinners Limited, renamed Unitex in 1982:

> To comply with the Federal Government's Policy of making the country self-sufficient in yarn by 1983, another subsidiary company, namely United Spinners Limited, was incorporated on 20th February, 1980. . . . United Spinners Limited will engage in the production of cotton and cotton/polyester blended spun yarn in Kaduna and supply most if not all its products to United Nigerian Textiles Limited (UNTL 1979).

By acquiring the Norspin mill's assets and opening the Unitex mill, UNTL management used a strategy of backward integration in order to avoid the expense of imported yarn and also to take advantage of local production of cotton. But as the number of textile manufacturing mills grew, local cotton producers could not supply sufficient raw cotton for textile production needs.

The problem of access to sufficient cotton for spinning and spare parts to repair old machines hampered initial production at Unitex:

> Production of yarn has started at this company with a total output of 1,832 tons of 24's for the year under review. The labour force was 600. It could not achieve full production due to shortage of new materials and necessary spare parts for renovation of the old machines. With availability of import licenses, it is hoped that we would reach our production target after the installation of 10,000 additional spindles. (UNTL 1982)

Despite this initial setback, Unitex was able to increase production: "in 1983, the total production was 2,127 tons of 25's Spun Yarn which reflects an increase of about 20% over the previous year" (UNTL 1983). Subsequently, the Cha Group was able to draw upon multinational companies for cotton, yarn, and dyeing supplies (Andrae and Beckman 1999, 109–10), unlike other textile manufacturers during this period of growth, which reflected the larger political economy, namely the "oil boom" years of the 1970s.

In 1983, UNTL became a major shareholder in Supertex Limited mill, which gave the company access to its printing facilities for UNTL bleached textiles. Due to economic constraints, however, the company's management was only able to open a single production line. Nonetheless, "the demand for its special feature high quality wax print . . . has been well established in the market. . . . Supertex Limited has plans to expand its existing production capacity and to diversify its finishing facilities" (UNTL 1984). Thus, by the late 1980s, the chairman was able to report increased production at the Supertex Ltd. mill, which reflected its production of a line of higher quality textile prints that were attractive to Nigerian consumers as well as to foreign buyers:

> The Company continues to perform well during the year, recording another 5% increase in production. Supertex Limited, with its reputation for superb quality products, already well established and highly patronized both in Nigeria and the neighbouring ECOWAS countries, has also recorded a 17% increase in export material. (UNTL 1989)

By 1990, the Supertex mill was reported to be exporting up to 25 percent of its products, but the continuing decline in textile manufacturing viability in Nigeria after 2000 led to the mill's closure in October 2007. The Supertex Ltd. mill was reopened after textile revival funds were distributed to UNTL in 2010, and in 2017 the mill manufactures polyester woven materials used in mattress covers and unbleached cotton baft sold in local markets and sent to the Nichemtex Industries Ltd. mill in lkorodu, Lagos, for printing.

Norspin, Nortex, Finetex

In 1963, Norspin, a cotton spinning mill with financial support from the British trading firm United Africa Company and the English Sewing Cotton Company, began production (Kirby 1975, 507). This mill was designed to supply handloom yarn for the United Africa Company's merchandise trade, specifically, to produce yarn for conversion into sewing thread in English Sewing Cotton's Lagos factory and cotton cord for the Dunlop tire factory. By 1980, however, the company closed its doors, as was noted by UNTL's chairman, Cha Chi Ming: "As you may have heard, Norspin Limited went into liquidation towards the end of 1980" (UNTL 1980).[10] As has been discussed, the plant's equipment was taken over by UNTL and used in its newly opened Unitex plant.

The Nortex textile mill was also opened in 1963, by a private investor, E. A. Seroussi, a Sudanese entrepreneur.[11] In the beginning of operations, the mill produced unbleached and bleached cotton cloth that was suitable for dyeing and printing. As was the case with other Kaduna mills in the early 1980s, Nortex production suffered from its inability to obtain new equipment and raw materials. In 1983, Mr. K. S. Wong (a Hong Kong Chinese businessman) became the principal shareholder as a result of his own holdings and his indirect holdings in Goldfort Co. Ltd., which served as a technical advisor to him. With this change in principal ownership, the Nortex mill continued production under the name Finetex. "Finetex Limited, incorporated in 1990 as a subsidiary Company of Nortex (Nig) Limited, started production in 1993 and specialized in production of printed textile fabrics using modern production facilities. . . . Goldfort Limited assisted Finetex Limited as technical partners in sourcing grey fabrics internationally and making available quality workforce for Finetex" (Gombe 2016).[12]

The Finetex mill specialized in cotton spinning, weaving, and printing super prints and wax prints for the Nigerian market. Alhaji Yusuf Iliyasu worked at both the Nortex and Finetex mills for eight years as a spinner; he was also one of the National Union of Textile Garment and Tailoring Workers of Nigeria (NUTGTWN) leaders. According to him, everything was going well until they were confronted with several problems. It began when the company management was unable to pay the suppliers of cotton lint, which

Fig. 4.1. Workers at the Nortex (Nig) Limited mill in Kaduna, overseeing spindles producing yarn, November 14, 1962. (Photograph by Bello, courtesy of the Kaduna State Ministry of Information.)

was used in the factory for spinning cotton thread. The second problem arose when wholesale customers, who were required to deposit a fixed amount of money before they could make orders, did not receive the textiles they had paid deposits for because production could not meet demand. The third problem was the nonsettlement services bills, such as water bills and electricity bills. The final problem was the nonpayment of workers' salaries. These problems brought about the closure of the Finetex mill in September 2005.

Chellco Textile Industries Limited

Unlike the others, the Chellco Textile Industries mill remains in production in Kaduna. The Chellco mill was opened in 1978, with 60 percent Indian ownership (Andrae and Beckman 1999, 115) and production began in 1980, with some workers recruited from the failing Nortex and Norspin mills (Andrae and Beckman 1999, 217). The company began with a focus on blankets of various grades and sizes. One group of blankets sold reflects consumer tastes for lighter-weight, colored striped and plaid blankets made with acrylic fiber, which is imported (Bashir 2013). Another group of solid-color blankets, referred to as "hospital blankets," are made for institutional users: hospitals, schools, military units, and prisons (Chellco Industries Ltd. 2017).

The Chellco mill is small compared with other textile mills in Kaduna such as KTL and UNTL, and in this sense it is more like the smaller, specialized textile mills in Kano discussed in chapter 6. Chellco also had more irregular labor relations as compared with other Kaduna mills, in part due to the seasonality of demand for blankets. Yet despite regular closures of the mill and repeated layoffs, the company has managed to continue production, expanding its offerings to bedspreads and acrylic yarns. In 2013, Chellco was one of the three companies in Kaduna State that received a Textile Revival Fund loan, and it has continued to manufacture blankets since that time (Agbese et al. 2016).[13]

TEXTILE/PRINT PRODUCTION: MILL WORKERS' EXPERIENCES

Various means of cotton print production have been carried out in Kaduna textile mills, as was discussed by Gideon Oloruntobi, who was in charge of printing maintenance at the Arewa Textiles mill. Other mills, such as Kaduna Textiles Limited (KTL), did not have printing facilities on site. Later, however, the Northern Nigerian Textiles Mill provided color print facilities for woven cotton cloths produced by the KTL mill until the company closed in 2002. Mohammadu Yahaya Waziri, one of the chapter authors, worked at the Northern Nigerian Textiles Mill as a designer during his National Youth Service Corps year, from August 1981 to August 1982. He described the equipment and techniques used in printing at the mill:

> Designs were brought to us and we enlarged them to the size of the screen or the circumference of the copper roller. [We were also responsible for] color separation. You see, the designs had to be enlarged on transparent films to the size of the screen before the colors are picked out using opaque paint. . . . I did everything manually, for about four different de-

signs. What I can say about Kaduna Textiles Limited is that its machinery is outdated . . . the weaving looms were using wooden attachments to throw the shuttles, so that the shuttle could fly off the loom at any time and harm the weaver. . . . When I was at KTL there was also the problem of raw materials and also management problems . . . the production manager, he trained as a colorist and rose to the rank of production manager—he got his experience on the job.

Waziri's experience of working at KTL enabled him to see firsthand the problems of the company. Northern Nigeria Textiles Mill continued to use the labor-intensive practice of screen printing until it closed.

However, other companies, such as UNTL, began using engraved rollers to print textiles. Another of this chapter's authors, Salihu Maiwada, who was an industrial design student with a specialization in textile design and who interned at UNTL during the early 1980s, explained the company's printing practices:

Beginning in 1983, I moved to the Engraving Department where I had to go through an orientation before beginning work. A number of processes were carried out before designs were transferred to rollers, which included color separation, photography, film processing, and the transfer of designs from film to copper rollers, after which designs were engraved on the rollers. As a design graduate, I only worked on color separation. As UNTL was owned by the Cha Group, a Hong Kong textile firm, there were many Chinese workers at the mill. . . . One man, Mr. Tung, from Hong Kong worked with me in the Engraving Department and we became friends, corresponding for several years even after he left Nigeria.[14]

The close collaboration between Nigerian and Chinese workers and management enabled UNTL to continue production, with exports to other West African countries comprising about 25 percent of its textile production by the early 1990s. While the indigenization of Nigerian industries promoted by the Nigerian Enterprises Promotion Decrees of 1972 and 1977 did not affect UNTL, which already had integrated Nigerian shareholders and managers within the company (Andrae and Beckman 1999, 34–35), they did affect KTL; by 1979, David Whitehead & Sons expatriate staff had left Nigeria. This loss of management and training expertise contributed to positions being filled by those with "on-the-job training," as Waziri noted.

PROBLEMS FOR THE KADUNA TEXTILE INDUSTRY:
POLITICAL AND ECONOMIC REFORMS

Onyeiwu (1997, 244) evaluated the situation of the Nigerian textile industry in 1997 and noted that while the textile mills in Kaduna were still operating, they were working with obsolete equipment, without the capital to obtain spare parts, and without a regular source of electricity. KTL was, as he put it, "on the verge of collapse." By 2002, KTL had closed.[15] Arewa Textiles literally shut its doors early in 2005. As one former worker explained, "We went for Christmas break in December 2004 and when we came back in January 2005, we found the front gate of the company locked."[16]

The closing of textile mills in Kaduna partly reflected the fall in international oil prices in the early 1980s (Andrae and Beckman 1999, 38), which contributed to a reduction in government support for textile manufacturing in northern Nigeria. Muhammed Buhari worked at Arewa Textiles, the other large textile mill in Kaduna founded through the efforts of Ahmadu Bello, who secured Japanese backing in the early 1960s. Buhari's observations of the problems of Arewa Textiles, where he worked for fifteen years until the mill closed in 2005, clarifies the particular problems of production that contributed to its closing:

> I began as supervisor, then I became a team manager, and then manager in charge of production control and maintenance. Most of the machines were from Japan, a few were from China and a few from Germany. Printed textiles (*atamfa*) were the main cloths we produced, both wax resist prints and roller prints, which were sold under the names Superprint, Africa Print, and Arewa Superwax. We also produced textiles for special requests such as army khakis. There were serious problems, even at the beginning in 1990 when I started. The major problem was obsolete equipment. . . . The problem started after SAP [Structural Adjustment Program] because the devalued naira made getting new machinery very expensive. So they could not compete with the price of foreign imported textiles but also the quality. They actually tried a private generator for power, but it was so expensive, their costs increased threefold. The black oil/fuel that they used was too expensive.[17]

Buhari noted that with the skyrocketing cost of imported spare parts for power stations and mill equipment, managers made do with obsolete equipment. One oft-cited reason for the mills' decline was that outdated textile equipment was neither repaired nor replaced because the foreign currency needed for spare parts and new equipment was not available. Yet even if spinning machines, winders, and looms had been replaced, they would have been prohibitively expensive to operate due to the irregular supply of electricity and the need to use "black oil" as a source of power. The problem of energy supply was cited in the literature, in newspaper articles, and by textile workers alike. As Gideon Oloruntobi, the former manager of printing maintenance at Arewa Textiles observed:

> It's a serious factor because even if the government provides money today, I will not deceive you, no textile mill can run successfully, no amount of money [will help], unless electricity is addressed. That one has to be addressed, otherwise you will waste the money on diesel, you will waste it on the black oil . . . which will make the cost of a yard or a meter uncompetitive.[18]

The economic constraints on textile production due to the lack of electricity and lack of spare parts led to temporary shutdowns and stoppages (Onyeiwu 1997, 244–45). These interruptions affected mill managers' ability to pay workers in a timely fashion and led to periods of compulsory leave. While the KTL mill continued operations (Andrae and Beckman 1999, 15–17), after 1984 a new manager was put in place who streamlined production by closing the third and fourth mills, refurbishing equipment through salvaging spare parts from decommissioned machinery, and putting fewer workers in charge of more machines (Andrae and Beckman 1999, 104). These actions improved production and even led to a slight profit in 1986. However, inefficiencies of production and the relatively high prices of KTL products undermined their competitiveness, particularly with respect to increasing contraband Chinese textile imports beginning in the 1990s and continuing through 2010 (Andrae and Beckman 1999, 286).

Trade: International Agreements and National Textile Import Policies

When Kaduna Textiles Limited began production in 1957, it was protected by customs tariffs that had been instituted by British colonial officials to prevent European and Japanese textile manufacturers from flooding the Nigerian market with their products. As a result, Hartley noted, locally manufactured textiles had a significant advantage:

We [at KTL] did have an important starting advantage in that there was a customs tariff for textile products entering Nigeria that amounted to eight pence per square yard. In pre-naira currency we planned to sell our baft at seventeen shillings and sixpence per ten-yard piece (twenty-one pence per yard), which gave us a substantial advantage over the imported product. The West Africa merchants knew that, given a satisfactory product, they would have to deal with us. (Hartley 2012)

This tariff of approximately 45 percent for less expensive textiles such as plain baft, piece-dyed, and printed cotton textiles remained in place until 1977, when a ban on imported textiles was implemented, replacing the unsustainable tariff system (Onyeiwu 1997, 243).

While most cotton textiles produced in Kaduna mills were sold domestically, a series of international trade agreements affected their production in some ways. The Multifibre Arrangement was put in place in 1974 to protect developing countries' nascent textile industries, with local quotas on imports being introduced. The 1977 Nigerian ban on imported textiles, while widely ignored, reflected this protectionist dynamic.[19] However, the World Trade Organization's General Agreement on Tariffs and Trade (GATT), which included the Multifibre Arrangement, was phased out in 1994 and the transitional Agreement on Textiles and Clothing ended in 2004 (GATT; World Trade Organization 2015). Thus quotas were largely ended in favor of local tariffs (Brambilla, Khandelwal, and Schott 2010, 350).

Yet, as Mohammadu Waziri has argued, the decision by the Nigerian government to accede to the World Trade Organization agreement was the main government policy that contributed to the collapse of the Kaduna textile industry. The editorial board of the northern Nigerian newspaper *Daily Trust* (2007) concurred: "Nigeria's once thriving textile industry has been particularly devastated by the cheaper imports from Asia due to the government's deregulation of foreign trade and capital investment in the name of globalization as Nigeria joined the World Trade Organisation (WTO)."[20]

THE SMUGGLING OF CHINESE COTTON PRINTS INTO NORTHERN NIGERIA

Chinese-made textiles had been widely available to Nigerian consumers, as Chinese and Nigerian brokers had brought them to Nigeria for sale before

Nigeria's signing of the WTO agreement in 2004. In the mid-1980s, there was an upsurge in textile manufacturing in mainland China, particularly in areas designated as Special Economic Zones (Zeng 2011), where foreign investors were given incentives to build new textile mills with updated equipment (Perkins 1997). This increased capacity, and Chinese business acumen in identifying the African textile market as one in which they could sell their textile products, prompted them to begin exporting large containers of their cotton textiles to northern Nigeria.

Border Crossings

Nigerian and Chinese textile dealers began bringing in massive quantities of Chinese cotton textiles mainly through Cotonou, Benin, in the late 1990s. Since textile imports were banned by the Nigerian government at that time, an elaborate system for smuggling textiles to Kantin Kwari market in Kano was developed (Burgis 2015). Nigerian cloth dealers would first go to China and select the textiles they wanted to ship to Cotonou. The containers were unloaded at the port but were not opened there. A small payment was made to Benin customs officials, then the containers were loaded onto trucks and taken north through Benin to the Niger border, crossing the bridge at Malanville and entering Niger at Gaya, where Nigerien customs officers would ask them to pay the customs fee.

While the Niger duty fee was half as much as the Nigerian duty fee, this amount was negotiable, so that when a driver would say he could not afford the required amount, he and his truck would be escorted to Birnin Konni, where the head customs officer was approached. The driver would give the customs official his passport with a certain amount of CFA currency inside "to reduce the duty you will pay" from the original amount quoted. If the customs official accepted the reduction, he would hand back the passport minus the CFA. This back and forth would continue until the officer returned the driver's passport with the CFA intact; this meant he had reached the limit of his deduction and that the driver must pay the agreed-upon remaining duty. After making this payment, he was free to continue through Niger to the Nigerian border south of Maradi.

Inhabitants of the numerous small villages along the border facilitated the border crossing just south of Dan Issa, Niger, on the road known as NR1 to Katsina.[21] Once at the border, the driver would then be asked to open a container to reveal its goods. During the time when imported textiles were banned in Nigeria, the customs officer would then arrest the driver, after

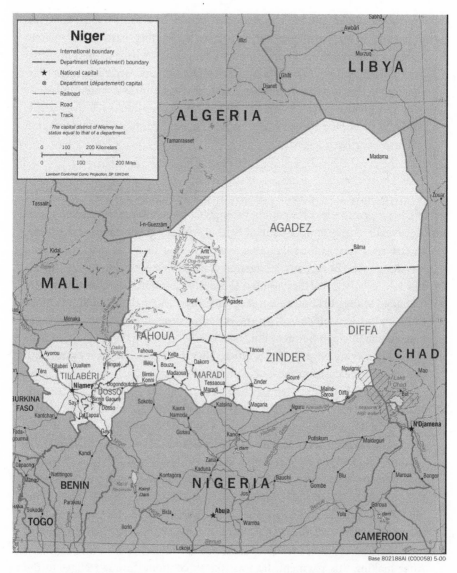

Map 4.1. Map of Niger showing smuggling route through Benin, Niger, and Nigeria. (Gaya-Birnin Konni-Maradi-Kano; produced by the U.S. Central Intelligence Agency, 2000.)

which the driver would make sufficient payments to customs officials. The customs people would distribute the payment amongst themselves and the truck would be allowed to pass between the hours of 2 a.m. and 4 a.m. By 8 a.m., the truck with its container of Chinese textiles would reach dealers (mainly Lebanese and Nigerian businessmen) in Kantin Kwari market in Kano.

THE COLLAPSE OF THE KADUNA TEXTILE INDUSTRY

In 2010, the Nigerian government announced its decision to abandon the textile import ban initially implemented in 1977. While this action further contributed to increased imports of Chinese-manufactured textiles to Nigeria, three of the major textiles mills in Kaduna had already closed before the lifting of the textile ban. With the closure of many Nigerian textile manufacturing firms in both Kaduna and Kano, cloth traders had fewer sources of cloth.

In the past, dealers working for trading companies such as Paterson Zochonis and UAC had made bulk purchases of cloth that were sold in small quantities to individual traders. The closing of the many mills ended this distribution system, and traders then obtained their cloth from Nigerian wholesale brokers who worked with Chinese trading firms in Kano. However, some of these Nigerian brokers have connections with textile firms in China and make purchases directly from them, either by setting up offices in China or through digital business communication (see chapter 6).

Nigerian traders are no longer going to China as before, though, because the N500 (approximately $3.00 or £2.00) profit per package is not enough to make the travel pay. The Chinese can send digital photographs of cloth samples to be duplicated in their mills, just as Nigerians did in the past.[22] With fewer Nigerian traders going to China to order and buy cloth, Chinese traders themselves have largely taken over the textile wholesale marketing of Chinese textiles, in Kaduna[23] but mainly in Kano.

While many Nigerians blame the Chinese for underselling Nigerian textiles and hence putting Nigerian mills out of business, "the collapse of Nigeria's local textile industry cannot be solely laid at the door of low-priced Chinese goods," as Ian Taylor (2007, 634) has observed. Rather, with the lack of a regular supply of electricity, despite government promises to improve the situation, "it is virtually impossible even for the most efficient Nigerian textile manufacturer to compete with Chinese products." The global dominance of Chinese and Indian textiles has been noted in reports from the early 2000s:

A WTO [World Trade Organization] study released in September [2004?] showed that China and India would probably come to dominate about eighty per cent of the global textile market in the post-MFA [Multifibre Arrangement] era, while the remaining twenty per cent would be shared by the rest of the world. (Phiri and Nduru 2005)

This situation raises the question of whether this dominance is in the interest of northern Nigerians. With a large youthful population and widespread unemployment in northern Nigeria (Ahmad and Akor 2012), some politicians and union activists have recommended reviving the textile industry, which historically has been a major employer in the region, as a way of addressing the unemployment problem. Several programs have been put forward in recent years to revitalize the textile industry, to improve the power infrastructure, and to increase cotton production.

The Textile Revival Fund and the Cotton, Textile, and Garment Development Fund

With the closure of KTL in 2002, Arewa Textiles in 2005, and UNTL in 2007, former president Olusegun Obasanjo announced a plan just prior to leaving office in 2007 to establish a N70 billion fund (which was later increased to N100 billion) that would provide moribund mills with loans to revive the industry. By September 2009, however, funds had not yet been disbursed, in part because the procedures for administering the loans had still not been finalized (Abubakar 2008).

The following year, Namadi Sambo, then the vice president of Nigeria, set up a committee to reorganize revival efforts (Shehu 2010). By the end of March 2011, Salisu Umar, chairman of the textile section of the Manufacturers Association of Nigeria, reported that "At least 60 per cent of textile companies in the country have accessed loans from the N100 billion textile revival fund" (Shosanya 2011). The textile revival committee facilitated the loan made to the largest Kaduna textile mill, UNTL, which was reopened in December 2010 (Aremu 2010).

This political support led to the Nigerian government's ongoing attempts to revive the industry with the N100 billion Cotton, Textile and Garment Development Fund in 2009. The reopening of UNTL in December 2010 raised the hopes of former UNTL workers (Daily Trust 2009). The fund enabled UNTL managers to hire more than nine hundred workers—involved in "Production, Administration, Accounts, Engineering, Computer, Spinning, and Weaving"—as well as to buy new spinning and weaving equipment (Ahmadu-Suka 2011b). This number reflects approximately a quarter of the mill's former work force. While producing textiles for the domestic market, UNTL continues to work with a skeleton staff, as the many and complex problems facing the Kaduna textile industry remain to be addressed.[24] By April 2013, some workers had been laid off due to poor market conditions, irregular electricity, and a shortage of cotton:

> A textile worker in Kaduna, Ibrahim Ezekiel, while speaking on the plight of textile workers said, 'Our company [UNTL] has sent us away. We are now on a three-week compulsory leave. Our company was reopened for business in 2010 by Vice President Namadi Sambo. Since that time, the company has not operated at optimal capacity. What we are doing here are spinning and weaving while the final printing is done in Lagos. There has been shortage of cotton and the situation in the country is so bad that the only option left for our management was to send us on a three-week compulsory holiday. We are on holiday because the company can't produce anything for now in spite of the intervention fund. . . . Unlike countries like China where government moderates importation of finished goods, Nigeria's borders are porous. . . . Another reason our companies can't compete with companies in other countries is the foreign companies have access to frequent electric supply with low bills. We don't have constant electricity in Nigeria and the bills are also high which makes our company, owned by Chinese, to run the business at a loss.' (Isuwa 2013)

In 2016, UNT Plc in Kaduna resumed cotton thread and textile manufacturing, albeit on an intermittent and reduced scale. Thus, despite the government's efforts to provide a textile revival fund in 2009, the textile manufacturing industry has not fully recovered (Olakitan 2015). In July 2016, the distribution of the remaining N40 billion from the Cotton, Textile and Garment Development Fund was suspended. Hadiza Olaosebikan, a Bank of Industry spokesperson, remarked that the government "realized that the challenges facing the sector is more than finance" (Agbese et al. 2016).

In addition to the problems of irregular electricity, outdated machinery, and smuggled textiles, the difficulty in acquiring raw cotton is another problem, as Usman Saulawa, director of the Kaduna Chamber of Commerce, Industry, Mines and Agriculture, observed:

> We seem to be much more concerned about textile industries and not giving emphasis to cotton production. If you observe, the cotton production has drastically gone down, a number of cotton farmers are either trying to survive or have directed their efforts towards doing other things. The cotton belt from Gusau in Zamfara State to Funtua in Katsina State, part of Kano, Bauchi, Gombe up to Maiduguri in Borno State is now a thing of the past. (Agbese et al. 2016)

The Raw Materials Research and Development Council, in collaboration with the Institute of Agricultural Research (at Ahmadu Bello University, Samaru), distributed improved cotton seeds to cotton farmers in nine states in 2015 and 2016 (Agbo 2016). It is hoped that cotton seed distribution and farming have been augmented by the introduction of two varieties of high-yielding genetically modified BT cotton (Sa'idu 2018).

Revival of Kaduna Textiles Limited

In August 2017, the Turkish textile firm SUR entered into an agreement with the New Nigerian Development Company to renovate the textile manufacturing company Kaduna Textiles Limited. Initially, the company was to refurbish the mill with updated equipment to produce military uniforms, then it was expected that other garments would also be manufactured. According to Alhaji Ali Gombe, chairman of the Restructuring Committee–KTL, "SUR will provide 35 percent of the total funds while the balance would be shared between the Federal Government and 19 Northern states" (*Daily Trust* 2017). While parties involved planned to move forward on this project, the SUR management's insistence that a large prepaid contract for uniforms from the Ministry of Defense be provided led to the abandonment of the project.[25] Nonetheless, other possibilities are being explored. In November 2017, the textile company Vlisco Group met with the Nigerian minister of finance about the possibility of investing in the Nigerian cotton and textile industries (Muhammad 2017). Also in November 2017, the speaker of the House of Representatives, Yakubu Dogara, opened public hearing on two bills organized by the Committee on Industry. The bills cover local participation in cotton, textiles, and garments as well as infrastructure buildup regarding the textile industry (Krishi 2017). These possibilities offer hope that eventually the textile industry will be revived in Kaduna (see epilogue).

CONCLUSION

In a way, textile manufacturing and distribution practices in Nigeria have come full circle, approximating the situation in the early 1950s, when Nigerians obtained their manufactured textiles from England (and to a lesser extent from France and Japan) and when European agents working for foreign marketing firms distributed textiles to Nigerian traders. With the decline of Kaduna textile manufacturing, imported textiles once again dominate the market, although they are from China, not England. Similarly, with the liberalization of imported textiles, Chinese textile companies and trading firms with overseas offices in Kano and Lagos now distribute to Nigerian wholesale brokers who sell textiles to Nigerian traders. Perhaps discussions to revitalize Kaduna textile manufacturing will succeed, following the earlier example of KTL, which represented the collaboration of Nigerian political leaders, government agencies, and foreign manufacturing partners. It is worth noting, though, that KTL's old partner, David Whitehead & Sons, is no longer manufacturing textiles either.[26] This situation raises the question of whether textile production for domestic markets by national textile industries using local labor and raw materials is a worthy social as well as an economic goal. That the Chellco Industries mill and some of the textile mills in Kano are still operating suggests that achieving such goals may be possible in smaller, more specialized factories, a subject which is examined in the following chapter.

NOTES

1. David Whitehead & Sons (1957).

2. Kano was considered first, based on its history as a major textile production center with an experienced management and labor force. However, Kaduna, as the regional administrative capital, located near cotton-growing regions, the Kaduna River and a rail service, was eventually chosen as the site of the first major mill in northern Nigeria (Paden 1986, 264).

3. As is discussed in chapter 5, the Structural Adjustment Program had a similar effect on the Kano textile manufacturing industry.

4. Hartley 2012; see also Onyeiwu 1997, 239.

5. As was discussed in chapter 3, the Department of Development and Welfare established textile training centers to encourage floor loom handweaving in Nigeria and to provide employment for returning soldiers (Renne 1997). Knowledge of handweaving, however, was hardly preparation for using industrial looms and the associated card-

ing, spinning, dyeing, and finishing equipment, nor were most veterans interested in handweaving as an occupation.

6. Nich Rutherford, interview with Jaclyn Kline, March 2, 2012, Minchinhampton, UK. This mill has since been transferred to a Zimbabwean firm in 2001 and subsequently closed (Nduna 2016).

7. Muhammed Buhari, interview with E. Renne, July 8, 2010, Samaru-Zaria.

8. Gideon Oloruntobi, interview with E. Renne, February 28, 2012, Kaduna.

9. Muhammed Buhari, interview with E. Renne, July 8, 2010, Samaru-Zaria.

10. According to one of the chapter authors, Mohammadu Waziri, the Norspin factory was closed by the Nigerian government when it was discovered that the Grade A cotton that was being spun into yarn was being exported to European textile industries.

11. He also opened the Zamfara Textiles Industries Ltd. Mill in Gusau in 1965 (Kirby 1975, 507). This mill, which produced unbleached, bleached, and dyed cotton cloth, was acquired by UNTL in the following year.

12. Mr. Wong eventually relocated to the Benin Republic. Based on his experience, Mohammadu Waziri explains the reason for his move. "In 1996, Finetex Textiles Company contacted me to meet with foreign traders (those who usually smuggle the textiles from Nigeria to their countries) to buy Finetex cloth directly from the company using a letter of credit because the value of the Nigerian currency (naira) had fallen in 1996. I traveled to Lagos and met with traders, offering the incentive of producing better quality products if they could pay with foreign currencies. This arrangement was made with Mr. Wong. The traders, however, confessed that none of them was rich enough to trade with his own capital; all of them borrowed money from their home governments with the agreement of sharing their profits. If they used a letter of credit their governments would know their volume of trade. Then they would need to share all their profits and pay tax on all their income, so they declined the arrangement. Mr. Wong moved to the Benin Republic so that he could sell Finetex materials with other currencies rather than the naira."

13. The other two companies are Zaria Industries Limited, which produces tarpaulin materials for tents (Zaria Industries Limited 2018) and United Nigerian Textiles Limited in Kaduna, which currently produces unbleached baft material and polyester woven materials, as has been discussed.

14. See CHA Textiles—History (Cha Group 2012). Information about Cha Textiles is also available from the company website: http://www.chatextiles.com/english/index.html (accessed September 2, 2012); see also Andrae and Beckman 1999, 109.

15. Kaduna Textiles Limited, the oldest mill in Kaduna, was using old looms with wooden fly-shuttles. Although KTL upgraded its weaving equipment, the Arewa Textiles and United Nigerian Textiles Limited had faster looms and better print textiles. Finetex wove finer textiles with looms that were even faster, although by 2007 these mills had all closed. They were unable to compete with high-speed Chinese looms.

16. Ayuba Mamman, interview with E. Renne, August 7, 2012, Kaduna.

17. Muhammed Buhari, interview with E. Renne, July 8, 2010, Kaduna.

18. Gideon Oloruntobi, interview with E. Renne, February 27, 2017, Kaduna.

19. Andrae and Beckman (1999, 34) note that the "smuggling [of textiles] was rampant" during the oil boom years due to the increased value of the naira, even after the 1977 textile import ban was implemented.

20. The editorial went on to add that "government should immediately intervene by banning the export of black oil to save the textile industry from total collapse, which could burden the labour market with an additional 33,000 job losses."

21. On Wednesday market days, traders would come from Nigeria to Dan Issa to sell their produce. This interborder trade was also a venue for the smuggling of various commodities including secondhand clothes. A similar situation is described by Paul Nugent (2002, 102), who discusses the active role that border villagers played in facilitating border crossings in colonial British Ghana to French Togoland and back. As he put it, "By shuttling between the two territories, border peoples could have their cake and eat it."

22. Alhaji Abubakar, interview with E. Renne, August 28, 2012, Kano.

23. In 2009, Chinese traders attempted to rent the Mungal Shopping Plaza in Kaduna so that a Chinese depot market would be established in Nigeria for online orders of Chinese textiles. The Kaduna and Kano traders united to resist this plan, otherwise the Chinese would have taken over the importation of textiles entirely. The Chinese wanted the plaza so that Chinese sales representatives would work with Nigerian customers in Kaduna to make orders. Once the goods were manufactured they would be brought back into Nigeria. This plan, however, was not successful.

24. In April 2013, UNTL-Kaduna workers were laid off for three weeks for lack of demand as well as the expense of cotton and electricity.

25. Wuese Iyorver, interview with E. Renne, November 13, 2017, Kaduna. There is the possibility, though, of a Chinese company getting involved in the renovation of this mill as well as Chinese and Pakistani assistance in improving the electricity supply in Kaduna State (Sani Hunkuyi, interview with E. Renne, November 27, 2017, Kaduna).

26. Bernard and Jill Laverty, the present co-owners of David Whitehead & Sons, bought the capital of David Whitehead & Sons in 1996 and currently operate the business from an office in Parbold, Lancashire (Bernard Laverty, interview with Jaclyn Kline, 27 February 27, 2012, Parbold).

REFERENCES

Abubakar, J. 2008. "N70bn Textile Fund on Hold." *Daily Trust*, 18 September 18.

Abubakar, J. 2010. "151 Textile Firms Close Shop in Nigeria." *Daily Trust*, January 4.

Agbese, Andrew, Christiana Alabi, Maryam Ahmadu-Suka, and Francis Iloani. 2016. "Why Textile Industry Remains Dormant Despite FG's N100bn Bailout." *Daily Trust*, July 3. https://www.dailytrust.com.ng/.

Agbo, Ahmed. 2016. "RMRDC Moves to Revive Cotton Farming, Distributes Seeds to Farmers." *Daily Trust*, July 7. https://www.dailytrust.com.ng/.

Ahmad, R., and O. Akor. 2012. "Effects of Youth Unemployment on Families." *Daily Trust*, August 24. www.dailytrust.com.ng/.

Ahmadu-Suka, M. 2011a. "United Textile Re-Opens After 4 Years of Closure." *Daily Trust*, November 17. www.dailytrust.com.ng/.

Ahmadu-Suka, M. 2011b. "How Far Has Intervention Fund Taken UNTL?" *Daily Trust*, November 27. www.dailytrust.com.ng/.

Andrae, Gunilla, and Björn Beckman. 1999. *Union Power in the Nigerian Textile Industry*. New Brunswick, NJ: Transaction Publishers.

Aremu, I. 2010. "Return of UNTL: In Praise of Governance." *Daily Trust*, December 6. www.dailytrust.com.ng.

Axelsson, Linn. 2012. *Marking Borders: Engaging the Threat of Chinese Textiles in Ghana*. Stockholm: Acta Universitatis Stockholm.

Bashir, Mishbahu. 2013. "How We've Controlled Blanket Market for 35 Years—Chellco." *Daily Trust*, December 22, 2018. https://www.dailytrust.com.ng/.

Brambilla, I., A. Khandelwal, and P. Schott. 2010. "China's Experience Under the Multi-Fiber Arrangement (MFA) and the Agreement on Textiles and Clothing (ATC)." In *China's Growing Role in World Trade*, edited by R. C. Feenstra and S.-J. Wei, 350. Chicago: University of Chicago Press.

Burgis, Tom. 2015. *The Looting Machine: Warlords, Tycoons, Smugglers, and the Systematic Theft of Africa's Wealth*. London: William Collins.

Cha Group. 2012. "Textiles Website, History." http://www.chatextiles.com/english/index.html.

Chellco Industries Ltd. 2017. "Chellco Industries Website." http://chellco.com/blankets.html.

Daily Trust. 2007. "Editorial: Avert Textile Industry Collapse." *Daily Trust*, July 20, 56.

Daily Trust. 2009. "Textile Fund Is Ready—Minister." *Daily Trust*, December 23. www.dailytrust.com.ng/.

Daily Trust. 2017. "Cheerful News About Kaduna Textile." *Daily Trust*, August 22. https://www.dailytrust.com.ng/.

David Whitehead & Sons. 1957. "Kaduna Textiles Limited." Brochure prepared for the opening ceremony of KTL, November 22, 1957, David Whitehead & Sons, Ltd, Archives, Parbold, Lancashire.

David Whitehead & Sons. 1973. "Kaduna: The Largest Spinning and Weaving Operation South of the Sahara." *Textile Month* (June).

Gombe, Abdullahi A. 2016. "Finetex, New Nigerian Development Company" unpublished letter, April 14.

Hansen, Karen T. 2000. *Salaula: The World of Secondhand Clothing and Zambia*. Chicago: University of Chicago Press.

Hartley, Gordon W. 2012. Unpublished report by former commercial manager, Kaduna Textiles Limited, February 18, 2012, in authors' possession.

Isuwa, Sunday. 2013. "Has FG's N100bn Textile Fund Gone Down the Drain?" *Sunday Trust*, April 14. www.sundaytrust.com.ng/.

Johnson, M. 1974. "Cotton Imperialism in West Africa." *African Affairs* 73, no. 291: 178–87.

Kirby, Peter. 1975. "Manufacturing in West Africa." In *Colonialism in Africa 1870–1960*, vol. 4, edited by L. H. Gann and Peter Duignan, 470–520. Cambridge: Cambridge University Press.

Krishi, Musa. 2017. "Dogara: Nigeria's Textile Sector Crucial to Economic Development." *Daily Trust*, November 18, 53.

Loimeier, Roman. 1997. *Islamic Reform and Political Change in Northern Nigeria*. Evanston, IL: Northwestern University Press.

Maiwada, S., and E. Renne. 2013. "The Kaduna Textile Industry and the Decline of Textile Manufacturing in Northern Nigeria, 1955–2010." *Textile History* 44, no. 2: 171–96.

Minchin, Timothy. 2013. *Empty Mills: The Fight Against Imports and the Decline of the U.S. Textile Industry*. Lanham, MD: Rowman & Littlefield Publishers Inc.

Mudashir, I. 2010. "Hopeful Ex-Workers Besiege UNTL, Kaduna for a New Lease of Life. *Sunday Trust*, December 19.

Muhammad, Hamisu. 2017. "Adeosun, Vlisco Hold Talks on Cotton, Textile Revival." *Daily Trust*, November 15, 13.

Nduna, D. 2016. "The Fall of David Whitehead Textiles." *The Herald*, April 6. http://www.herald.co.zw/the-fall-of-david-whitehead-textiles.

Nugent, Paul. 2002. *Smugglers, Secessionists and Loyal Citizens on the Ghana-Toga Frontier: The Lie of the Borderlands since 1914*. Athens: Ohio University Press.

Olakitan, Yemi. 2015. "Nigeria's Troubled Textile Industry." *Sunday Mirror*, February 15. http://nationalmirroronline.net/.

Olukoshi, A. O., ed. 1993. *The Politics of Structural Adjustment in Nigeria*. London: James Currey.

Onyeiwu, S. 1997. "The Modern Textile Industry in Nigeria: History, Structural Change, and Recent Developments." *Textile History* 28, no. 2: 234–49.

Paden, J. 1986. *Ahmadu Bello: Sardauna of Sokoto*. Zaria: Huda Huda Press.

Pedler, Frederick. 1974. *The Lion and the Unicorn in Africa: A History of the Origins of the United Africa Company 1787–1931*. London: Heinemann Educational.

Perkins, F. C. 1997. "Export Performance and Enterprise Reform in China's Coastal Provinces." *Economic Development and Cultural Change* 45, no. 3: 501–39.

Phiri, F., and M. Nduru. 2005. "Asia Strips Africa's Textile Industry." *Asian Times*, April 26.

Renne, E. 1997. "'Traditional Modernity' and the Economics of Handwoven Cloth Production in Southwestern Nigeria." *Economic Development and Cultural Change* 45, no. 4: 773–92.

Renne, Elisha. 2019. "United Nigerian Textiles Limited and Chinese-Nigeria Textile Manufacturing Collaboration in Kaduna, Nigeria." *Africa* 89, no. 4: 696–717.

Sa'idu, Isa. 2018. "Our GMO Cotton Is Targeting Textile Revival—IAR." *Daily Trust*, August 19. https://www.dailytrust.com.ng/.

Shehu, M. 2010. "FG Sets Up Committee on Textile Revival." *Daily Trust*, July 28. www.dailytrust.com.ng/.

Shosanya, M. 2011. "60% of Textile Coys Have Accessed Loan." *Daily Trust*, March 24. www.dailytrust.com.ng/.

Taylor, Ian. 2007. "China's Relations with Nigeria." *The Round Table* 96, no. 392: 631–45.

UNTL (United Nigeria Textiles Limited). 1979. "Cha Chi Ming, Chairman's Report, Annual Report and Accounts." Unpublished document.

UNTL (United Nigeria Textiles Limited). 1980. "Cha Chi Ming, Chairman's Report, Annual Report and Accounts." Unpublished document.

UNTL (United Nigeria Textiles Limited). 1982. "Cha Chi Ming, Chairman's Report, Annual Report and Accounts." Unpublished document.

UNTL (United Nigeria Textiles Limited). 1983. "Cha Chi Ming, Chairman's Report, Annual Report and Accounts." Unpublished document.

UNTL (United Nigeria Textiles Limited). 1984. "Cha Chi Ming, Chairman's Report, Annual Report and Accounts." Unpublished document.

UNTL (United Nigeria Textiles Limited). 1989. "Cha Chi Ming, Chairman's Report, Annual Report and Accounts." Unpublished document.

World Trade Organization. 2015. "Textile Monitoring Body: The Agreement on Textiles and Clothing. http://www.wto.org/english/tratop_e/texti_e/texintro_e.htm.

Zaria Industries Limited. 2018. Zaria Industries Limited website. http://zariaindustries. bloombiz.com/.

Zeng, D. 2011. "How Do Special Economic Zones and Industrial Clusters Drive China's Rapid Development?" Policy Research Working Paper No. 5583. Washington DC: The World Bank.

CHAPTER 5

The Kano Textile Industry and Trade during the Independence Era

ABDULKARIM UMAR DANASABE

Textile manufacturing in Kano began in 1952 with the opening of the Kano Citizens Trading Company (KCTC) mill. The KCTC mill was financed by investments from local Kano businessmen, unlike the beginning of the Kaduna textile industry, which was founded with government involvement, as discussed in chapter 4. Indeed, this pattern of local businessmen's investment—both Nigerian as well as Lebanese and Syrian—in Kano's textile manufacturing industry has persisted. Thus, after independence, while some foreign investors, such as the French firm MNC, collaborated with Kano manufacturers to establish the Northern Textiles Manufacturers mill (Gidan Bargo) in Kano, the majority of mills operating in the Bompai, Challawa, and Sharada industrial areas were medium-sized mills, often founded by members of Kano's leading merchant families. As Andrae and Beckman note (1999, 82):

> The contrast between Kaduna and Kano is sharp. Kano had more than twice the number of enterprises (19 as compared to 9 for Kaduna in 1985) but all small and medium sized, except for Gaskiya, the newcomer, a large integrated mill with spinning, weaving and finishing. . . . [However,] most of the Kano mills were single function/product units, spinners and weavers or more specialized firms, producing e.g. blankets, and embroidered lace.

At the height of the textile manufacturing in these three areas in the late 1970s, there were more than twenty mills in operation and more than ten thousand workers (Andrae and Beckman 1999, 82). They were producing plain weave, unbleached baft (known as *akoko*) and twill cotton materials, cotton knit garments, uniform materials, bedsheets, blankets, towels, and other specialty textiles. Nonetheless, the Kano mills followed a trajectory similar to that of the Kaduna mills, closing in the late twentieth century. Nonetheless, some mills have remained in operation, with some even expanding following the release of grants and loans associated with the Textile Revival Fund in 2010.

The chapter begins with an extended discussion of the earliest textile mill established in northern Nigeria by the Kano Citizens Trading Company. The founding of this mill reflected the foresight of the emir of Kano, Alhaji Abdullahi Bayero, along with members of Kano Native Authority and prominent Kano businessmen who realized the importance of developing a local textile manufacturing industry. Following Nigerian independence in 1960, additional mills were built in Kano, several of which reflected the collaborative efforts of Hausa-Fulani and Lebanese businessmen living in Kano. The origins of twelve of these mills, and the particular products they manufactured and how those products were sold and distributed, are discussed. The origins, products, and longevity of twelve of these mills is also considered. Among these mills, only five are currently in operation.

The reasons for the closure of eight of these mills (including the Kano Citizens Trading Company mill) are then examined. While many of the factors that contributed to the decline of textile mills in Kano and Kaduna were the same, there were some differences, such as a smaller scale of operation, local patterns of collaborative ownership, fewer partnerships with the New Nigeria Development Company Ltd. (formerly the Northern Nigerian Development Corporation), and political violence. Also, as Andrae and Beckman note, Kano textile mills tended to specialize in particular types of textiles and apparel, which have affected continued textile and garment manufacturing in distinctive ways in Kano. After a consideration of the factors that enabled some mills to remain in operation while others failed, the chapter concludes with a consideration of the current situation of textile manufacturing in Kano. It examines the consequences of the ending of the Cotton, Textile and Garment Development Fund in 2016, the possibilities for cotton-growing and cotton-manufacturing collaborations, and the continuing quantities of Chinese textile imports shipped to Kano markets.

ESTABLISHMENT OF TEXTILE MANUFACTURING IN KANO:
THE KANO CITIZENS TRADING COMPANY

The idea of establishing a modern textile mill in Kano was conceived during the reign of the progressive emir of Kano, Alhaji Abdullahi Bayero Ibn Abbas (1926–1953), by the Kano Native Authority (NA)—the major shareholder—and by Kano businessmen such as Alhaji Alhassan Dantata (DanAsabe 1987, 2000), who contributed property worth £10,200, along with Alhaji Muhammad Nagoda, who invested £200. Many others, including petty traders, laborers, and small farmers from all over Kano Province, also invested small amounts of cash, between one and five shillings. Their contributions were a sort of compulsory levy collected by district heads in 1949 after the emir of Kano—the executive head of the Native Authority (NA) of the former Emirate of Kano—had directed every poll-tax-paying adult to contribute five shillings or more toward the establishment of the Kano Citizens Trading Company Ltd. textile mill.

The mill was located at Gwammaja, in Kano City (*Gaskiya Tafi Kwabo* 1949). The foundation stone for the building of the company was laid by the emir on January 19, 1950. Mill equipment was imported from the United Kingdom, with installation carried out by British engineers. The mill started operations in 1952. The KCTC mill was producing nearly two million yards of high-quality Bedford cords and unbleached and bleached cotton textiles in various colors annually (Ministry of Information, *Kano State of Nigeria* 1969, 46). Consumers considered the textiles produced by the KCTC mill to be excellent, especially the baft shirting cloth known as *akoko*. Its crisp whiteness was compared favorably with the imported bleached white cotton cloth. The mill also manufactured khaki textiles that were used for uniforms worn by the Native Authority police and prison guards, as well as blue material that was used for girls' school uniforms in Kano. Indeed, the clarity of this blue material was considered to be excellent and this cloth was popular throughout the former Northern Region (Gwazaye 2013, 27).

The KCTC mill was a busy operation with three shifts: morning, afternoon-evening, and night. At its inception, the company was administered by an appointee of the emir, Alhaji Yunusa Wakilin Masaka. The technical staff was headed by a Muslim Indian named Mr. Hussain. He was assisted by a southern Nigerian Muslim man from the present-day Edo State known as Mamman Auchi, and some Hausa men such as Muhammad Wawu, Bako Lamido, and others. The financial department was manned by southern Nigerians and

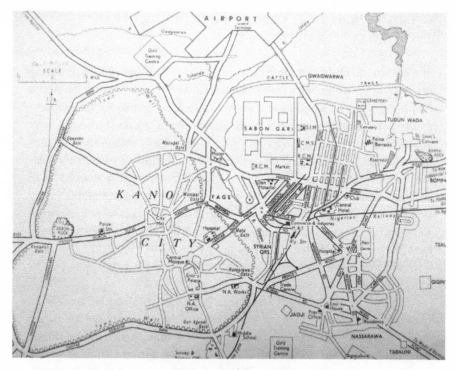

Map 5.1. Map of Kano metropolis, indicating Syrian Quarters, City Market (Kasuwa Kurmi), and Bompai Industrial Area. Drawn and reproduced by Federal Drawing Department, Lagos, Nigeria, 1958. (Courtesy of the University of Michigan Library, Stephen S. Clark Map Library.)

Christian Northerners from Southern Zaria. The bulk of the laborers, however, were northern Nigerian Hausas. The main raw material was Nigerian cotton and the entire range of products from this mill were sold in Nigeria.

In 1967, Kano Province became Kano State, and the investment of the Kano Native Authority in the Kano Citizens Trading Company was taken over by the Kano State government. The late Alhaji Baba DanBaffa, a Kano businessman, became the managing director of the company. Other members of board were prominent Kano people representing various interests such as Malam Aminu Kano, a left-wing politician; the late Malam Nasiru Kabara, a leader of the Qadiriyya brotherhood; the late Malam Tijjani Usman Zangon Bare-Bari, leader of the Tijaniyya brotherhood; and the late Muhammad Nagoda, a prominent businessman (Ministry of Information, *Kano State of Nigeria* 1969).

The Kano Citizens Trading Company mill, which was subsequently known as the Kano Textile Mills–Gwammaja, did well during the 1960s and 1970s. While the company only manufactured several thousand yards of fabric per annum during the 1950s, by 1960 it produced 1,056,522 yards (Bashir 1989, 108). Although the mill was not set up for textile printing, the continued popularity of its bleached white cotton shirting material meant that its products were in great demand. But on December 31, 1986, during his military regime, Gen. Ibrahim Babangida introduced the Structural Adjustment Program, as was discussed in chapter 4. The Structural Adjustment Program (SAP) compelled state governments and their agencies to sell their interest in profit-making ventures to private individuals. It was under this arrangement that the Kano Textile Mills–Gwammaja was sold to Alhaji Uba Leader, a Kano businessman, in 1987. While he sold the old, obsolete looms and other equipment as scrap and replaced them with more up-to-date weaving equipment, he was unable to maintain this company. He closed the company down in 2010 after filing for bankruptcy.

In the years following the establishment of the Kano Citizens Trading Company mill, several textile mills opened, mainly in the Challawa, Sharada, and Bompai industrial areas of Kano. These industrial areas had been established through government initiatives begun in the 1950s. Soon after the opening of the Kano Citizens Trading Company mill in 1952, "a loan of £30,000 was granted by the Northern Regional Development Board to establish an industrial estate in Kano" (Bashir 1989, 107). The industrial zones, Sharada and Challawa, were established as part of this initiative. After independence, the Bompai Industrial Estate was created by the emir of Kano, Alhaji Muhammadu Sanusi I. The Bompai Industrial Estate grew to include several cotton textile mills, such as Magraps Textiles and Universal Textile Industry Ltd., mills that were backed by Lebanese Kano-based businessmen, as well as Gaskiya Textile Mills Ltd., jointly funded by the Kano businessman Nababa Badamosi, the Nigerian Industrial Development Bank, and the Bank of the North (Andrae and Beckman 1999, 129). These mills and others operated during the heyday of textile manufacturing in Kano in the 1970s. The following twelve mills, along with the Kano Citizens Trading Company, which also operated at that time, exemplify the types of textile manufacturing industries found in Kano. The mills that are still operational are described first, followed by mills that have ended production, mainly in the beginning of the twenty-first century.

TEXTILE MILLS STILL OPERATING IN KANO

Adhama Textiles and Garment Industry Ltd.

The founder and owner of Adhama Textiles, Alhaji Sa'idu Dattijo Adhama, had the idea of opening a textile manufacturing plant in 1977. In December 1978, he concluded preparations and on January 1, 1979, the company began operations. It has remained in operation since that time. The Adhama Textiles and Garments factory specializes in knitting cotton jersey materials, dyeing, and sewing. The head of state, Gen. Yakubu Gowon, started the National Youth Service Corps (NYSC) program in 1973, which placed recent university graduates for one year of service in communities throughout Nigeria.

After its founding, Adhama Textiles produced T-shirts worn by many NYSC workers between 1983 and 1984. When General Buhari became the head of the Nigerian state, Alhaji Adhama was the only NYSC supplier who was not arrested during Buhari's earlier efforts at eliminating widespread corruption in Nigeria. As Alhaji Adhama put it, "We were paid exactly for what we did—we supplied quantity and quality." Aside from cotton knit fabric used to construct T-shirts for commissioned special orders, Adhama Textiles also produces underwear, men's sports shirts, and women's blouses, all using Nigerian-grown cotton.

In 2011, the company was able to access funds from the N100 billion Cotton, Textile and Garment Development Fund established by the Nigerian government to resuscitate the textile industry.[1] This fund was organized through a bond issued by the Debt Management Office (Agbese et al. 2016).[2] The Bank of Industry distributed Cotton, Textile and Garment Development Fund loans to a number of companies in Kano State, which included Adhama Textiles and Garments Industry, Ltd.[3] The fund enabled the company to purchase new knitting machines, sewing machines, printing equipment, and dyeing vats. Adhama Textiles and Garments sells its products through orders from organizations that need specially printed shirts and through Kano-based dealers.

Tofa Textile Mills Ltd.

Like Adhama Textiles, the Tofa Textile Mills Ltd. company was opened by a prominent local businessman, Alhaji Isyaku Umar Tofa, a former Kano civil servant who achieved great business success.[4] In 1990, he purchased the ailing Northern Textiles Manufacturers–NTM (Gidan Bargo) mill and renamed it Tofa Textile Mills Limited.

Fig. 5.1. Production of jersey materials and custom printed T-shirts at the Adhama Textiles & Garment Industry Ltd. mill, Bompai Industrial Area, Kano, January 24, 2017. (Photograph by E. P. Renne.)

The Northern Textile Manufacturers–NTM (Gidan Bargo) was established in the Bompai industrial area of Kano in 1962 by the Kano North African businessman Mahmoud Gashash, who held the largest number of company shares.[5] By 1976, the company was taken over by a French conglomerate, La Compagnie Française de l'Afrique Occidentale (CFAO) (Pedler 1974). The original technical partners, the Japanese company, Nishizawa, were retained by CFAO and held an 11 percent share of NTM by 1980. However, with the implementation of indigenization of Nigerian industries promoted by the Nigerian Enterprises Promotion Decrees of 1972 and 1977, ownership was opened to local businessmen and to the Kano State government. Mahmoud Gashash invested in 24 percent of the capital, while the state Northern Nigerian Investments Company Ltd. held 16 percent of the company capital. CFAO retained a 41 percent share of the company and was also in charge of its management.

Northern Textile Manufacturers (NTM) specialized in the production of blankets (see chapter 8). As a vertically integrated plant, it also included facilities for both spinning and weaving. The installed machinery consisted of 620 spindles, 120 automatic and 42 shuttle-less looms, which at full capacity could weave 5.6 million meters of cloth per annum. In the mid-1970s, employment was as high as 2,500 but it dropped considerably by 1985 to as few as 374 workers. After its sale to Alhaji Isyaku Umar Tofa in 1990, this mill has continued operation of under the name of Tofa Textile Mills. The company has continued NTM's specialization in the production of blankets of several sizes as well as baby shawls. This integrated mill also produces polyester thread for its automatic and shuttle-less looms, which it inherited from the NTM plant. This mill has remained in operation.[6]

African Textile Manufacturing Ltd.

African Textile Manufacturing Ltd. (ATM), another important textile mill that continues to manufacture textiles, was established by a Lebanese businessman, Suhail Akar, in January 1980 and began production in 1998. The company produces high-quality textiles with brand names such as Crowntext, Wazobia, Dunia, Queen Text, Festac Wax, and Aboda Real. ATM has produced many attractive printed cotton textiles, including the cloth called *abada*.[7] Its detailed design consists of curvilinear forms in gold, yellow, black, and red, which are highlighted with fine black lines. The company also produces textiles for family occasions such as weddings and for politicians during political campaigns. For example, in 2015, the People's Democratic Party (PDP) gubernatorial candidate, Senator Ifanyi Athur Okowa of Delta State, commissioned the ATM mill to produce textile material that was used during his political campaign. The yellow foundation material includes a photograph of the senator along with the PDP logo, a large umbrella with the party colors of green, white, and red. This material was distributed to the senator's supporters during his campaign, who had it sewn in various ways.[8] The mill was still operating as of August 25, 2015, although due to the erratic power supply and the high cost of raw materials and spare parts for machinery, it was producing at half capacity.[9] Nonetheless, its attractive website illustrates some of the company's offerings.[10]

Angel Spinning and Dyeing Limited, Kano

This company was established in 1981 by a Lebanese businessman, known as Mr. Dyke, with support from the late Alhaji Dan Magaji Sheshe, a Kano-based businessman. Mr. Dyke continues to run the company as the managing director. Angel Spinning and Dyeing Ltd. began with the manufacture of mosquito netting, and in 1986 it expanded to produce cotton and polyester textiles. In 1996 and 1997 the company won federal government awards for the excellent quality of its products. In 2017, it employed 2,100 workers and produced 40 million meters of plain poplin, polyester, cotton prints, and tie-dyed materials as well as brocade (Ghalila *shadda*) Angel brand textiles. The company is still in operation.[11]

Terytex Nigeria Ltd. (NTL)

Terytex Nigeria Ltd. was established in 1980 by Mr. P. K. Haryany, an Indian businessman, as a small-to-medium-scale manufacturer of towels and bed sheets. The technical section of the firm was headed by Mr. Amand Ghate. In 1998, the company commissioned its spinning unit. Mr. Haryani owned 40 percent of the share capital, while Chief H. B Chanrai, another Indian businessman, the Northern Nigerian Investments Company Ltd., and Terytex Employees Trust owned 19.47 percent; other investors held the remaining shares. Maj. Gen. Mukhtar Muhammad, who took over the company,[12] worked closely with Alhaji Sa'idu Adhama of Adhama Textiles, especially when either company had a large commercial order that needed to be filled. Although Major General Muhammad died recently, the company as of 2018 is still functioning (Muhammad 2010).

While these five mills remain in operation, providing textiles to the Kano market and beyond, the majority of textile mills that were established in the 1960s and 1970s have since closed. They are described in the following section.

TEXTILE MILLS THAT HAVE CLOSED IN KANO

Bagauda Textile Mill Limited, Kano

Bagauda Textile Mill Limited was established in 1972 by Alhaji Isyaku Rabi'u, a Kano businessman (Muhammad 1979; Forrest 1990, 47), together with a Lebanese businessman. The company specialized in manufacturing high-quality materials such as terylene, worsted wool, terylene viscose, and shirting materials. The mill produced woven cloths for uniforms, mainly from synthetic materials. Bagauda Textile Mill was so renowned that the head of the Federal Military Government of Nigeria, Yakubu Gowon, visited the mill in 1974. By 1979, the company had acquired modern weaving and printing machinery and by 1980 employed between 350 and 420 workers.

Bagauda Textile Mill was considered to be one of the best textile mills in the country. The products of the company, particularly its suiting material made from a blended cotton-polyviscose yarn, could be found in many markets in Northern Nigeria and in the neighboring nations of Niger, Chad, and Cameroon. But the mill was adversely affected by "the foreign exchange squeeze . . . as Bagauda was 100 per cent dependent on imports of its synthetic (polyviscose) and blended yarns as well as for chemicals and dyes" (Andrae and Beckman 1999, 125). These problems continued through the 1980s and by 2009 the company was closed. Some of the reasons for its closure were trade liberalization on textile imports (as was discussed in chapter 4), consumers' preference for foreign textiles over locally made textiles, neglect of the agricultural sector (specifically cotton), an unstable electric power supply, and a lack of technical proficiency relating to mill upkeep. These problems also affected several other mills in Kano.

Universal Textile Industries Limited, Kano

This company was jointly founded by Alhaji Aminu Dantata and the Lebanese businessman George Akle and his wife Françoise (Albasu 1995, 173; Forrest 1990, 46). It was commissioned in the 1980s and produced cotton yarns of various qualities used by local weavers, good quality white yardage, and printed cotton cloth (*atamfa*). At the height of the mill's production, the labor force had more than a thousand workers. But due to many of the factors affecting other Nigerian textile mills at the time, Universal Textile Industries Ltd. closed its doors on November 31, 2009. Alhaji Aminu paid off the Lebanese partners, George and Françoise Akle, who were leaving the country. While the company remains closed, the machinery and other equipment are still there.[13]

Gaskiya Textile Mills, Limited, Kano

Gaskiya Textile Mills is located in the Dakata Industrial Area of Kano. It was established by the late Alhaji Nababa Badamasi, a Kano-based businessman, with a loan of more than N80 million from the Bank of the North, and with funding from the Nigerian Industrial Development Bank (Andrae and Beckman 1999, 129). The company was commissioned by the then military president of Nigeria, Gen. Muhammadu Buhari, in 1983 and began production in 1985 (Andrae and Beckman 1999, 128), with local partners and an Indian-based partner, Arvind Mills of Ahmedabad. The mill initially had nine hundred workers, many of whom had been laid off from other textiles mills in Kano. Gaskiya Textiles eventually came to employ more than five thousand workers. The main products of the company were unbleached (*akoko*) and bleached white cotton shirting (*alawayyo* or *zauwati*), print cotton cloth (*atamfa*) of various colors and patterns, and white and brown khaki mainly from cotton and nylon.[14] High-quality wax print and plain weave textiles were its most popular products. Yet the company ceased operations in 1996.[15] As of 2017, the company is a shadow of its former self. Indeed, the administrative buildings have been taken over by rats and snakes, while the weaving machinery in the half-kilometer-long warehouse is rotting away. Since the Gaskiya Textile Mills closed, it has been extensively vandalized, so it is unlikely that it will open again unless the Northern Nigerian Development Corporation (in collaboration with the Bank of the North) can find a buyer who is willing to renovate the plant.

Holborn Nigeria Textile Ltd.

The Holborn Nigeria Textile Ltd. mill was established by a group of Indian businessmen who had worked with Alhaji Aminu Dantata at the Universal Textile Mills, Kano. After they were compensated by Aminu Dantata in the early 1980s for their shares in the company, they established the Holborn Nigeria Textile Ltd. textile mill, where they produced knitting materials of various sizes and colors. The mills also produced towels and handkerchiefs. They sold the company's materials to Kano traders who sold them in local markets. They were doing well until the introduction of the Structural Adjustment Program in 1986, which undermined their ability to buy spare parts and dyes for printed produced. The company was forced to close down in 1998.[16]

Magraps Textiles Mill Limited, Kano

This company was established by a Lebanese businessman in Kano to produce baby blankets, towels, and surgical papers in 1970. As was the case with the Holborn Nigeria Textile Ltd. mill, this mill was doing well but declined with the introduction of the 1986 Structural Adjustment Program. It is now closed.[17]

Dangote Textiles Mills Ltd., Kano

Dangote Textile Mills, Ltd., Kano, was established by the Dangote group. The company produced 600,000 meters of cloth and 150 million tons of yarn per month. The mill included facilities for spinning, weaving, printing, and bleaching. In 1990, the company established a cotton ginnery in the cotton belt of southern Katsina, known as Dangote Ginnery Ltd. at Kankara LG, near Malumfashi. The Dangote Cotton Ginnery is ginning to sell to other spinning and textile companies and was still functioning as of December 2017. Farmers also may take their cotton to this ginnery to have their cotton ginned for them to sell outside.

The Dangote Textile Mills in Kano, however, as well as the Dangote Textile Mill in Lagos had stopped production by 2009 because they could not compete with textile materials imported from China, India, and Japan. The Dangote group is now using the facilities for the production of sacks for its flour mills located in Kano, Lagos, and Ilorin. They are also being used as warehouses for its products.[18]

DECLINE IN TEXTILE MANUFACTURING IN KANO

There were various problems that led to the closing of many of the textile mills in Kano. Many Kano textile traders blame the influx of unregulated Chinese cotton textiles as undermining the sale of Nigerian-manufactured textiles (Adamu 2010; Habib 2012; Lere et al. 2012; also as discussed in chapter 6). Yet as Alhaji Adhama observed: "You know, the disaster in the textile industry, a lot was man-made, especially by the Northerners . . . whoever is in textiles today can hardly forgive some of the Northern leaders who surrendered it."[19] As he explained, the focus on oil wealth "has spoiled the nation." The large sums of naira from oil sales at the unregulated disposal of politicians led to various forms of corruption that affected the textile manufacturing industry, both nationally and in Kano State (Wakili, Mudashir, and Opoola 2016). For example, when the Nigerian textile import ban was lifted in 2010 and replaced with textile duty fees and a 5 percent textile levy, the bulk of the N130 billion levy fee that was collected and which was to be spent on improvements for the national textile industry mysteriously disappeared, with only N13 billion remaining.[20] In addition, when the Chinese government agreed to observe WTO rules concerning world trade in 2001 and the World Trade Organization phased out the Agreement on Textiles and Clothing in 2004 in favor of local tariffs (GATT) (World Trade Organization 2015), huge shipments of Chinese textile imports were smuggled into Kantin Kwari market in Kano (see chapter 6). After 2010, when the Nigerian textile import ban was lifted, these increased imports were also subject to import duties, which were to have contributed to improvements in Kano textile manufacturing equipment and higher prices for Chinese textiles as they absorbed duty fees. However, such was not the case. With several companies operating with obsolete equipment and with inadequate supplies of cotton thread and dyes, these companies could not compete with the efficiencies of Chinese textile production as well as digital printing and trading practices.

REASONS FOR TEXTILE COMPANY CLOSURES IN KANO

The closures of the eight companies that ended textile production (including the Kano Citizens Trading Company) cluster around two time periods, namely 1997–1998 and 2009–2010. The former period reflected the aftereffects of the devaluation of the Nigerian currency associated with the 1986 Structural Adjustment Program, while the latter period reflected the ending of the textile import ban in 2010. The latter period was also one of increasing violence associated with Islamic reform group known as Boko Haram. By 2012, several deadly bombings took place in Kano. On January 24, 2012, 185 people were reported killed as a result of the violence:

> A powerful blast destroyed the Sheka Police Station while sporadic gunfire was heard around the Bompai area, where the state police headquarters is located, residents said. The fresh bombing and shooting spree started at about 6.30 pm at Sheka when gunmen riding motorbikes stormed the neighbourhood and attacked the police station. (Umar and Aliyu 2012)

The growing fear surrounding this situation led many Lebanese and Indian families to move from Kano (Lere et al. 2012). Of the eight companies that closed, four were wholly or partly owned by Lebanese or Indian families, although two of the remaining mills—African Textile Manufacturing Ltd. and Angel Spinning and Dyeing Ltd.—still have Lebanese directors. Some Kano-born Lebanese, however, have remained in Kano. As one man explained, "I cannot leave Kano because I have nowhere to go. I can't go back to Lebanon since I don't know anybody there. We would always stay here no matter what" (Lere et al. 2012).

This situation differs from that of the Kaduna mills, which closed their doors in the period from 2002 to 2007. Yet some of the same factors affected these companies' ability to continue textile manufacturing. Aside from increasing importation of smuggled Chinese textiles after 1990 and trade liberalization agreements after 2010, a system for the legal importation of

Chinese textiles was established. While some traders preferred to deal with Nigerian textile mills, many consumers preferred Chinese-made textiles over locally made ones on the basis of price and quality (as is discussed in chapter 6). For example, in 2014, a new type of *atamfa* material appeared in Kano and other northern Nigerian markets.[21] Referred to as *yar da atamfa* ("throw-away" *atamfa*) in Kano and *mai roba* (or *roba-roba*, rubber-rubber, referring to its plastic, rubbery feel) in Kaduna and Zaria, these less costly Chinese textile imports reflected the need for lower-priced *atamfa* offerings. By substituting polyester for cotton thread in their manufacture, such cloths are sold at approximately a third of the price of imported Chinese cotton *atamfa*.[22]

Problems of Cotton Production

It is not only pricing that has contributed to Chinese production and Nigerian consumption of polyester *atamfa* textiles. Chinese manufacturers have begun to face shortages of raw cotton produced in China (Tabuchi 2015).[23] Indeed, a delegation of Chinese officials visited Nigeria to assess the possibilities of sending raw cotton to China. The Dangote Ginnery Ltd. in southern Katsina state continues to process raw cotton for sale to textile mills in Kano and Kaduna, although cotton production in Kano, Kaduna, and Katsina states, which would normally provide northern Nigerian textile manufacturers with this important raw material, has declined in recent years. While General Buhari, during his tenure as head of state (December 1983 to August 1985), supported research on improved cotton seed with funds from the Petroleum Trust Fund, this program was abandoned after Babangida came to power in 1985.[24] The difficulty of obtaining long-staple raw cotton necessary for the most recent cotton ginning equipment has grown more acute. Indeed, in 2016, farmers in Zamfara and Katsina states cited low cotton prices and the difficulties in obtaining improved long-staple cotton seeds as the main problems they faced (Mahmud 2016; Umar 2016). Furthermore, the better prices paid for soybeans, sorghum, and maize have led some to abandon cotton farming altogether. However, government programs and the recent bumper cotton crop and higher prices reported by Katsina farmers in 2017 (Mahmud 2017) may encourage more farmers in the cotton-belt to return to cotton farming. In any event, the reorganization of cotton farming and buying procedures is needed to enable Kano textile and garment manufacturers to maintain and even expand their production and sales. For as Alhaji Sa'idu Adhama has noted, "The whole world believes that cotton is a necessity for human existence—it is a poverty-freeing commodity. A country that can produce cotton will not be a poor nation. But cotton was neglected because of oil, oil has spoiled the nation."[25] As discussed in chapter 4, government programs to distribute cotton seed to farmers and to improve cotton production are now in place.

Other Factors Impeding Textile Manufacturing in Kano

As in Kaduna, the erratic supply of electricity that contributed to the demise of textile manufacturing in Kaduna has also affected many of the mills operating in Kano. While there have been several plans for improving the provision of power, they have largely been unsuccessful. Two recent projects in Kano State, however, have improved this situation. First, on August 30, 2017, the federal government approved a contract with a consortium of Chinese companies for construction of the Mambilla Hydro Power Plant, which will be connected to three dams across the Donga River in Taraba State, Nigeria (*Daily Trust* 2017). When completed, this plant will improve power provision in northern Nigeria. While this project has been long in coming, it is hoped that it, unlike other past projects, will improve the supply of electricity (Daka, Adepetun, and Opara 2018). Second, in May 2017, the Kano State government entered into agreement with three companies, each of which will construct 100 mw solar energy power plants in Kano State (Ibrahim 2017).[26]

Several Kano textile mills that had been prospering in the 1960s and 1970s were affected by the Structural Adjustment Program implemented by Gen. Ibrahim Babangida during his tenure as head of Nigeria. Implemented at the insistence of the International Monetary Fund, this program was based on the assumption that devaluing the naira, the Nigerian currency, and reducing government spending would lead to an improved economy through accessing local inputs and increasing export sales (Olukoshi 1996). However, even before the introduction of the Structural Adjustment Program in 1986, the steep decline in oil prices in the early 1980s made it increasingly difficult for textile companies in Kano to access spare parts for weaving and spinning equipment. One of the consequences of this situation was to reduce factory work and output. As Olukoshi (1996, 17) noted:

In a survey covering 34 companies in six subsectors of manufacturing and with ownership spread among foreign, indigenous, and Levantine manufacturers, the Kano branch of MAN confirmed the devastating effects of the crisis on industry. The survey, spanning the period from January to October 1984, found that the seven textile companies it covered were all, on average utilizing only about 14 per cent of their installed capacity. They had also re-trenched over 2,000 workers and the foreign exchange allocation which they received through import licenses issued by the federal government in 1984 met only 20 per cent of their total requirements.

Conditions for accessing imported spare parts and other supplies, such as chemical dyestuff used in the production of cotton textile prints, became increasingly expensive after the devaluation of the naira in 1987. Three of the Kano textile manufacturing companies that closed or were sold during the period immediately following the implementation of the Structural Adjust-ment Program included Holborn Nigeria Textiles, Ltd., Magraps Textiles Mill Limited, Kano, Northern Textiles Manufacturers–NTM (Gidan Bargo). These mills had all been established by Lebanese, North African, and Indian businessmen who adapted to these economic difficulties by moving onto other sources of livelihood.

CONCLUSION

As was seen with regard to the initial textile mill established by the Kano Cit-izens Trading Company in Kano, there was and remains considerable textile manufacturing and marketing expertise among Hausa and Fulani, as well as Lebanese and Indian, businessmen living in Kano. After all, Kano was the major center for the handwoven textiles and dyeing trade in West Africa in the nineteenth century (Candotti 2010; Shea 1975), as Heinrich Barth noted in his visit to Kano in 1851 (see introduction). Thus, despite the present dom-inance of Chinese textile imports in Kano markets, there are economic textile niches that smaller Kano companies have continued to fill. As is the case with Nigerian-Chinese collaboration in the generation of electricity, as suggested by plans for completion of the Mambilla Power Plant project, there may be future possibilities for Nigerian-Chinese collaboration in textile manufactur-ing in Kano State. Indeed, the many smaller textile-manufacturing operations in Kano, associated in the past with the initiative of local Nigerian and Leb-anese businessmen as well as collaborations between Kano businessmen and government institutions, may eventually be revived. While the production of textiles has diminished, trade in a wide range of textiles has continued in Kantin Kwari market in Kano. The establishment, growth, and subsequent dominance of Chinese-manufactured textile imports into this market, with its attendant problems and solutions, are discussed in the following chapter.

NOTES

1. In 2015, an interview with Alhaji Adhama was aired on YouTube in which he explains the founding of the company and also his collaboration with the Terytex Nigeria (see https://www.youtube.com/watch?v=3MP6z2nJTZE).

2. Beginning in late 2007, former president Olusegun Obasanjo initiated the N70 billion Textile Revival Fund (Ahmed 2008; see chapter 4).

3. In Kaduna State, Zaria Industries Limited, United Textile (UNTL), and Chellco Industry (Agbese et al. 2016; Bashir 2013) also received loans.

4. Before he ventured into textile manufacturing, he was involved in stationery manufacturing, of exercise books, attendance registers, and tissue paper. Alhaji Sa'idu Dattijo Adhama, interview with A. DanAsabe, January 16, 2018, Kano.

5. See also Forrest 1990, 48.

6. Both Alhaji Umar Tofa, the head of Tofa Textile Mills Ltd., and the mill's managing director, Suleiman Umar, are featured on YouTube (https://www.youtube.com/watch?v=YZLXh8lGpd4), as part of Bank of Industry, Nigeria's program to improve textile manufacturing in Nigeria through their Cotton, Textiles, and Garments Fund.

7. According to Bargery (1993 [1934], 1), *abada* is defined as "a European trade-cloth, so called because, although of many colours and shades, these are fast and do not fade."

8. Ebiteh Godwin, Personnel Manager, African Textile Manufacturing Ltd., interview with A. DanAsabe, September 10, 2018, Kano.

9. Ebiteh Godwin, interview with A. DanAsabe, August 24, 2015, Kano.

10. See the African Textiles Manufacturing Ltd. 2018 for images of wax prints and special-order prints as well as weaving and spinning equipment.

11. Personnel manager, Angel Spinning and Dyeing Mills, interview with A. DanAsabe, September 2, 2015, Kano.

12. Alhaji Sa'idu Dattijo Adhama, interview with A. DanAsabe, February 2, 2018, Kano.

13. Muhammad Kwaru, AGM personnel, interview with A. DanAsabe, November 16, 2016, Kano.

14. Ibrahim Isma'il, Gaskiya Textiles worker, interview with A. DanAsabe, January 30, 2018, Kano.

15. *Leadership Weekend* 2015, 19–21; Andrae and Beckman 1999, 118–34.

16. Alhaji Sa'idu Dattijo Adhama, interview with A. DanAsabe, February 11, 2018, Kano.

17. Alhaji Sa'idu Dattijo Adhama, interview with A. DanAsabe, February 11, 2018, Kano.

18. Murtala Muhammad, personnel officer, Dangote Group, interview with A. DanAsabe, August 22, 2017, Kano.

19. Alhaji Sa'idu Dattijo Adhama, interview with A. DanAsabe, January 23, 2017, Kano.

20. As Alhaji Adhama put it when speaking with a Central Bank of Nigeria manager, "we don't need a government loan, we need the textile levy monies."

21. In 2014, a Zaria woman bought six yards of *mai roba* cloth (for N900) for her daughter, who was wearing it as a group cloth when attending a wedding with her friends, who were all wearing it in the same pattern.

22. In January 2017, Elisha Renne purchased six yards of *mai roba atamfa* manufactured by MtL Fashion, a textile firm in Nabo, China, for N1,300 at Zaria City market. A similarly patterned cotton *atamfa* cloth was selling in the market for N4,600 for six yards.

23. One Chinese manufacturer, the Keer Group, has established a cotton mill in Indian Land, South Carolina, and is producing cotton thread from abundant and subsidized American-grown cotton. The thread is being exported to Asian countries (Tabuchi 2015).

24. Ten years later, however, the Kano Agricultural Development Agency established a demonstration farm for growing new types of cotton with longer staple.

25. Alhaji Sa'idu Dattijo Adhama, interview with A. DanAsabe, January 23, 2017, Kano.

26. In January 2018, as part of this agreement, "the Kano state government has handed over 150 hectares of land to Dangote Group for the development of $150m Dangote/Black Rhino solar power plant in Zakirai, Gabasawa local government area of the state" (Ibrahim 2018).

REFERENCES

Adamu, Lawan. 2010. "Chinese Exploit Us, Threaten Local Industries—Kano Bizmen." *Weekly Trust*, July 10. www.weeklytrust.com.ng/.

African Textiles Manufacturing Ltd. 2018. http://atmng.com.

Agbese, Andrew, Christiana Alabi, Maryam Ahmadu-Suka, and Francis Iloani. 2016. "Why Textile Industry Remains Dormant Despite FG's N100bn Bailout." *Daily Trust*, July 3. https://www.dailytrust.com.ng/.

Ahmed, Idris. 2008. "Why the N70bn Textile Fund got Stalled." *Daily Trust*, June 25. www.dailytrust.com.ng/.

Albasu, S. A. 1995. *The Lebanese in Kano: An Immigrant Community in a Hausa Society in the Colonial and Post-Colonial Periods*. Kano: KABS Print Services.

Andrae, Gunilla, and Björn Beckman. 1999. *Union Power in the Nigerian Textile Industry*. New Brunswick, NJ: Transaction Publishers.

Bargery, G. P. 1993 [1934]. *A Hausa-English and English-Hausa Dictionary*, 2nd ed. Zaria: Ahmadu Bello University Press.

Bashir, Ibrahim. 1989. "The Growth and Development of the Manufacturing Sector of Kano's Economy, 1950–1980." In *Kano and Some of Her Neighbors*, edited by B. M. Bakindo, 104–23. Zaria: Ahmadu Bello University Press.

Bashir, Misbahu. 2013. "How We've Controlled Blanket Market for 35 Years—Chellco." *Daily Trust*, December 22, 2013. https://www.dailytrust.com.ng/.

Candotti, Marisa. 2010. "The Hausa Textile Industry: Origins and Development in the

Precolonial Period." In *Being and Becoming Hausa: Interdisciplinary Perspectives*, edited by A. Haour and B. Rossi, 187–211. Leiden: Brill.

Daily Trust. 2017. "Gigantic Break in Mambilla Power Project." *Daily Trust*, September 3. https://www.dailytrust.com.ng/.

Daka, Terhemba Daka, Adeyemi Adepetun, and Stanley Opara. 2018. "Buhari Seeks China's Support for Mambilla Power Project." *The Guardian*, September 6 https://guardian.ng/news/.

DanAsabe, Abdulkarim. 1987. "Comparative Biographies of Selected Leaders of the Kano Commercial Establishment." PhD dissertation, Bayero University, Kano.

DanAsabe, Abdulkarim. 2000. "Biography of Select Kano Merchants, 1853–1955." *FAIS, Journal of the Humanities* 1, no. 2: 45–60.

Forrest, Tom. 1990. "The Advance of African Capital: The Growth of Nigerian Private Enterprises," No 24. Oxford: Queen Elizabeth House Development Studies Working Papers.

Gaskiya Tafi Kwabo. 1949. May 27.

Gwazaye, Yusuf A. 2013. *Rayuwata!* Kano: Gidan Dabino Publishers.

Habib, Hisham. 2012. "Kano Traders Send SOS to Kwankwaso over Chinese 'Invasion.'" *Daily Trust*, April 18. www.dailytrust.com.ng/.

Ibrahim, Yusha'u. 2017. "Kano Seals Deal with 10 Companies on Power, Infrastructure." *Daily Trust*, May 25. https://www.dailytrust.com.ng/.

Ibrahim, Yusha'u. 2018. "Dangote Receives Land for $150m Solar Power Project in Kano." *Daily Trust*, January 22. https://www.dailytrust.com.ng/.

Leadership Weekend. 2015. October 17, 19–21.

Lere, I., H. Musa, N. D. Khalid, and I. M. Giginyu. 2012. "As Lebanese, Indians Retreat, Chinese Fill the Void in Kano." *Daily Trust*, September 9. www.dailytrust.com.ng/.

Mahmud, Idris. 2016. "Why Cotton Farming Is Declining in Katsina." *Daily Trust*, June 30. http://www.dailytrust.com.ng/.

Mahmud, Idris. 2017. "Bumper Cotton Harvest in Katsina, Price Rises in Markets." *Daily Trust*, November 23. https://www.dailytrust.com.ng/.

Ministry of Information. 1969. *Kano State of Nigeria*. Kano.

Muhammad, Hamisu. 1979. "Focus on Isyaku Rabi'u." *New Nigerian*, February 22.

Muhammad, Musa. 2010. "Globalization and Nigeria Textile Factories. An Analysis of Three Kano Textile Factories." PhD dissertation, Bayero University, Kano.

Olukoshi, A. O. 1996. "Economic Crisis, Structural Adjustment, and the Coping Strategies of Manufacturers in Kano, Nigeria." UNRISD Discussion Papers, DP77. New York: United Nations.

Pedler, Frederick. 1974. *The Lion and the Unicorn in Africa: A History of the Origins of the United Africa Company 1787–1931*. London: Heinemann Educational.

Shea, Philip J. 1975. "The Development of an Export-Oriented Dyed Cloth Industry in Kano Emirate in the Nineteenth Century." PhD dissertation, University of Wisconsin, Madison.

Tabuchi, Hiroko. 2015. "Chinese Textile Mills Are Now Hiring in Places Where Cotton Was King." *New York Times*, August 2. www.nytimes.com.

Umar, Shehu. 2016. "Why Cotton Farming Is in Decline: Ginneries Shutting Down in Zamfara." *Daily Trust*, September 24. https://www.dailytrust.com.ng/.

Umar, Auwalu, and Ruqayyah Aliyu. 2012. "Fresh Bomb Blasts in Kano." *Daily Trust*, January 25. www.dailytrust.com.ng/.

Wakili, Isiaka, Ishmael Mudashir, and Latifat Opoola. 2016. "FG Recovers N115bn From Looters." *Daily Trust*, June 5. https://www.dailytrust.com.ng/.

World Trade Organization. 2015. 'Textile Monitoring Body: The Agreement on Textiles and Clothing." http://www.wto.org/english/tratop_e/texti_e/texintro_e.htm.

CHAPTER 6

Chinese Printed Textiles and Traders in Kantin Kwari Market, Kano

HANNATU HASSAN

Kantin Kwari market, located in central Kano, is the largest textile market in northern Nigeria. Due to its reputation and location, it has become a center for textile trading and marketing between the Nigerian traders and the Chinese textile manufacturing representatives. During the late twentieth century, Nigerian textile industries faced a number of challenges, which brought about the closure of many textile mills in Kano and Kaduna, as was discussed in chapters 4 and 5. These closures, which were exacerbated by increasing importation of Chinese textiles in the 1990s, have resulted in the presence of Chinese textiles, along with Chinese representatives of several firms, in Kano's Kantin Kwari market. This chapter, based on personal interviews and newspaper accounts, examines this situation whereby Chinese textiles and firms have entered Kantin Kwari market and how Nigerian wholesale and retail cloth traders have responded to their presence in Kano in the early twenty-first century. The chapter begins with a discussion of the early history of Kantin Kwari market, during the period when Lebanese businessmen were selling textiles in the Syrian Quarters, after which Lebanese and Nigerian partners established textile businesses within the market. It continues with a description of the market during the 1960s and 1970s, when Nigerian textile mills in Kano and Kaduna were fully operational and supplied the market with a range of different cotton textiles. Following an examination of Chinese textile traders' entry into the market, the chapter then considers how Kano traders have interacted with Chinese textile manufacturing representatives who have set up offices in Kano. Consequently, there have been several recent disputes, which included the traders' use of warehouses to avoid customs officials' scrutiny and Chinese companies' attempts to manufacture and market copies of local indigo-dyed, resist-print textiles. In light of the importance of the textile trade for Kantin Kwari market's viability and the continued importation of Chinese manufactured textiles, the chapter concludes with a consideration of the possibility of Nigerian-Chinese textile collaborations in Kano.

BACKGROUND ON KANTIN KWARI MARKET, KANO

The city of Kano has a long history as a center of commerce in the West African subregion (Mahadi 1984). The textile market, Kantin Kwari, is one of the busiest markets in Kano State, with several thousand cloth traders from all over Nigeria and neighboring West African countries doing business there on a daily basis. It is also one of the largest textile markets in sub-Saharan Africa, with a daily turnover running into several million naira.

The beginning of Kantin Kwari market dates back to the 1930s, when "commercial transport services which gave rise to the establishment of Fagge taxi park (opposite Kantin Kwari)" (Fagge 1970, 88) facilitated transport of traders and textiles. In 1949, the British colonial resident created an official market area in Fagge-Ta-Kudu that was to be controlled by the Kano Native Authority. "Only indigenous Kano traders were to be given plots there. African Arabs who lived in Kano for many years were considered 'Natives' and were to be given plots there as well" (Albasu 1995, 134). In 1950, Lebanese traders who did not already have plots in the adjacent Syrian Quarters bought plots in the Fagge-Ta-Kudu area, which came to be known as Kantin Kwari.[1] In 1953, many certificates of occupancy were issued to Lebanese businessmen who were trading in textiles. As S. A. Albasu (1995, 138) explains:

> Nearly all the Lebanese shops in Fagge-Ta-Kudu dealt in retailing textiles. They bought imported cloth in bulk and sold to Africans in pieces. Many of the European firms preferred supplying the Lebanese whom they knew very well and whose performance in the groundnut trade they appreciated. Thus while the Europeans dominated the import trade the Lebanese traders established a stronghold over the distribution trade.

This situation gradually changed as some Kano businessmen joined Lebanese traders in Kantin Kwari in opening shops. Sani Buhari Daura was the first Kano businessman to open a shop, known as the Bayajida Trading

Company in the Kantin Kwari market area.[2] He began as a dealer for Kaduna Textiles Limited (KTL), which had started manufacturing unbleached baft cotton cloth in 1957 (Maiwada and Renne 2013). He brought this unbleached baft (*akoko*) and later bleached (*zauwati* or *alawayyo*) cotton cloth from KTL in Kaduna as a wholesaler and sold it to retailers in the market at Kano. Kantin Kwari market later expanded when Alhaji Sanusi Dantata built shops in the market along the main thoroughfare of Unity Road.[3] Alhaji Nababa Badamasi, another textile businessman in Kantin Kwari market, later went on to establish the Gaskiya Textile Mills in Kano, which manufactured unbleached white shirting material (*akoko*), cotton print textiles (*atamfa*), and tan khaki materials. These textiles were sold in Kantin Kwari market until the company ended operations in 1996 (see chapter 5).

THE INTRODUCTION OF CHINESE TEXTILES AND TRADERS IN KANTIN KWARI MARKET

While some have described the extensive presence of Jega traders from Kebbi State in Kantin Kwari market after 2000 as facilitating the movement of Chinese traders into the market with manufactured textiles,[4] Chinese textile traders had shown interest in this market earlier, in the 1990s. In 1997, according to Alhaji Sa'idu Adhama, "I saw Chinese in Cotonou—they were eyeing Nigeria and the Kano Kantin Kwari market. I said that if we don't do anything they will come and take over."[5] Yet nothing was done, and by 2012 most of the textiles sold in Kantin Kwari market were imported from China (Eneji et al. 2012).

A particular configuration of factors contributed to immense growth in Chinese textile imports to Kantin Kwari market in early twenty-first century. The demise of the textile manufacturing industry in northern Nigeria by the beginning of the twenty-first century was a critical element. But the opening up of China in the mid-1980s—after state trading companies were abolished (Haugen 2011, 165)—to foreign textile firms, which introduced improved textile equipment, contributed to efficiencies of production and lower costs. Furthermore, there were changes in World Trade Organization textile trade agreements, which included the ending of the Multifibre Arrangement (in 1994) and of the transitional Agreement on Textiles and Clothing (in 2004), in accordance with the rules of the General Agreement on Tariffs and Trade (GATT) (World Trade Organization 2015). After the Chinese government agreed to observe WTO rules concerning world trade in 2001 (Yeung and

Mok 2004), Chinese textile exports expanded exponentially, particularly after the Nigerian government abandoned its textile import ban in 2010 (Mudashir 2010). Finally, an expansion of digital business communication—the use of smartphones, express courier services, and websites to provide information on Chinese textile companies and their products (discussed in chapter 7)—and the movement of people (through expanded flights between Nigeria and China)—facilitated the presence of Chinese traders and textile company representatives.

TEXTILE TRADE IN KANTIN KWARI MARKET IN THE TWENTY-FIRST CENTURY

At Kantin Kwari market, Chinese textiles are sold through several venues: by Chinese company agents, by Nigerian wholesale traders, by local Nigerian trading companies, and by independent textile retail traders with stalls in the market. Chinese textile firms have offices on the main roads on the outskirts of the market, where a select group of Nigerian wholesale textile buyers meet with Chinese personnel to order bales of cloth. One textile firm, Senfiertex Jacquard Manufacturers, for example, has a company office in a building on Unity Road that was established in 2008. Buyers may examine samples of cotton damask fabrics produced in its factory in Zhuji, Zhejiang Province.[6] As part of Nigerian government requirements, this company has Nigerian employees, which include its Nigerian manager, who has an office in an adjacent part of the building, and a Nigerian guarantor, who sells to Nigerian wholesale customers at a business office elsewhere in Kano. Additionally, Nigerian wholesale buyers who have long-standing trade relationships with this company may be invited to visit the company's factory in Zhuji, both to reward them for their business and to encourage company loyalty. For example, Alhaji Nuhu Yakubu Abubakar traveled to China in 2009:

> From Kano, we started going to China, getting orders from China because we have Chinese people in the market, Kantin Kwari. I started meeting them there. I used to give orders for *shadda* [cotton damask], but sometimes *atamfa* [printed textiles]. But 80 percent of my orders were for *shadda*. The *atamfa* I used to order was not expensive, it's low quality, it's sold from N1,500 to N3,000. You know, if you are educated, there is no problem with global business. I went to China only once in 2009 but after that, all our transactions

are through the internet or handset. Since I went to their factory and saw how they were doing their work, we are only communicating through handset. And I will communicate to them what I want and they will send it to me.[7]

Many Nigerian wholesale buyers, like Alhaji Abubakar, now carry out business with Chinese companies mainly by phone, the Internet, and by FedEx. Chinese companies send electronic images of textile patterns and colors and physical samples upon which Nigerian traders make order decisions. On placing an order, buyers are expected to pay a percentage of the total cost of the materials, and once they have arrived buyers pay the balance. Some Nigerian traders have offices near Kantin Kwari market where they sell wholesale lots (by the bale or bundle), mainly of cotton damask or cotton print textiles purchased directly from Chinese firms.

There are also Nigerian-owned trading companies that buy textiles indirectly through guarantor-brokers from several Chinese companies, which produce popular brands such as ABC, Sunstar, and MBTX textiles. One such company sells these textiles in a large shop on the edge of Kantin Kwari market. As the company manager, Alhaji Sadiq, explained, his group decided to place wholesale orders with Nigerian guarantors associated with particular Chinese firms and then to sell textiles in a spacious showroom with adjacent parking. In instances when he has special orders—a request for a particular wax print textile, perhaps with an adaptation of another textile design in a different color scheme—he deals directly with company guarantors.[8]

Nigerian Traders Conducting Business in China

While Alhaji Abubakar traveled to China at the invitation of the textile company he worked with, some textile traders consider traveling to China to shop for textiles they want, either by placing orders with companies in Guangzhou, China, or through communication with Kano-based brokers who work there. Several northern Nigerian textile traders from Kano work with Chinese textile brokers in particular areas of Guangzhou and nearby Foshan, where they have established a system of trade connections. By working closely with a trusted Chinese broker, they are able to choose particular patterns to be manufactured by the factory. By sending the finished bales of cloth by container to Kano, traders can avoid (or at least forestall) other traders marketing their new patterns before they do (see also Haugen 2011).

Two northern Nigerian traders, Alhaji Shafi'u Abdulkadir and Alhaji Musa Bala, travel to Guangzhou, China, where they order textile materials directly from Chinese brokers (Renne 2015). In Kano, Alhaji Shafi'u and Alhaji Musa share the same shops, and they reach their customers there and through other agents, as the two of them are away at Guangzhou much of the time. Alhaji Shafi'u started his business with his uncle, initially clearing goods for customers in Kano before venturing into cloth trading in China. More recently, however, he observed that work in China is not the same as it was, as customers were not buying as they did in the past. For example, he used to send at least fifty containers or more to Nigeria but now he hardly gets enough orders to send two or three containers weekly.[9] With the decline in oil prices and the weak Nigerian economy, consumption of textiles has fallen in recent years.

Retail Nigerian Traders in Kantin Kwari Market

Kantin Kwari market is filled with many stalls and shops rented by retail textile cloth traders that sell different types of textiles, such as damask (*shadda*), cotton print (*atamfa*), and plain unbleached cotton (*akoko*) cloths, along with headscarves and other garments. There are also some traders without shops that display their textile goods by the side of the road or in front of some shops. These traders are often small agents for some of the big shop owners such as Alhaji Shafi'u. Mallam Umar Idris is one such cloth trader without a stall who has direct contract with wholesale traders. Mallam Idris started his cloth trading twenty years ago as an apprentice. Without a shop or stall, he makes rounds in the market looking for buyers. Since a shop or stall costs more than N1,000,000 or more, depending on the location in Kantin Kwari market, he has continued to trade in this way.

Most of the traders who were interviewed started cloth trade as apprentices; some are still apprentices going to school and coming back to the market in the afternoons to work. Bello Abdullahi Usman is an apprentice who works in a shop belonging to Musa Bala and Alhaji Shafi'u Abdulkadir. Two other apprentices work with him in the shop, but he is the most senior of them all. He also travels with cloth to sell in other parts of Nigeria, such as towns in Niger State and in Abuja, the Nigerian capital.

EMERGING DISCORD IN CHINESE-NIGERIAN TEXTILE TRADE IN KANO

The current ascendancy of Chinese manufactured textiles in Kantin Kwari market in Kano as well as the presence of Chinese textile company representatives there have led to a series of disagreements. For example, following the ending of the 2010 textile import ban and the liberalization of Nigerian-Chinese trade, Kano market traders have faced growing problems with the presence of Chinese traders selling directly in Kantin Kwari market. This situation was a source of continuing friction, such that the Kantin Kwari Traders Association restricted the number of days that Chinese traders could enter the market to Wednesdays and Saturdays, thus reducing their ability to undersell Nigerian textile traders' prices (Mudashir and Yaya 2014).[10] Consequently, Chinese traders and factory representatives sought to continue textile trading but outside of the market proper. For the representatives of Chinese textile factories who work there, they deal exclusively with their companies' Nigerian guarantors and long-standing Nigerian wholesale buyers. Nigerian wholesale and retail traders in Kantin Kwari market buy their materials from these Nigerian men, not directly from the Chinese, reflecting the hierarchy of control of Chinese textile procurement within Kano, with smaller Nigerian retail traders at the bottom of this trading pyramid.

Smuggling of Textiles to Kano: Reactions of Kano Textile Workers and Dealers

The earlier practice of truckers bringing textiles from Cotonou, Benin, to the market in Kano discussed in chapter 4 has continued despite various efforts to curtail it. In 1999, the Textile Workers Union pressured the Obasanjo administration to stop the smuggling of Chinese textiles into Kano because they believed they were undermining Nigerian-manufactured textile sales. During a raid conducted in the Kano area that year, any imported printed textiles found in Kantin Kwari market were confiscated (although European textiles were said to have been left undisturbed); one Lebanese businessman lost millions of naira worth of textiles. Following the raid, textile dealers negotiated an informal system for importing textiles with government officials, who discontinued the practice of market raids.[11]

This raid nevertheless gave dealers the idea to use warehouses away from Kantin Kwari market. Rather than having trucks deliver containers close by with textiles being taken directly to the market, the dealers built large warehouses with tall walls around them so that trucks with containers could enter and no one could see them offloading the containers with the contraband textiles inside. A limited number of textiles would then be brought to the market for buyers to sell. More textiles could be brought from distant warehouses if they were needed. As was the case in eighteenth-century France when the government sought to impose a ban in the import of Asian textiles in order to protect the nascent French textile industry (Gottman 2016), the popular demand for textiles from China and India supported the massive smuggling of these textiles despite government efforts.

Continued Smuggling After 2010

These practices continued even after 2010 when the Nigerian government opened the country to imported textiles, with associated tariffs and duties to be paid. Some dealers sought to avoid paying duty whenever possible.[12] Smugglers might disguise a container's contents by putting items without duty charges in front. For example, there was a lace company in Kano without one lace machine that was essentially a front for Chinese lace textile imports. When they brought containers with lace fabrics from China, they were packed in such a way that the back of the container was packed with thread so that customs officials let them pass without paying the required 20 percent duty. Indeed, the word for smuggler in Hausa, *yi fasa kwauri*, literally, "breaking the shin" refers figuratively to incapacitating a customs officer (with cash) so that he would allow a shipment to pass.

More recently, imported Chinese textiles have been being sent to the enormous container entrepot in Lomé, Togo (Sylvanus 2016). Alhaji Isyaku Shittu, a Zaria City cloth trader, explained this situation in July 2010:

> Everything comes from Kano, in the market, not [Nigerian] companies. And those who bought it in Kano bought it from those selling it in Niger. Niger gets it from Togo and Togo gets it from China—they don't go to Cotonou now. And even though we have customs, if they give customs something, they will just allow them to enter. Even in Kano, when they bought the material to Zaria, customs officers will check it, but when they see the 'Made in Nigeria' printed on the selvage, they don't say anything.[13]

Thus, even when it was in place, the textile import ban had been largely ineffective due to Nigeria's porous borders and malleable customs officials. As one cloth trader in Zaria noted: "The ban is there but it is not enforced. Most of the textiles sold in Kano and Lagos are from China and most of the people bringing them are top politicians. This is widely believed."[14] Indeed, since the early 2000s, Chinese textiles have come to dominate the Nigerian textile market. As one man observed, there is no way that this smuggling could go on without government approval or looking the other way.[15] In

2015, though, customs officials decided to investigate the smuggling situation in Kano.

The Warehouse Raid by Customs Officials in 2015

After the 1999 raid on textile traders in Kano and the subsequent unofficial settlement, Chinese textiles brought into the country via Benin and Niger were often stored in large warehouses. As has been noted, these warehouses served as a way of avoiding customs agents' inquiries about large shipments of cloth without documentation. But on May 8, 2015, officials of the Nigerian Customs Service (NCS) began raiding warehouses where suspected smuggled textiles were being stored. Seventy-five warehouses containing smuggled textiles were raided and sealed up. Accord to the comptroller-general of the Nigerian Customs Service, Abdullahi Dikko Inde, "I initiated the raid of the warehouses from my office in Abuja based on information in order to salvage our economy. Only one of the warehouses' worth is N4.2bn and if you multiply it by 75, you will get the worth of the seizure we have made" (Mudashir 2015a). As it turned out, the amount of smuggled materials was estimated at N315 billion (Mudashir 2015c). This raid associated with smuggled textiles was not the first. As was discussed, "During the Obasanjo administration, over 200 trailers of contrabands were burnt here in Kano and over 400 others were burnt in Lagos," Inde observed (Mudashir 2015a).

Two weeks later, customs officials began to de-seal the closed warehouses after warehouse owners paid the requisite duties. As one senior customs official observed, "The Chinese traders are responding more than the local ones. Out of the 25 Chinese-owned warehouses, owners of 15 warehouses have responded and we realised over N1 billion as duties from them" (Mudashir 2015d).[16] Nonetheless, five Chinese nationals who were involved in the operation of illegal warehousing of textiles in the Gandun Albasa area of Kano were arrested, and three were deported (Ogwu 2015):

> The Comptroller-General of Immigration, David Parradang, disclosed that investigations by his service found that three out of the five Chinese nationals do not possess valid travel documents to reside and engage in any business in Nigeria beyond the scope of their admission, adding that immediate steps will therefore be taken to effect their deportation.

Upon settlement of the warehouse textile smuggling predicament, Comptroller-General Inde further stated that the service would intensify routine mop-up operations of smuggled textiles to identify illegal immigrants involved in the trade. He added that those who are law abiding and are contributing to the national economic development through foreign direct investment (FDI) will be encouraged and given any assistance they may need (Ogwu 2015).

What is particularly interesting about the dispute over the closure of the textile warehouses is that many Kano businessmen were opposed to this action. As the secretary of the Kano State Traders' Union, Alhaji Aliyu Lamin Gwale, put it:

> It was the closure of the textile factories that pushed us to China and we have been doing this for over 15 years. We are surprised that suddenly they went after our warehouses and sealed 75 so far. . . . It is unfortunate that after we overcame the insecurity challenge in Kano and traders started coming from within the country and beyond, the Customs are now doing this to us. (Mudashir 2015b)

While the government did deport three Chinese traders involved in smuggling imported textiles without paying duties, many who did pay customs duties and whose papers were in order remained. Similarly, many Nigerian traders paid customs duties for their imported cloth and are continuing in business, for, as they observed, the closure of the Nigerian textile mills forced them to import cloth. In a sense, then, Chinese and Nigerian traders are in some agreement about Chinese textile imports.

CONTROVERSY OVER RESIST-DYED AND PRINT TEXTILES IN 2015

Nonetheless, other problems have arisen. Nigerian traders working with Chinese company representatives in Kano continue to worry about Chinese copies of pattern designs associated with Hausa resist-dyeing and embroidery work. The Chinese trade and investment in Nigeria have made goods cheaper and spurred infrastructure projects, but the relationship has also exacted a cost. This cost affects not only cloth traders in Kantin Kwari market but also those using synthetic dyes for tie-dyeing in their compounds and for dyers in the older indigo dye pit centers, many of whom still use methods dating back more than five hundred years. The local dyers accused the Chinese of copying their products and selling the inferior cloth at a low price. On May 14, 2015, the Kano

Dyers Association, popularly known as Masu Rini Progressive Association (MARIPA), staged a protest march, as Abdulkadir Muktar (2015) explained:

> Barely 24 hours after the Emir of Kano, Mallam Muhammadu Sanusi, sought the help of the Chinese government for more investment in Nigeria, thousands of residents of the city yesterday protested against what they described as Chinese "invasion" and dominance of the tie and dye business in the state. The emir had received the Chinese Ambassador to Nigeria, Mr. Gu Xiaojie in his palace on Monday, asking him to help buoy the nation's economy by encouraging more Chinese investment in the country. But protesters yesterday blocked the road to the emir's palace for hours, with placards which said: "No more China Ghalila," "We are not foreigners," "Mu da rini muke alfarma," meaning "We are proud of our dyeing business."

The secretary of the Kano Dyers Association, Yakubu Lawal Ishaq, said that the Chinese will soon cause thirty thousand dyers and traders in Kano to lose their jobs if imported textiles are allowed to flourish without restrictions in Kano. The emir of Kano, Muhammadu Sanusi II, cautioned the protesters to refrain from any act that might cause violence in the course of agitating over their plight. The emir promised that the state government would look into the situation. On August 31, 2015, a memorandum of understanding was signed at the office of Alhaji Rabi'u Bako, the state commissioner of commerce, trade and investment, which the local dyers said would help preserve a trade the city of Kano prides itself upon. Based on the agreement, the Chinese traders would no longer bring the ready-made dye materials into Kano. Similarly, dyers would henceforth purchase good chemicals from the Chinese along with face masks, gloves, and white cotton fabric. The Chinese traders were given three months to dispose of all the materials they had brought to Kano. The dyers association secretary, Malam Ishaq, said that after signing a memorandum of understanding with the Chinese traders, the Chinese agreed to stop imitating the local dyers products.

In addition to copying locally made indigo-dyed cloths, the Chinese were selling imitation embroidered garments, which are much cheaper than machine-embroidered local products. Consumers buy what they refer to as "Chinese brocade" because of the price difference. Mallama Aishatu, a trader who sells textiles in Kantin Kwari market, said that her customers were happy with the Chinese brocade as most of them could not afford the local embroiderers' products, which are expensive.

Fig. 6.1. Women's dress top and wrapper, made with textile materials imported from China, with imitation of embroidery along the sleeve edges, November 2017, Kano. (Photograph by Hannatu Hassan.)

TEXTILE TRADING NETWORKS AND SOCIAL DYNAMICS

The different perspectives of government customs officials, Kantin Kwari traders, and Chinese textile manufacturer representatives reflect the particular economic interests of those involved in the textile trade between China and Northern Nigeria. Their positions are not equal: Chinese brokers and factory managers have a product that is manufactured efficiently and in a range of qualities and prices that could not be matched by Nigerian textile mills even before the protections provided by the WTO treaties on textile trade were dismantled and the Kaduna and Kano textile mills collapsed. While the illegal importation of Chinese textiles at lower prices may have undermined Nigerian textile sales during the 1970s and 1980s, the industry's decline also reflected Nigerian internal problems, such as frequent changes in political leadership, which contributed to abrupt shifts in industrial policy and a failure to maintain the power infrastructure, as well as external factors, such as the introduction of the World Bank/IMF Structural Adjustment Program in 1986 that led to the deregulation of the Nigerian currency and made imports of spare parts and modern weaving equipment prohibitively expensive (Akinrinade and Ogen 2008, 164–67).

Yet however unequal, the Chinese factory representatives and the Nigerian wholesale and retail traders are in a relationship as sellers and buyers and therefore need one another. Rather than Nigerians vilifying the Chinese for taking away their business or Chinese implying that Nigerians cannot compete, some, like Alhaji Sadiq, suggest considering the possibility of making the most out of this situation:

> I know that almost all over the world, [people] they buy from China. . . . Because if you look at the cost of production . . . it's another problem. . . . I don't want to challenge the government or challenge anybody here but here the truth is this. If only our companies would have less problem . . . what I mean there is NEPA [electricity], there are many things they need [in order to] . . . be able to produce all these things. . . . Most of the Chinese people if they know that these companies now can survive, then they will be ready to bring their money to come and invest in the country. I know that most of the Chinese people will do it, because it is business, everyone is looking for how to make something [money]. So this thing is a collective something but it has to start from our government . . . this way, maybe it will work.[17]

His comments suggest the possibility of some sort of Chinese-Nigerian collaboration.

CONSEQUENCES OF CHINESE TEXTILES AND MANUFACTURING REPRESENTATIVES IN KANTIN KWARI

The presence of the Chinese investors at the market initially was seen as beneficial. The Chinese came with a considerable amount of capital to push the market forward, and they guaranteed production of the latest designs of textile materials that were in high demand. The Chinese provided the seed money to those in need and partnered with them in the textile business. But as time went on, the Chinese manufacturing representatives took over the market, and fortune then turned into misfortune, according to a local businessman.

The local traders in Kantin Kwari market complain that the Chinese are recruiting Nigerian traders to conduct business on their behalf in return for some of the profits. Nigerian cloth traders in the market also complain that the Chinese are taking over Kantin Kwari market. Some cloth traders claim that the Chinese representatives in the cloth market are putting them out of business, leaving them nothing but huge debts and heaps of goods in their shops. Members of the Nigerian textile traders association reminisced that when they were dealing with the Lebanese they operated almost on an equal footing, but with the Chinese the situation is different. Now, because only a few dealers go to China to bring goods, 80 percent of textile goods are brought directly by Chinese representatives. The remaining 20 percent are brought in by wholesaler traders such as Alhaji Shafi'u who compete in the market with the Chinese wholesalers whose capital cannot be compared with their own.[18] Thus, after repeated complaints from the local traders, the government began to take action in May 2012, with immigration officials arresting forty-five Chinese nationals over retail trading in Kano State.

Interactions between Kano and Chinese Traders

According to Alhaji Awalu Gambari Jakada, who has been in the textile business and market since 1979, relations between Kano and Chinese traders in the textile market are not good. He explained that the Chinese have not kept their promise of restricting themselves to wholesale trade. Chinese traders have ventured into retailing alongside the Nigerian traders, which was not part of the agreement when the Chinese entered the cloth market. One problem is that orders that are made by the Nigerian businessmen are not delivered in good time. According to Alhaji Awalu, the Chinese take orders of textile prints from Nigerian businessmen, but instead of sending the orders in a timely fashion, Chinese traders fill the market with their Nigerian customers' orders. The Chinese traders then sell these print textiles at a low price before bringing the Nigerian customer's orders to Kano for sale. This situation results in the Nigerian traders losing millions of naira.[19] Yet some Chinese businessmen, such as Mr. Lee, observe the original agreement rules. Mr. Lee only gives goods to Nigerian wholesalers and does not retail his textiles at all. Alhaji Awalu and the other Kano traders who were interviewed said that if all the Chinese traders and company representatives would do business like Mr. Lee then all would be well.

THE FUTURE OF KANTIN KWARI MARKET

Kantin Kwari textile market in Kano does have a future according to most of the local traders in the market, although some traders have closed their shops due to lack of funds and to competition from Chinese textile manufacturers' representatives in the market. These traders believe that the Nigerian government can help to ensure the market's future through various interventions. According to Hajiya Halima, a local trader in the market, such interventions will encourage the Chinese traders to invest in building textile industries in the country instead of importing textiles into the country. Government should also try and repair the country's infrastructure, such as roads, while the power supply should be adequate so that the industries would not be running at a loss. The textile mills that have closed should also be reopened through government assistance.[20]

The market can still survive, according to some wholesale businessmen like Alhaji Shafi'u, if the Chinese were restricted to the wholesale business and would leave the retailing to the local traders, who cannot compete with the Chinese in terms of goods and finance.[21] Smuggling of textile goods could also be more effectively stopped if the Nigerian Immigration and Customs Services would monitor Chinese activities in the country. Furthermore, Chinese traders in Kano, such as Mr. Lee, should be recognized for his ethical business practice. He has even been given a business site along Maiduguri Road, near Kantin Kwari market, which is currently under construction. Nigerian traders are not worried, though, as he will restrict his business to wholesale trading as he has done in the past.[22]

Possibilities of Nigeria-Chinese Textile Collaboration

While the Chinese have many business ventures in Nigeria, the Chinese prefer to manufacture finished products in their country and ship them to Nigeria. This situation has led to a huge trade imbalance between China and Nigeria (Iloani 2017). Yet Nigerian traders in Kantin Kwari market who were interviewed all agreed that there can be collaboration between Nigerian and Chinese textile manufacturers. Many, including the emir of Kano, Muhammadu Sanusi II, have called for assistance from the Chinese for help to rebuild the textile industry in Nigeria.

One possible joint venture involves a textile industrial park. The Kano State government has signed a memorandum of understanding with the Shandong Ruyi Group of China for establishment of a $600 million textile industrial park in Kano, which would be one of the biggest in Africa upon its completion. This MOU was signed by Alhaji Usman Alhaji, secretary of the Kano State government on its behalf, and Mr. Ya Fu Quion on behalf of the Ruyi Group, in the presence of his Excellency Dr. Abdullahi Umar Ganduje OFR and the chairman of the Shandong Ruyi Group at the headquarters of the Shandong Ruyi Group, a multibillion-dollar Chinese textile conglomerate based in Jining, China (Adewale 2017).[23]

The possibility of successful joint Chinese-Nigerian development projects, which could include textile manufacturing, raises the question of whether such efforts will be a South-South "win-win situation" for the two countries. Taylor (2007) has observed that the Chinese government, which has invested considerable funds for improving infrastructure in Nigeria, has a vested as well as ideological interest in seeing such projects through. Textile traders in the Kantin Kwari market area believe that in order to increase the amount of Nigerian-made textiles, the government should reopen textile mills that have closed. Some argue that there is a need for Nigeria to reduce its dependence on exports through the diversification of domestic production such as textiles.

Some northern Nigerians, such as Alhaji Isyaku Umar, the chairman of the Tofa Group of Companies, are not categorically opposed to Chinese participation in the Nigerian economy. While Alhaji Umar wants Chinese traders to be restricted from directly trading in Kantin Kwari market, he approves of the establishment of a plastics factory by Chinese investors, as it provides Nigerians with employment. As he observed, "You know the participation of the Chinese in the country's economy can be categorised into two. One commercial and the second industrial. The government should discourage the commercial and encourage the industrial because it assists in boosting our economy" (Mudashir and Yaya 2014). As Alhaji Nuhu Yakubu Abubakar, the Kano-based wholesale textile trader who deals directly with a Chinese factory in Zhejiang Province, pragmatically observed:

You can take a new UNTL [United Nigeria Textile Ltd.] sample and send it to China and they will produce the same textile at a lower cost. Because our people are going for the cheaper-priced cloth and we the business people, we like only profit. But if they put the textile industry in order, we prefer to deal with our own people in Nigeria. Because our country will improve and people will get more work to do. And sometimes we don't like to go outside to buy things but if we can't get it in our country, we have to.[24]

For all the potential problems, he is not opposed to working with Chinese textile manufacturers in establishing mills in special economic or free trade zones in Nigeria for their mutual benefit.

CONCLUSION

Kano State has long been known as the center of commerce and industry, in which textiles played a major role. In 1851, Heinrich Barth (1857, 1:511) traveled to Kano and observed indigo dyeing and cloth production there:

> There is really something grand in this kind of industry, which spreads to the north as far as Múrzuk, Ghát, and even Tripoli; to the west, not only to Timbúktu, but in some degree even as far as the shores of the Atlantic, the very inhabitants of Arguin dressing in the cloth woven and dyed in Kanó; to the east, all over Bórnu, although there it comes in contact with native industry of the country; and to the south it maintains a rivalry with the native industry of the I'gbira and I'gbo, while toward the southeast it invades the whole of Adamáwa.

Long-distance traders from northern Nigeria as well as trans-Saharan traders from Tripoli carried Kano cloth to many places.

By the beginning of the twenty-first century, however, the closure of most of the textile mills in Kano and Kaduna states has led to textile traders finding it hard to survive, as they are at the mercy of the new giants of textile production, the Chinese. According to Villoria (2009), Nigeria has been a net loser in textile trading with China as the rapid growth in China's manufactured exports has reduced African manufactures' market share in both domestic and foreign markets for clothing industries.

The extensive imports of inexpensive new and used textiles have undermined the textile production in the country and endangered its self-sufficiency. According to Aibueku (2016), more than twenty-five textile mills have shut down and many others are running at less than 40 percent capacity. Many textile traders in Kano blame the decline of the Nigerian textile industry on the influx of cheaper fabrics from China and India. Yet there are other problems that remain, such as an inadequate infrastructure, a shortage of raw materials, an unreliable electricity supply, the smuggling of Chinese textiles to avoid customs duties, and the copying by the Chinese of Nigerian textile patterns. Recent discussions for reopening textile mills in Kaduna reflect efforts to encourage the use of locally made materials for Nigerian uniforms (Agbese and Alabi 2017). For many Nigerians, the rebuilding of the Nigerian textile industry, in collaboration with Chinese textile manufacturing companies—using up-to-date machinery, well-trained staff, and moderately priced products—would be worth the effort needed to accomplish this goal. According to one Nigerian trader interviewed in 2015, "We are in total support of the efforts by the federal government to revive our textile industries. Our partners in China are ready to come to the country and establish factories in the country but what they want is improved security and electricity" (Mudashir 2015b). There is also a need for improved textile printing machinery including digital resources and equipment, which is discussed in the next chapter.

NOTES

1. This area was not attractive to Hausa businessmen who already owned plots in the area because it was a *kwari* (depression) area and was liable to flooding(Albasu 1995, 136).

2. Abdulkarim DanAsabe, interview with Hannatu Hassan, November 10, 2017, Kano.

3. Alhaji Hassan Dantata, interview with Hannatu Hassan, November 10, 2017, Kano.

4. See *Leadership* 2015.

5. Alhaji Adhama, interview with E. Renne, January 23, 2017, Kano.

6. Senfiertex Jacquard is a branch of a larger company, Zhejiang Guoshen Textile Co., Ltd., in Zhejiang, China. http://www.chinatexnet.com/ChinaSuppliers/25196/Senfiertex-Jacquard-223696.html.

7. Alhaji Nuhu Yakubu Abubakar, interview with E. Renne, August 28, 2012, Zaria.

8. Alhaji Sadiq Yusuf, interview with E. Renne, November 13, 2012, Kano; see also Renne 2015.

9. Alhaji Shafi'u, interview with H. Hassan, August 7, 2015, Kano. He also travels to Hong Kong and Egypt.

10. Alhaji Sadiq Yusuf, interview with E. Renne, November 13, 2012, Kano.

11. Mohammadu Waziri, one of this volume's authors, strongly opposed this action by the government. He notes that the government not only banned the importation of foreign textiles but went further to instruct custom officials to storm the market and confiscate the already imported goods of the textile marketers. In 2003, Comrade Yahuza of Zamfara Textiles, a textile mill in Gusau affiliated with UNTL, questioned the authority of customs officials who enabled illegal foreign textiles to enter the country

in the first place. In other words, while textile importers who were dealing in smuggled textiles were punished, customs officers who permitted the passage of these smuggled goods were not.

12. This strategy was particularly the case for secondhand clothing, which traders planned to sell cheaply. Customs officers in 2017 reported intercepting several shipments of secondhand clothing bales (Giginyu and Auwal 2017).

13. Alhaji Isyaku Shittu, interview with E. Renne, July 4, 2010, Zaria City. "If the NDLEA can detect traffickers with drugs in their stomach, why is it difficult for the Customs to prevent smuggling of textile materials through the widely known 176 smuggling routes along Nigeria's porous borders?" asked Adams Oshiomhole, the former president of the Nigeria Labour Congress, who was, more recently, the governor of Edo State (Babadoko 2008).

14. Alhaji Isyaku Shittu, interview with E. Renne, July 4, 2010, Zaria City.

15. Many people knew the name of one well-known and well-connected smuggler, Alhaji Dahiru Mangal, who formerly organized convoys of as many as one hundred trucks carrying Chinese textiles from Benin to Kano. According to Tom Burgis (2013), "Mangal is said to charge a flat fee of N2m (about $13,000) per cargo, plus the cost of goods. In 2008 Mangal was estimated to be bringing about 100 40-ft. shipping containers across the frontier each month."

16. See chapter 4 on the association of some Kano textile traders with the smuggling of imported textiles through Nigeria's northern border with Niger, which are subsequently kept in large warehouses in Kano.

17. Alhaji Sadiq Yusuf, interview with E. Renne, November 13, 2012, Kano.

18. Alhaji Shafi'u, Kano, interview with H. Hassan, September 7, 2014, Kano.

19. Alhaji Awalu, interview with H. Hassan, November 20, 2017, Kano.

20. Hajiya Halima, Kano, interview with H. Hassan, May 14, 2016, Kano.

21. Alhaji Shafi'u, Kano, interview with H. Hassan, July 9, 2015, Kano.

22. This assessment of Mr. Lee contrasts with traders' worries about the decision taken by the Kano State government to give other Chinese traders land to build their own market. They fear expanding the Chinese presence, as they do not want Chinese to be both wholesalers and retailers of Chinese textile imports.

23. The Shandong Ruyi Technology Group Co., Ltd. was founded in 1972.

24. Alhaji Nuhu Yakubu Abubakar, interview with E. Renne, August 28, 2012, Zaria.

REFERENCES

Adewale, Murtala. 2017. "Kano, Chinese Company Sign $600 Million Deal on Textile Hub." *The Guardian-Nigeria*, September 27. https://guardian.ng/.

Agbese, Andrew, and Christiana Alabi. 2017. "NNDC Raises Fresh Hope on Kaduna Textile Industry." *Daily Trust*, September 3. https://www.dailytrust.com.ng/.

Akinrinade, S., and O. Ogen. 2008. "Globalization and De-Industrialization: South-

South Neo-Liberalism and the Collapse of the Nigerian Textile Industry." *The Global South* 2, no. 2: 159–70.

Aibueku. U. 2016. "Textile Industry a Hidden Gold Mine in Nigeria." *The Guardian*, February 16. https://guardian.ng/.

Albasu, S.A. 1995. *The Lebanese in Kano: An Immigrant Community in a Hausa Society in the Colonial and Post-Colonial Periods*. Kano: KABS Print Services.

Babadoko, S. 2008. "N70bn Grant Can't Save Textiles unless . . . Oshiomhole." *Sunday Trust*, April 27 www.dailytrust.com.ng/.

Barth, Heinrich. 1857. *Travels and Discoveries in North and Central Africa*, vols. 1–3. New York: Harper & Brothers.

Burgis, Tom. 2015. *The Looting Machine: Warlords, Tycoons, Smugglers, and the Systematic Theft of Africa's Wealth*. London: William Collins.

Eneji, M., I. Onyinye, D. Kennedy, and S. Rong. 2012. "Impact on Foreign Trade and Investment on Nigeria's Textile Industry." *Journal of African Studies and Development* 4, no. 5: 130–41.

Fagge, Tahir A. 1970. *A History of Fagge Town*, unpublished mimeograph, Nigeria.

Giginyu, I., and A. Auwal. 2017. "Customs Intercepts Smuggled Rice, Bales of Second-Hand Clothes." *Daily Trust*, November 18. https://www.dailytrust.com.ng/.

Gottman, Felicia. 2014. *Global Trade, Smuggling, and the Making of Economic Liberalism: Asian Textiles in France 1680–1760*. Basingstoke Hampshire: Palgrave Macmillan.

Haugen, H. 2011. "Chinese Exports to Africa: Competition, Complementarity, and Cooperation Between Micro-Level Actors." *Forum for Development Studies* 38, no. 2: 157–76.

Iloani, Francis. 2017. "Nigeria-China Trade Imbalance Hits N6tr in 4 Yrs." *Daily Trust*, June 12. https://www.dailytrust.com.ng/.

Leadership. 2015. "Jega Traders in Kano." *Leadership*, July 11. www.leadership.ng.

Mahadi, Abdullahi. 1984. "The Genesis of Kano's Economic Prosperity in the 19th Century: The Role of the State in Economic Development up to 1750." *Journal of the Historical Society of Nigeria* 12, no. 1/2: 1–21.

Maiwada, S., and E. Renne. 2013. "The Kaduna Textile Industry and the Decline of Textile Manufacturing in Northern Nigeria, 1955–2010." *Textile History* 44, no. 2: 171–96.

Mudashir, I. 2010. "Why FG Lifted Ban on Textiles—Finance Minister." *Daily Trust*, December 6. www.dailytrust.com.ng/.

Mudashir, Ismail. 2015a. "Customs Seize N315bn Textiles in Kano." *Daily Trust*, May 15. www.dailytrust.com.ng/.

Mudashir, Ismail. 2015b. "Kano traders seek govt intervention on seized textiles." *Daily Trust*, June 1. www.dailytrust.com.ng/.

Mudashir, Ismail. 2015c. "Customs releases N315bn seized textiles." *Daily Trust*, June 18. https://www.dailytrust.com.ng/.

Mudashir, Ismail. 2015d. "Customs rakes N1bn from Chinese smugglers." *Daily Trust*, June 29. https://www.dailytrust.com.ng/.

Mudashir, I., and G. H. Yaya. 2014. "In Kano, Textile Traders Lament the Chinese Are Driving Them Out of Business." *Daily Trust*, November 9. www.dailytrust.com.ng/.

Mukhtar, Abdulkadir. 2015. "Protest in Kano Over Foreign Control of Dye Business." *Daily Trust*, May 13. https://www.dailytrust.com.ng/.

Ogwu, Sunday. 2015. "FG to Deport Chinese Textile Smugglers." *Daily Trust*, May 28. https://www.dailytrust.com.ng/.

Renne, E. 2015. "The Changing Contexts of Chinese-Nigerian Textile Production and Trade, 1900–2015." *Textile: Cloth and Culture* 13, no. 3: 211–31.

Sylvanus, Nina. 2016. *Patterns in Circulation: Cloth, Gender, and Materiality in West Africa*. Chicago: University of Chicago Press.

Taylor, I. 2007. "China's Relations with Nigeria." *The Round Table: The Commonwealth Journal of International Affairs* 96, no. 392: 631–45.

Villoria, N. B. 2009. "China and the Manufacturing Terms of Trade of African Exporters." *Journal of African Economics* 18, no. 15: 781–823.

Yeung, G., and V. Mok. 2004. "Does WTO Accession Matter for the Chinese Textile and Clothing Industry?" *Cambridge Journal of Economics* 28: 937–54.

World Trade Organization. 2015. "Textile Monitoring Body: The Agreement on Textiles and Clothing." http://www.wto.org/english/tratop_e/texti_e/texintro_e.htm.

CHAPTER 7

Nigerian-Chinese Connections and Digital Textile Designs in the Twenty-First Century

DAKYES SAMAILA USMAN

Nigerian-Chinese textile design work in Nigeria began with the establishment of the United Nigeria Textiles Limited (UNTL) mill by the international Chinese corporation known as the Cha Group in 1964. As was discussed in chapter 4, Chinese textile specialists worked with Nigerian students and workers at the UNTL mill to train textiles designers and to develop prints appropriate for the Nigerian market. At the same time, the Cha Group—under the leadership of Cha Chi Ming—contributed to the growth of the Department of Industrial Design, at Ahmadu Bello University in Zaria, by providing funds for equipment and opportunities for many student interns who came to UNTL. Initially, textile printing at the UNTL mill (as well as at other Kaduna mills such at Kaduna Textiles Ltd.) was carried out using screen and film methods. Later, UNTL began using engraved copper rollers. Eventually, however, the Cha Group moved toward digital textile designs for printed cotton textiles, and screen and roller printing were abandoned. In 2003, the Cha Group established a partnership with the Italian printing company Maver Sri, which is a leader in digital textile printing. Subsequently, inkjet printers were introduced to the Cha Group textile mills where printing was carried out.[1] Because the facilities at the UNTL plant in Kaduna had insufficient space for its digital printing operations, when the mill reopened after 2010 this work was moved to their textile mill, Nichemtex Industries Ltd., at Ikorodu in Lagos State in southwestern Nigeria. Now, however, much of the company's printing in West Africa is carried out at its ATL textile mill in Akosombo, Ghana (Miescher 2017), while computerized textile design work is confined to the ABC facilities at Hyde, near Manchester in the UK (Elands 2017).[2] Thus, for Nigerian design students at Ahmadu Bello University who have received training in computerized digital textile design techniques, numerous obstacles have impeded their use of these techniques in textile production in northern Nigeria.

This chapter focuses on textile printing processes to clarify textile printing practices taught at Ahmadu Bello University and current trends in digital textile printing (*Textile World* 2018). The chapter begins with an examination of printing techniques used by textile mills in Kaduna: block printing and screen printing, which are still being taught at Ahmadu Bello University. It then considers the consequences of the lack of computers and digital printing equipment at the university. It continues with a discussion of the findings of interviews conducted with textile industry designers who formerly worked for several Kaduna and Kano textile mills. I conclude with a brief discussion of my experiences of digital textile printing, which I learned as a faculty member in the printing section of the Department of Industrial Design at Ahmadu Bello University. As of 2018, however, the future for ABU design students trained in textile printing is quite limited; they have few opportunities to carry out digital printing work in Nigeria. This is due to the lack of functioning textile mills that would require their services as well as the intermittent electrical power supply that impedes freelance computer digital design work. Perhaps in the future, students will be able to utilize the digital images of earlier, beloved textile patterns such as "Stars" and to develop them in new creative ways for the production of contemporary cotton print textiles in the Nigerian market.

ABU TEXTILES/DESIGN DEPARTMENT INTERACTIONS WITH UNTL OFFICIALS

The Cha Group chairman, Cha Chi Ming, made a point of contributing to textile production education in Kaduna and Zaria, both of company workers—by sending them for overseas training—and of students from local universities, polytechnics, and colleges. In his 1974 Annual Report, the director, Cha Chi Ming noted that:

The company continued to sponsor 156 employees on training courses both in Nigeria and overseas, as well as providing increased in-service-training facilities, and as a result our Nigerianisation programme is progressing steadily. Every effort is still being made to recruit qualified Nigerian staff from all known sources in Nigeria and overseas. Five senior Nigerian staff have been promoted to managerial status and twenty Nigerian employees were promoted to supervisory grade staff in both the technical and administrative sections. (UNTL 1974)

In addition to UNTL's sponsorship of employees at local educational institutions, the company also provided weaving, printing, and dyeing equipment and supplies that could be used in this training. In recognition of his contribution to Nigerian educational institutions and to the development of northern Nigeria, Cha Chi Ming was awarded an honorary doctorate from Ahmadu Bello University, Zaria, in 2005.

OLDER PRINTING METHODS TAUGHT AT AHMADU BELLO UNIVERSITY

Ahmadu Bello University faculty have taught several older direct printing methods, which have been used to familiarize students with some of the general concepts of printing (Collier 1970; Kadolph 2007). Traditional textile printing techniques are categorized into two methods: Direct printing, in which colorants containing dyes, thickeners, and the mordants or substances used for fixing the color on the cloth are printed in same spot where the dye is expected to adhere. The other method is resist dyeing, in which a wax or other substance is printed onto fabric by means of a stencil, brush, or block that is subsequently dyed. When the fabric is dyed, the waxed areas do not accept the dye, leaving uncolored patterns against a colored background. Traditional textile printing techniques taught in the Department of Industrial Design at ABU have focused on direct printing methods, which include hand block printing, stencil printing, and screen printing.

Hand Block Printing

The hand block textile printing process is one of the earliest, simplest, and slowest printing methods. The design to be printed is drawn on, or transferred to, prepared wooden blocks. All the colors are separated by transferring each color to a separate block. The designer carefully cuts the shape of the motif on the wood block. The dexterity of the designer at this point is put to test; the quality of the cut-out motif determines to an extent the final

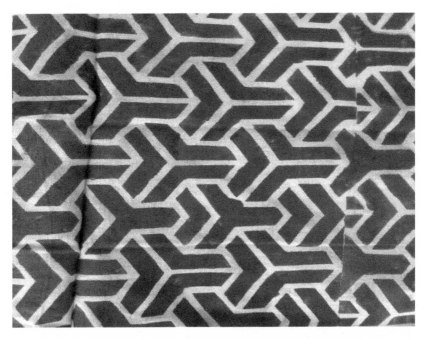

Fig. 7.1. Stencil-printed cotton textile, Ahmadu Bello University, Zaria, 2018. (Courtesy of the Dept. of Industrial Design Ahmadu Bello University, Zaria.)

quality of the impression. Fine details, difficult to cut in wood, are built up in strips of brass or copper, which is bent to shape and driven edgewise into the flat surface of the block. The designer applies color to the block and presses it firmly and steadily on the cloth, striking it with a wooden mallet. The designer ensures that registration marks are kept visible, as they are useful in taking the next impression so that the pattern can continue without a break. Each succeeding impression is taken in the same way until the length of cloth is fully printed. The cloth is then wound over drying rollers each time the printing of one color is over. When the four impressions are all taken, the printed fabric is ready for finishing treatments.

Stencil Printing

Stencil printing is another technique taught in the department. It is one of the oldest forms of printing used both in graphic and textile design. The method is simple: The motif is designed and repeated to form patterns on heavy paper. The colors to be printed are carefully separated by tracing the patterns for each color out on separate pieces of heavy paper. Registration marks are created at the four corners of each stenciled paper to facilitate pattern repeats when printing. Fabric is then treated and laid flat on the printing table and the desired color is applied by dabbing brushing. The other colors are then taken one after the other until all the colors are printed and the fabric is ready for final treatment.

Screen Printing

There are various terms used for what is essentially the same technique. Traditionally the process was called *screen printing* or *silkscreen printing* because silk was used in the process prior to the invention of polyester mesh. Currently, there are special-use mesh materials of nylon and stainless steel available. Manual screen printing is carried out as follows: The design to be printed is transferred onto a screen mesh that is stretched on a wooden or steel frame. Starch paste is then applied to the screen to block the areas of the mesh that are not to be printed. The prepared screen is used to apply the desired color with a squeegee blade, which presses the ink through the unblocked areas of the screen; this process is repeated for subsequent colors to be applied. As in the case of stencil printing, registration marks are used to produce multiple-color impressions.

INDUSTRIALIZED TEXTILE PRINTING

These printing techniques form the basis of more sophisticated printing techniques that were used in the textile mills in Kaduna, such as automated stencil printing. This technique uses photosensitive solutions to transfer the design from a transparent film to the screen mesh. Depending on the quality of the print being made, a particular density of screen mesh is selected; it is then coated with emulsion and dried. The overlay film is placed over the screen in the darkroom and expose with a light source usually ultraviolet in the 350–420 nanometer spectrum. The screen is then washed, and the unexposed areas dissolve and wash away, leaving the negative stencil image areas. The mesh is now ready for use when mounted on a flatbed screen printing machine; thousands of impressions can be obtained in hours.

Rotary Screen Printing

Rotary screen printing is similar to the flatbed printing method, the difference being that in the case of rotary screen printing, the screen is wrapped around a copper roller. The roller rotates at the same speed as the cloth to be printed. In this way, numerous impressions are taken in a short time with high definition.

One textile printing specialist, Gideon Oloruntobi, who taught at Ahmadu Bello University, described his experience of copper roller printing at the Arewa Textile Mill in Kaduna:

> As I told you about copper roller printing machine, we send the bleached material either to copper roller printing machine or we send it to rotary machine. The difference is that the copper printing machine will use copper, the design is engraved on the copper roller and this one we attach it to the machine by means of pressure, then we mount it on a drum. Depending on the number of colors we want on the cloth, if we want two rollers which means there will be two designs on the cloth, if you want three, there will be three designs—at that time, we had a machine that could take about eight. All these things will have a different roller that runs at the same time, eight, six, five, or three times, according to what the customer requires.
>
> After that we have another called a rotary screen printing machine. It was from Poland for doing printing. . . . The rotary machine we can print wax on the printing machine and that one is the same but we are using screen instead of roller, a transparent screen and it's on a flat base, then it has a roller type that has a screen that with a little pressure applies a chemical. After that as we print it will be wet so we send it inside a dry chamber. . . . It dries and it comes out again, we send it to machine to steam it up. There are some dyes that the color we treat with a certain chemical . . . so it will not fade. So after leaving that process . . . then it goes back to washing machine, drying again.[3]

The Arewa Textile Mill has since closed. If it were to reopen, such obsolete printing equipment would need to be replaced with facilities for the production of digitally designed textiles.

DIGITAL PRINTING DEVELOPMENTS AT AHMADU BELLO UNIVERSITY

The process of digital printing has been developed in the past fifty years as the use of computers has increased the options for design work. According to Susan Carden (2016, 20), "a computer program was written at Dundee University that allowed digital images, created by simple programming, to be an output as color separation from a dot matrix printer, using RGB (red, green, blue) chemicals." This equipment and technique were subsequently improved upon so that large rolls of plain fabric could be printed, much like continuous paper printing is done with an inkjet desktop printer. There are currently several programs that can be easily installed on computers that enable textile designers to create new patterns and adapt older ones. Thus, in Kaduna or Kano, a customer coming to the mill with a desired textile print that she or he wants replicated can see the image on the computer screen, which can then be printed on paper for the customer's final deliberations. At the textile design workshop at Ahmadu Bello University–Zaria, one room is devoted to computers, which unfortunately are outdated and cannot be used with updated digital textile design programs. Indeed, students are advised to bring their own laptop computers to class to learn about digital textile design work. As several students noted, even training in the use of digital printing programs is no guarantee of employment in textile mills in Nigeria today.

Nigerian Textile Designers' Work

In February 2015, I interviewed seven textile designers who had been working in textile mills in Kano, Kaduna, and Lagos about their experiences as designers and their appraisal of the future of such design work in Nigeria. One young man, who had been a student in the Department of Industrial Design at Mautech, Yola, worked for some time at the African Textile Manufacturing Ltd. mill in Kano (see chapter 5). There he used a computer "to create or trace a design as well as to separate the colors before the design was taken to the darkroom [to make film prints]." At that time, this mill did not use digital printing but rather used films for screen printing. When asked about patterns being sent digitally to China for the production of cotton print textiles there, he observed: "Everything is digital these days so the design can be emailed or in a situation where the client is physically present [and perhaps traveling to China], they can go with the printed hardcopy." Another man who trained in Yola also worked at the African Textile Manufacturing Ltd. mill in Kano, although he designed patterns both by hand and by computer. This situation was also the case for two other men, one who had trained at Ahmadu Bello University, Zaria. He worked at UNTL as a designer, where he used manual and digital textile printing methods.[4] The other man, who trained at Obafemi Awolowo University in Ile-Ife, worked at the Western Textile mill in Lagos. There were only two who worked solely by hand tracing designs and both had been women students at Ahmadu Bello University, Zaria.

Of these designers, some were pessimistic about the prospects of textile design work in Nigeria. One simply said, "Bleak," while another stated, "Sincerely speaking, I will say there is no hope for the textile industry." Yet the others were more optimistic, particularly if the problem of electricity could be addressed:

> Textile design is a thing that applies to people daily, people cannot do without cloth. Even though some textile companies have packed up of late, I would say it was due to mismanagement and misuse of funds. It's not because the products do not sell. Although raw materials and light availability are some of the excuses used, we have to be sincere so that these issues can be curbed.

Alhaji Sa'idu Dattijo Adhama, chairman of the Adhama Textiles and Garment Industry in Kano (see chapter 5), who uses updated equipment for printing T-shirts, would heartily agree with this assessment.

CONCLUSION

Teaching at Ahmadu Bello University has been a worthwhile experience, though not without challenges. Some of the problems that militate against effective teaching and learning include administrative bottlenecks and the difficulty of keeping abreast of the latest technology. The textile design and production processes since the opening of the university in 1962 had been of the analog variety until 1994. At that time, Dr. Hattie Hilliard came to Ahmadu Bello University with the Fulbright Scholar Program. She introduced computer graphic design techniques to members of the Department of Industrial Design faculty. I, along with one of my colleagues in the graphic unit, was selected to start training on digital textile design on computers. Unfortunately, we only had a short time for training so we had to build on it with subsequent training opportunities.[5] The late introduction to computer applications in digital textile methods and design work in the department has affected the quality of teaching and learning and, by extension, the quality of students who will eventually graduate and work in the industry. While the textile design and printing industry has become highly digitized and even includes e-textile innovations,[6] design programs at Ahmadu Bello University are not tailored to prepare graduates for the future of textile design work. For "human beings cannot be in charge of a situation until they have first conquered it; to work with advanced technology, a practitioner must first begin by mastering it" (Carden 2016: 36). Teaching design in an environment that does not have basic teaching facilities is discouraging, to say the least. Keeping up with the continuing innovations in digital textile design and printing has been a difficult challenge. Fortunately, though, the Department of Industrial Design has recently acquired some state-of-the-art equipment for both graphic and textile design and production. Once the facilities become functional, there will be need for staff retraining. With that, we are hopeful that things will change for the better and that we will produce design graduates who will find employment in Nigeria, possibly with Chinese-Nigerian textile firms such as the Cha Group mills in Ikorodu or in the proposed textile industrial park in Kano, on collaborative graphic and textile design work.

NOTES

1. See Cha Group 2012.

2. By restricting the production of new designs to offices at Hyde, Cha Group managers hope to limit their use by competitors (Elands 2017).

3. Gideon Oloruntobi, Arewa Textiles, interview with E. Renne, February 28, 2012, Kaduna.

4. This man was laid off from UNTL in Kaduna and then went to work at the UNTL mill at Ikorodu, Lagos. He is now a student in the College of Education at Ahmadu Bello University in Zaria.

5. Dr. Hilliard died in an automobile accident on her return from a gallery exhibition in Lagos in January 1995.

6. E-textiles include attractive textile materials and apparel with "embedded computational and electronic elements" (Buechly et al. 2013, 1).

REFERENCES

Buechley, Leah, Kylie Peppler, Michael Eisenberg, and Yasmin Kafai, eds. 2013. *Textile Messages*. New York: Peter Lang.

Carden, Susan. 2016. *Digital Textile Printing*. London: Bloomsbury Academic.

Cha Group. 2012. 'Textiles Website, History." http://www.chatextiles.com/english/index.html.

Collier, Ann M. 1970. *A Handbook of Textiles*. Oxford: Pergamon Press.

Elands, Helen. 2017. "Designing for Wax Prints at ABC." In *African-Print Fashion Now! A Story of Taste, Globalization, and Style*, edited by S. Gott, T. Loughran, B. Quick, and L. Rabine, 66–69. Los Angeles: Fowler Museum.

Kadolph, Sara J. 2007. *Textiles*, 10th ed. Upper Saddle River, NJ: Prentice-Hall.

Miescher, Stephan. 2017. "'Bringing Fabrics to Life': Akosombo Textiles Limited in Ghana." In *African-Print Fashion Now! A Story of Taste, Globalization, and Style*, edited by S. Gott, T. Loughran, B. Quick, and L. Rabine, 86–95. Los Angeles: Fowler Museum.

Textile World. 2018. "Digital Textile Printing: Explosive Growth Continues." *Textile World*, February 28. http://www.textileworld.com/textile-world/features/2018/02/digital-textile-printing-explosive-growth-continues/.

UNTL (United Nigeria Textiles Limited). 1974. "Cha Chi Ming, Chairman's Report, Annual Report and Accounts." Unpublished document.

CHAPTER 8

Textiles, Fashion, and Time

SALIHU MAIWADA AND ELISHA RENNE

Take Time
No Hurry in Life
Sorry Baby No Time for Love
 —Sayings painted on backs of Nigerian buses, taxis, and trucks

The question of how the intersection of textile aesthetics, fashion tastes, production practices, and trade, as well as changing socioeconomic and political contexts, have contributed to the decline in textile production in northern Nigeria relates to time. Fashion, in particular, reflects certain conceptions of time; a textile design is considered to be "out of date," while a certain style of embroidered robe is considered to be "timeless." Yet certain textiles may return to their past fashionable glory, as when the patterns and structure of earlier strip-woven cloths are represented on cotton print fabrics, or when the glossy surface of the expensive indigo-dyed and beaten *kore* robes from Wudil (southeast of Kano), which were transported by trading caravans throughout West Africa, are visually akin to the recent fashion in men's kaftans made with highly polished manufactured cotton damask materials and embroidered with industrially spun rayon thread.

Aside from these visual aesthetic and material qualities, trends in textile fashions also reflect time in relation to production. The labor-intensive handwork involved in the making of hand-embroidered robes during the nineteenth century—which included the hand-spinning of cotton thread, handweaving and sewing of narrow-strip textiles, embroidery work, tailoring, indigo dyeing, and beaten finishing—took time (Freeman 2018, 20). Even with the introduction of industrially spun thread, which increased the speed of handweaving and contributed to the decline in the slow process of hand-spinning, handweavers could not compete with the speed of manufactured plain weave, twills, and printed cloth production and the expansion of fashionable options. The most recent developments in digital textile weaving and printing have taken these changes in time and fashion even further, with inexpensive printed textiles—in Kano known as *yar da atamfa* ("throw away" print cloth)—worn for a short time and then discarded (see chapter 6). Indeed, this sense of time in terms both of being fashionably up-to-date and of fast-paced industrial textile production associated with modernity is reflected in contemporary young men's lack of interest in old-fashioned and slow handweaving in Sabon Garin Kayyu, Kano State.

The chapters in this volume have examined these changing conceptions of the aesthetics and production of textiles in relation to time but also in relation to the larger social order and to global trade. The stately and careful slowness associated with the dignity of traditional rulers was mirrored in the heaviness of robes made with handwoven materials of cotton and silk, which were sometimes worn in several layers (Douny 2011). Additionally, the myriad types of named handwoven cloths produced, which were also evaluated with terms that represented their quality, reflected the fineness of social distinctions made between royals (the *sarauta* class), commoners (*talakawa*), Islamic scholars (*malamai*), farmers (*manoma*), and slaves (*bayi*), a point made by Candotti (2010, 194). The types of robes that were distributed during Sallah also reflected these discerning perceptions of a person's social worth. With the enactment of British colonial rule and the eventual end of slavery, these distinctions were challenged (to some extent) as those with cash, regardless of their background, could buy and wear expensive, fashionable garments. Nonetheless, the British system of indirect rule also underwrote the continued power and resources of traditional rulers, who maintained demand for handwoven *babban riga* robes and shiny blue-black *turkudi* strip-cloth turbans, even as imported British manufactured textiles became more common. Yet the imported British manufactured cotton print cloths, referred to as *'yar* Onitsha cloth by Zaria women, were only initially affordable by wealthy, royal women within these emirs' court. The long-standing aesthetic ideal that associates beauty with wealth in Hausa-Fulani society is an important finding derived from this study. One coveted nineteenth-century cloth produced in the Kano Emirate attests to this configuration of value. Known as *saki da kudi* (literally, black/white "guinea fowl" cloth and money), it consisted of alternating panels of indigo-dyed blue-black handspun, handwoven cotton and *alharini* magenta silk (Shea 1975, 95; see chapter 2). If the deep blue-black indigo and brilliant magenta colors were thought to be particularly beautiful, that these colors were obtained at considerable expense contributed to their beauty as well.

This cultural dynamic equating wealth with beauty helps to explain the extensive efforts British and Dutch manufacturers went to in registering particular trademarks for their manufactured textiles. For example, the British firm A. Brunnschweiler & Co. (ABC; originally Swiss), used several exclusive trademarks on cotton print textiles (Pedler 1974). The history of this firm and the many ways consumers confirmed the identity of these textiles underscores the importance of distinctive marks.[1] ABC cotton print textiles were manufactured in Manchester and were sold in Kano's Kantin Kwari market, where Hajiya Amina's husband purchased an ABC cloth for her marriage. This cloth has the ABC trademark clearly printed along its selvage along with the words "Guaranteed English Wax," which reinforces its worth in the eyes of consumers.

In December 2005, however, after the company was acquired by the Hong Kong–based Cha Group, President John Kufuor of Ghana inaugurated ABC wax textile production at Akosombo Textiles Limited, Accra, Ghana (Miescher 2017). The successful production of wax print textiles in Ghana "led to the transfer of the remaining ABC products such as Superwax, Handblock and Premium which resulted in the final closure of the Manchester production facility in December 2007" (Cha Group 2012).[2] ABC cloths produced in Ghana have subsequently been exported to Nigeria, where they are referred to either as "big English wax" or "little English wax," depending on the trademark and information printed on the selvage. According to Hannatu Hassan:

> The "little English wax" is the cloth with the ABC trademark that has "Made in Ghana" on the selvedge edge. It sells for N6,000–8,000 for six yards, while the ABC "big English wax" sells for N10,000–12,000 for six yards. We have been told that it is made in the UK. But while it has the ABC trademark, "Made in England" is <u>not</u> written on the selvage—there isn't any reference to the country of origin.
>
> "So why do you think it comes from the UK?" (ER)
>
> "Because that's what they've told us—and it's more expensive."[3]

The unexamined assumption here is that products made in the UK are superior to those made in West Africa (Pierre 2012).

Fig. 8.1. *ABC* cotton print textile referred to as Leaves, with the phrase "Guaranteed English Wax" printed on the margin. This cloth is owned by Hajiya Amina, Tudun Wada, Kaduna. (Photograph by E. P. Renne, November 24, 2017.)

In addition to price, trademarks, selvage information, and cloth traders' claims, the "big English wax" may be distinguished by smell, according to some Hausa women. For example, among the cloths at Muntari Sada's well-stocked textile store in Tudun Wada, Zaria, there was a "big English wax" cloth for sale. Hassana Yusuf insisted that she could smell its distinctive perfume-like odor, which is not present in "little English wax" cloths. Indeed, the printed label on the cloth included the phrase "Guaranteed ABC Wax," but the phrase "Made in Ghana" was not printed on its selvage.

Such assessments made between the trademarks, price, odor, and quality of cloth helps to explain the considerable efforts of twenty-first-century Chinese textile manufacturers to copy these marks and textile designs. Indeed, while the hand of a cloth—its feel and softness, odor, and clarity of printing— might distinguish a genuine Vlisco cloth for the discerning consumer, for others it would only be the price that differentiated a genuine Vlisco cotton print from a Chinese copy. For if others assume that one is wearing a genuine Vlisco cloth, its expensive beauty enhances the status of its wearer.

INDEPENDENCE, MODERNITY, AND TEXTILE MANUFACTURING IN KADUNA AND KANO

Just as the value of manufactured textiles is often associated with a genuine trademark and the clarity of designs and colors as well as price, the status of a textile-manufacturing company was often associated with mill size, types of equipment, extent of operations (spinning and weaving, dyeing and printing), and number of workers employed. This view was prevalent in nineteenth-century England, when huge textile mills were seen as signs of progress and prestige by many (but not all). Indeed, during the initial phases of industrialization in the UK, textile mills operated alongside handweavers working from their homes. By the late eighteenth century, however, cotton, woolen, and linen textiles were manufactured in multistory buildings, surrounded by walls, in integrated mills with carding, spinning, weaving, and finishing facilities. While economic efficiencies of scale figured into the decisions to construct larger and larger textile mills, other aspects of these mills were important, as large mill owners amassed wealth, prestige, and political power (Freeman 2018).

But there was an ideological side to this shift from handweaving to large-scale industrial textile production that reflected a growing association of progress with machine-produced cloth. The finely spun cotton thread made in textile mills was used to weave yards of baft cloth, which was subsequently subjected to a succession of bleaching, dyeing, and printing techniques. These processes contributed to the production of cloth that was preferred for its hand (its softness yet durability), its light weight, its attractive designs, and its fast colors. Despite the noisy, dusty conditions and the emphasis on timely efficiency and rigid schedules associated with working in such mills, wearing the cloths these mills produced marked one as a member of the modern age.[4] As Freeman (2018, xvii) has observed, "In the age of the factory, modern increasingly came to connote improved, desirable, the best that can be. Modern entailed a disavowal of the past, a rejection of the old-fashioned for the most up-to-date, an embrace of progress."

The establishment of textile mills, particularly in Kaduna under the auspices of Ahmadu Bello, the premier of the Northern Region, reflected a similar rationale and interpretation, although the socioeconomic and historical context of the textile industrialization of Northern Nigeria differed somewhat from industrialization elsewhere. First of all, building large-scale textile mills in northern Nigeria was associated with the end of British colonial rule, a period when large mills operated in the UK, and Nigeria provided raw materials, namely cotton. Opening such mills represented pride in Nigeria's emergence as an independent modern state. Second, Ahmadu Bello's vision of textile manufacturing in the north reflected his hopes for an economically vibrant Northern Nigeria that could compete with businesses, factories, and universities already established in the southern part of the country, a situation that had both ethnic and religious connotations. With the opening of Ahmadu Bello University in Samaru, near Zaria, he anticipated that the textile industry in Kaduna would provide training and employment for northern Nigerian students. Through their work and exposure to urban living, they would become, like New England textile mill workers, part of "a morally uplifting and culturally enlightening community [that was] developing a system of cheap, standardized manufacturing . . . [and] the efficient production of consumer goods" (Freeman 2018, 44). By introducing the professional production of textiles in large mills in Kaduna and Kano, political and business leaders hoped to establish Northern Nigeria's place in the modern world.

By following the trajectory of one particular product, blankets, and the processes by which they have been woven and sold in northern Nigeria, one can see the changes in consumer preferences for new styles of blankets, indirectly reflecting their assessment of new types of textile production. In other words, we suggest that an appreciation of the aesthetics and material qualities of particular styles of blankets—their colors, softness, warmth, weight, and durability—also reflects an admiration for the modern industrial processes by which machine-woven blankets have been made.

A SUCCESSION OF BLANKETS IN NORTHERN NIGERIA

During the harmattan season, from approximately November to March, the dry, dusty winds from the Sahara Desert move southward, obscuring the sun, which results in cold temperatures (Kwaifa 2017). In the past, northern Nigerians have kept warm during the night, and at times during the day,[5] by using thick, cotton strip-woven blankets known as *luru*, which have been produced in villages in Kano, Katsina, and Gombe state (Lamb and Holmes 1980). These cloths have largely been replaced by industrially woven blankets produced in Kaduna and Kano and, more recently, by blankets manufactured in China and imported to Kano. A consideration of the social lives of these blankets suggests how the intersection of textile aesthetics, fashion, politics, and economics reflects ideas about tradition and modernity, which have implications for the future of textile manufacturing and production in northern Nigeria.

Luru Handwoven Blankets from Kano State

In Kano State, *luru* blankets have been made in several villages just northwest of the city of Kano, near Bichi and Kwatarkwashi, and to the south of Kano, near Makole and Gano (Lamb and Holmes 1980, 108–13). This weft-faced strip-woven cloth was made mainly with handspun and industrial natural white cotton, with some indigo-dyed cotton thread used to make weft-faced patterns. Aside from plain blue-black bands, one of the most common patterns was referred to as *aska* (knife), which is also a pattern commonly found on men's *babban riga* robes.[6] On the best *luru* blankets, the strip patterns were carefully woven so that when they were sewn together, the pattern matches across the width (or part of the width) of the cloth.

As with other specialized handwoven or dyed textiles, the *luru* industry had its own distribution system. "Weavers from the villages bring blankets to certain regular markets where they can sell their produce and buy yarn. There is such a market at Dambata; but perhaps the largest is the market in Bichi, held every Friday" (Lamb and Holmes 1980, 113). Cloth traders from Kano frequently attended the Bichi market to buy *luru* blankets to sell in

Kurmi market in Kano City (Lamb and Holmes 1980, 125). One *luru* blanket purchased at the Kurmi market in Kano in November 1994 consists of nine handwoven strips six inches wide, woven with natural white and indigo blue-black handspun cotton weft threads, with a knife design. This configuration of pattern and thread colors suggest that it was likely produced in the Bichi area and referred to as a *luru zubwa* (Lamb and Holmes 1980, 112). The unfinished warp edges show the very fine, stiff cotton warp threads that are entirely covered by the thick weft threads.

 Luru cloths, however, have become increasingly rare. Alhaji Usman Kayyu does not know of anyone who was weaving *luru* blankets in the Kano area in 2018. Indeed, he said he had not seen them in the market in the past ten years. It is possible that with the demise of cotton hand-spinning in the Kano area, the lack of the thick cotton handspun thread used for weft has led to the decline of *luru* weaving as well (Lamb and Holmes 1980, 113). It is also possible that certain qualities of *luru* blankets are seen by Hausa consumers as "out of fashion," woven on handlooms with thick cotton thread. *Luru* blankets provide warmth but are also heavy and, because they are predominantly white, they become dirty easily and are difficult to wash. They thus have the disadvantage of being seen as both impractical and "traditional."

Northern Textile Manufacturers/Tofa Textiles

Beginning in the 1960s, northern Nigerian consumers had the opportunity to purchase locally made, industrially woven blankets from mills in Kano and Kaduna. In Kano, the mill that presently is known as Tofa Textiles began production as Northern Textile Manufacturers (NTM–Gidan Bargo, literally, the House of Blankets), which was established in the Bompai industrial area of Kano in 1962 (discussed in chapter 5). Initially, blankets manufactured by the Northern Textile Manufacturers mill in the 1960s attracted buyers who appreciated their figurative and floral designs and their durability. In addition to these patterned blankets, dark gray blankets with intermittent bands of red, gray, and white were also made. With the acquisition of the company by Alhaji Umar Tofa in 1990, new equipment was subsequently purchased for the continued manufacture of the dark gray blankets, which are popular among working-class consumers.[7] These dark gray, red, and white blankets are made primarily of local cotton that is carded and spun at the mill. While plainly patterned, the visual appearance of these blankets may appeal to older customers, as they are reminiscent of military blankets imported to Nigeria during the colonial era.

Chellco Industries Limited

Chellco Industries is the other major blanket manufacturer in Nigeria, and it began production in Kaduna in 1980 (discussed in chapter 4). According to Chellco's senior human resource manager, Timothy Majidad, "Chellco was the largest manufacturer of blankets in Nigeria between 1980 and 1990 and was exporting unfinished products to Ghana" (Bashir 2013). Over the years, Chellco Industries has provided more "modern" choices, as it sells a larger range of industrially woven blankets in different patterns, colors, and styles. There are plain checked blankets in white and red, white and blue, and white, along with jacquard-woven blankets with geometric, floral, and figurative patterns. These lofty, lightweight blankets are made of imported acrylic yarns that are spun at the Kaduna Chellco mill. There are also attractive institutional blankets, twill weave blankets in a single color and plaids in several combinations of blue, red, black, and white. Referred to as "hospital blankets," these cloths are also sold in the market to low-income customers, who like their warmth, their softness, and their durability. Blankets may also be custom ordered as the Chellco website states: "We can produce any design and colours as per needs; Chellco blankets are available in different sizes i.e., single bed, double bed, executive & luxury bed."[8] The lower prices of some Chellco blankets make them competitive with similarly patterned acrylic blankets from China.

Chinese Fleece Blankets

A large Chinese blanket factory, Baoding Hanzhe Blanket Co., Ltd., Xinxing Industrial Zone in Shandong, China, produces fleece polyester and acrylic blankets for African customers. In 2014, Alhaji Musa Bala, an associate of Alhaji Shafi'u Abdulkadir (their textile import business is discussed in chapter 6) traveled with his Chinese broker to Baoding, where they inspected blankets being made for an order of two large containers that Alhaji Shafi'u had made earlier that year in time for the harmattan season in northern Nigeria (Renne 2015). The red and white acrylic blankets made for Alhaji Shafi'u were decorated with circular abstract patterns. Other blankets in red, blue, and black or in different shades of blue were also available. The colors and patterns of these blankets contribute to their attractiveness, as do their lightness and their soft, fleecy loft. As well as being beautiful, they are practical; they are comfortably warm and wash and dry easily.

These attractive fleece blankets from China, introduced in the early twenty-first century, have come to dominate blanket sales in Kano. There, imported Chinese acrylic and polyester blankets in Kantin Kwari market come in three types, which are differentiated by price. Those selling for approximately N5,000 are the cheapest. While produced in attractive colors, they are lightweight, but because they are thin, they are not as warm as more expensive blankets. These sell for N10,000 and are soft and twice as thick as the cheaper blankets. The latest large fleece blankets from China, which come with matching pillowcases and a small bedside rug, are the most expensive, selling for around N20,000. Here again, price and beauty intersect as these blankets are considered to be part of fashionably beautiful interior décor.

This shifting material preference—from heavy, handwoven cotton *luru* blankets to fashionable, industrially made fleece blankets (both locally made and foreign-made)—corresponds with the overall preference for lighter weight and softer textiles, which are rapidly manufactured in modern textile mills. These textiles—both blankets as well as dress materials— are available in myriad colors and designs that are continually changing, with the newest cloths considered to be the latest in beautiful fashions. Additionally, industrially manufactured textiles are appreciated for their practical qualities; they are easily washable and are colorfast, unlike older handwoven cloths. As is the case with *luru* blankets, demand for other indigo blue-black and white cotton handwoven textiles such as the famous *saki* cloth has also declined, as Kriger (2006, 109) has noted: "For reasons that have yet to be fully explained, elegantly tailored and embroidered garments of *saki* cloth, which signified the caliphate administration and its elites, are now only rarely made now by special order." While worn for special ceremonial events, heavy, handwoven *saki* cloth is no longer "in fashion." Rather, the imported lighter-weight and later locally manufactured cotton textiles that became commonplace by the second half of the twentieth century have been used by Hausa embroiderers and tailors to produce machine-embroidered robes and kaftans. Such garments, made more quickly by machine than by hand, are seen as keeping pace with more quickly changing fashions. Nonetheless, the demand for hand-embroidered robes and caps made with traditional embroidery patterns persists, suggesting the ways that even new kaftan fashions are embedded in the long textile history of northern Nigeria.

CONCLUSION

Textile production and trade in northern Nigeria over the past two centuries has reflected changes in the manufacture of woven cloth as well as in dyeing and printing processes. Initially manifested in the massive production and trade in handwoven and indigo-dyed cloth, the association of large-scale textile manufacturing with modernity and progress contributed to the emergence of numerous textile mills opened in the mid-twentieth century in northern Nigeria.

The decline in textile production in Nigeria in the early twenty-first century reflects the current predominance of the Chinese textile manufacturing industry, with its up-to-date spinning, weaving, and digital printing equipment. Indeed, there have been several accounts of the decline of textile manufacturing elsewhere in the world in the early twenty-first century. For example, histories of textile manufacturing in the United States document its origins in New England, the movement of these mills to the South in search for a less costly labor force, and their final closings:

> In the first decade of the twenty-first century, the U.S. textile and apparel industry collapsed at a dramatic and unprecedented rate. Between January 2001 and January 2005, for example, the BLS [Bureau of Labor Statistics] reported that the industry lost a remarkable 373,800 jobs, or 35.7 percent of its total capacity. . . . If job losses continue at their current pace, an industry that has existed in the American Republic since its foundation will soon be virtually extinct. (Minchin 2013, 211)

Northern Nigeria provides another account of the rise and fall of the textile industry, with similarities to the decline of the textile industry in the United States, but also with differences. One difference was that these mills were not part of a process of mill development as was seen in the US and English textile industries. Rather, they were established in the north as full-blown entities where mill workers had little exposure to industrial manufacturing and where the power infrastructure on which efficient mill operation depended was also new. Thus, while mill closures and textile imports following new international trade agreements have affected the industry in Nigeria (Maiwada and Renne 2013), the United Kingdom (Toms and Zhang 2016), and the United States (Minchin 2013), the lifespan of large-scale textile manufacturing in Nigeria has been much shorter.

Perhaps that is why the history of the Nigerian textile industry does not figure into the many accounts of textile manufacturing decline. Despite Kano's centrality in textile manufacture and trade in the nineteenth century in West Africa and the establishment of industrial textile mills in northern Nigeria in the mid-twentieth century, this history is not widely known despite being part of this global process.[9] By the beginning of the twenty-first century, large-scale textile manufacturing in northern Nigeria, as in many parts of the world, had ended. Including Nigeria in this global textile historical narrative is important, however, since as Freeman (2018, xv) has observed:

> Understanding the history of giant factories can help us to think about what kind of future we want. . . . Today, as we may well be witnessing the historic apogee of the giant factory, economic and ecological conditions suggest that we need to rethink the meaning of modernity and whether or not it should continue to be equated with ever more material production in vast, hierarchically organized industrial facilities of the kind that were the bane and the glory of the past.

Yet as Orwell ([1937] 1958, 203) astutely remarked, "the machine has come to stay." Government and industry officials as well as textile workers and foreign investors are hoping to see the machines and related technologies—weaving equipment, solar panels, and digital communication—put into place to revitalize textile production and trade in Northern Nigeria in the coming years.

NOTES

1. While acquired by the British firm Calico Printers Association, Lancashire, in 1959, the company continued to be known as ABC (van der Laan 1983, 293). It was later acquired by the Cha Group–Hong Kong in 1992 and retained its trademarks.

2. Nonetheless, print designers in the UK continue to produce digital designs for printing on these cloths (Elands 2017).

3. Interview with E. Renne, November 21, 2017, Kano.

4. Freeman (2018, 62–65) makes a similar point about the young women who came from rural communities "in their plain, country-made clothes" to work in the urban textile mills in Lowell, Massachusetts.

5. Several types of blankets have been handwoven across the Sahel, with blankets produced in Burkina Faso, Niger, and Mali being among the most well-known (Picton and Mack 1979, 106–10).

6. The most common knife pattern designs embroidered on robes are *aska biyu* (two knives) and *aska takwas* (eight knives).

7. See the Bank of Industry (2015) Youtube video on the Tofa Industries Mill, Kano.

8. See Chellco Industries Ltd., 2017.

9. Additionally, several textile firms in the UK, Hong Kong, Japan, India, France, and Pakistan participated in the development of industrial textile manufacturing in Northern Nigeria (Andrae and Beckman 1999).

REFERENCES

Andrae, G., and B. Beckman. 1999. *Union Power in the Nigerian Textile Industry*. New Brunswick, NJ: Transaction Publishers.

Bank of Industry. 2015. "Tofa Textiles." https://www.youtube.com/watch?v=YZLXh8lG-pd4.

Bashir, Misbahu. 2013. "How We've Controlled Blanket Market for 35 Years—Chellco." *Daily Trust*, December 22. https://www.dailytrust.com.ng/.

Candotti, Marisa. 2010. "The Hausa Textile Industry: Origins and Development in the Precolonial Period." In *Being and Becoming Hausa: Interdisciplinary Perspectives*, edited by A. Haour and B. Rossi, 187–211. Leiden: Brill.

Cha Group. 2012 "Textiles Website, History." http://www.chatextiles.com/english/index.html

Chellco Industries Ltd. 2017. "Chellco Industries Website." http://chellco.com/blankets.html.

Douny, Laurence. 2011. "Silk-Embroidered Garments as Transformative Processes: Layering, Inscribing and Displaying Hausa Material Identities." *Material Culture* 16, no. 4: 401–15.

Elands, Helen. 2017. "Designing for Wax Prints at ABC." In *African-Print Fashion Now! A Story of Taste, Globalization, and Style*, edited by S. Gott, T. Loughran, B. Quick, and L. Rabine, 66–69. Los Angeles: Fowler Museum.

Freeman, Joshua. 2018. *Behemoth: A History of the Factory and the Making of the Modern World*. New York: W. W. Norton & Company.

Kriger, Colleen. 2006. *Cloth in West African History*. Lanham, MD: AltaMira Press.

Kwaifa, Aliyu. 2017. "As Harmattan Sets In." *Daily Trust*, November 15. https://www.dailytrust.com.ng/.

Lamb, Venice, and Judith Holmes. 1980. *Nigerian Weaving*. Roxford: H. A. and V. M. Lamb

Maiwada, S., and E. Renne. 2013. "The Kaduna Textile Industry and the Decline of Textile Manufacturing in Northern Nigeria, 1955–2010." *Textile History* 44, no. 2: 171–96.

Miescher, Stephan. 2017. "'Bringing Fabrics to Life': Akosombo Textiles Limited in Ghana." In *African-Print Fashion Now! A Story of Taste, Globalization, and Style*, edited by S. Gott, T. Loughran, B. Quick, and L. Rabine, 86–95. Los Angeles: Fowler Museum.

Minchin, Timothy. 2013. *Empty Mills: The Fight Against Imports and the Decline of the U.S. Textile Industry*. Lanham, MD: Rowman & Littlefield Publishers Inc.

Orwell, George. [1937] 1958. *The Road to Wigan Pier.* New York: Houghton-Mifflin Harcourt.

Pedler, Frederick. 1974. *The Lion and the Unicorn in Africa: A History of the Origins of the United Africa Company 1787–1931.* London: Heinemann Educational.

Picton, John, and John Mack. 1979. *African Textiles.* London: British Museum.

Pierre, Jemima. 2012. *The Predicament of Blackness: Postcolonial Ghana and the Politics of Race.* Chicago: University of Chicago Press.

Renne, E. 2015. "The Changing Contexts of Chinese-Nigerian Textile Production and Trade, 1900–2015." *Textile: Cloth and Culture* 13, no. 3: 211–31.

Shea, Philip J. 1975. "The Development of an Export-Oriented Dyed Cloth Industry in Kano Emirate in the Nineteenth Century." PhD dissertation, University of Wisconsin, Madison.

Toms, Steven, and Qi Zhang. 2016. "Marks & Spencer and the Decline of the British Textile Industry, 1950–2000." *British History Review* 90, no. 1: 3–30.

van der Laan, Laurens. 1983. "A Swiss Family Firm in West Africa: A. Brunnschweiler & Co., 1929–1959." *African Economic History* 12: 287–97.

Epilogue

ELISHA RENNE AND SALIHU MAIWADA

This volume builds upon earlier art historical, anthropological, and historical studies of various aspects of the textile history of northern Nigeria. By considering how the aesthetic evaluations of the materiality and visual qualities of textiles and dress intersect with textile production and the constitution of social identities within a particular socioeconomic, political, and historical context, the authors have sought to explain why textile-related production has declined in northern Nigeria over the past two hundred years. This volume thus provides information for the comparative study of the decline of textile manufacturing elsewhere in the world. It also suggests the conundrum considered by Orwell concerning the benefits and disadvantages of "mechanical progress," and, we would add, digital progress, for human existence. For while "No human being ever wants to do anything in a more cumbrous way than is necessary . . . the tendency of mechanical progress, then, is to frustrate the human need for effort and creation" (Orwell [1937] 1958, 200). While textile mill workers in northern Nigeria were proud to participate in the mechanization of weaving, the "tendency for the mechanization of the world" represented by more efficient looms and printing equipment in China has contributed to the closing of Nigerian mills, unemployment, and the decline of local handweaving.

This study of the ascendancies of different types of textiles, aesthetic preferences, textile production and finishing, and textile trade raises the question of whether local textile production might be revived in northern Nigeria. Several possibilities for reviving textile production through special government programs, as was mentioned by Alhaji Sa'idu Adhama (see chapter 5), have been proposed in recent years. Other means are also being considered.

There is possible Chinese interest in establishing a joint textile manufacturing venture with the Kano State government (discussed in chapter 6), which is particularly attractive given the recent bumper cotton harvest in the Katsina area in 2017 (Mahmud 2017). And in November 2017, members of the Vlisco Group, the Dutch textile and design firm, met with the minister of finance to discuss possibilities for improved cotton production, textile printing and design, and garment manufacturing in Nigeria (Muhammad 2017).

Several government initiatives were mentioned in 2018. They included the establishment of the Kano Zonal Office for the Implementation of the Nigeria Agribusiness and Agro-Industry Development Initiative (NAADI), which focuses on the production of textiles and garments as well as agricultural goods in Kano State (Iloani 2018); a Department for International Development (DFID)–funded initiative in Kaduna State for a training program in garment production and computer literacy at El-Jahab Mubarak Nigeria Ltd. (Ahmadu-Suka 2018); the construction of "an automated rapier weaving machine for the commercial production of aso-oke fabrics," jointly sponsored by the Raw Materials Research and Development Council (RMRDC) and the National Research Institute for Chemical Technology (NARICT); and the distribution of improved varieties of cotton seed to Nigerian farmers (Yahaya 2018; Yahaya, Yusuf, and Mahmoud 2019). Nonetheless, in October 2018, members of the National Union of Textile Garment and Tailoring Workers of Nigeria (NUTGTWN) staged a rally in Lagos to protest the slow pace of the revival of textile manufacturing. As the national president of the union, John Adaji, put it, "We need constant electricity and it must be affordable. . . . We need a local market [e.g., for the sale of material for uniforms] which means government should walk their talk to patronise what we produce in Nigeria" (Aliyu 2018).

Most recently in 2019, additional government initiatives have been promoted to support the revival of textile manufacturing in northern Nigeria. On March 5, 2019, the Central Bank of Nigeria issued a ban on the sale of foreign exchange to those importing textiles for sale in Nigeria (Agabi et al. 2019). The bank also approved support for the importation of cotton lint until 2020 in order to provide mills with sufficient material for producing cotton thread; the bank has also provided loans to cotton farmers through the Anchor Borrowers Program. Last but not least, the bank is working to guarantee the supply of electricity to textile mills: "the CBN began discussions with the Kano and Kaduna state governments to establish textile industrial areas in a bid to guarantee stable electricity in those industrial areas" (Agabi et al. 2019).

These important initiatives nonetheless face many hurdles, as was the case with the federal government's N100 billion Cotton, Textile and Garment Development Fund, which ended in 2016 (Agbese et al. 2016; see chapter 4). Furthermore, the policy that ordered military, paramilitary agencies, and government schools to purchase only textiles and garments made in Nigeria has yet to be enforced (*Daily Trust* 2018). Indeed, some local clothing manufacturers have objected to the CBN's ban on textile importers' access to foreign exchange (through the bank), arguing that textile manufacturing—mills, infrastructure, electricity, and availability of cotton—should be in place first before implementing the foreign exchange ban (Yahaya, Yusuf, and Mahmoud 2019). Otherwise, local tailors, seamstresses, and clothing manufacturers would find it difficult and expensive to access materials for their trade (Ekundayo 2019). Despite these challenges, textile industry officials and investors are hopeful that if the federal government is able to address the problems of regular electricity and the production of raw cotton (*Daily Trust* 2019), textile manufacturing will make a comeback in northern Nigeria (Iloani 2019).

Furthermore, if these plans move forward, they will constitute a new era in the ascendancies of textile production and trade in northern Nigeria. For when considering the production of textiles in northern Nigeria in the early twenty-first century, it should be remembered that the few factories in Kano and Kaduna that remain in full operation are smaller and more specialized operations. The digitization of textile-production processes discussed in chapter 7 also has contributed to this downsizing and specialization of textile production. Indeed, smaller operations that are attuned to local demand may be the way that textile manufacturing in Nigeria—and elsewhere in the world—will continue. While unemployment associated with the closure of the large textile mills in Kaduna and Kano continues to be a social and political challenge for northern Nigerians, these mills are, perhaps, entering a new era of textile production, textile aesthetic appreciation, and textile trade. Conceivably, the way forward for the sustainable production of textiles that are considered to be both beautiful and functional, that provide employment for people, and that are environmentally sound, may be gleaned from the extant practices of smaller, specialized textile manufacturing firms and handweaving operations that have continued working in the early twenty-first century in northern Nigeria. These as well as other mechanical and digital gains raise the question of whether and how a new era of textile production in northern Nigeria might be attained.

REFERENCES

Agabi, Chris, Zakariyya Adaramola, Francis Arinze Iloani, Hussein Yahaya, Kayode Ekundayo, Sunday Michael Ogwu, Abdullateef Aliyu, Ibrahim Musa Giginyu, and Yusha'u A. Ibrahim. 2019. "CBN Bans Forex Sale to Textile Importers." *Daily Trust*, March 6. https://www.dailytrust.com.ng/.

Agbese, Andrew, Christiana Alabi, Maryam Ahmadu-Suka, and Francis Iloani. 2016. "Why Textile Industry Remains Dormant Despite FG's N100bn Bailout." *Daily Trust*, July 3. https://www.dailytrust.com.ng/.

Ahmadu-Suka, Maryam. 2018. "Firm, MAFITA Train 32 Persons on Garment Production in Kaduna." *Daily Trust*, February 14. https://www.dailytrust.com.ng/.

Aliyu, Abdullateef. 2018. "Textile Manufacturers Oppose Levy-Free Import for Foreign Investors." *Daily Trust*, December 26. https://www.dailytrust.com.ng/.

Daily Trust. 2018. "Textile Manufacturers Decry Non-Implementation of Local Content Order." *Daily Trust*, January 20. https://www.dailytrust.com.ng/.

Daily Trust. 2019. "Expect 15,000 Tonnes of Cotton in Kaduna this Year, Farmers Promise." *Daily Trust*, February 17. https://www.dailytrust.com.ng/.

Ekundayo, Kayode. 2019. "Forex Textile Exclusion Threatens Fashion Industry LCCI." *Daily Trust*, March 18. https://www.dailytrust.com.ng/.

Iloani, Francis. 2019. "Nigeria Yet to Meet $2bn Textile Targets 4 yrs after Policy." *Daily Trust*, March 11. https://www.dailytrust.com.ng/.

Mahmud, Idris. 2017. "Bumper Cotton Harvest in Katsina, Price Rises in Markets." *Daily Trust*, November 23. https://www.dailytrust.com.ng/.

Muhammad, Hamisu. 2017. "Adeosun, Vlisco Hold Talks on Cotton, Textile Revival." *Daily Trust*, November 15. https://www.dailytrust.com.ng/.

Orwell, George. [1937] 1958. *The Road to Wigan Pier*. New York: Houghton-Mifflin Harcourt.

Yahaya, Hussein. 2018. "Why We Must Revive Cotton Farming in Nigeria—DG, RMRDC." *Daily Trust*, February 4. https://www.dailytrust.com.ng/.

Yahaya, Hussein, Vincent Yusuf, and Idris Mahmoud. 2019. "Why FG Should Solve Issues in New Textile Policy." *Daily Trust*, March 14. https://dailytrust.com.ng/.

Research Methods and Sources

Many archival and photographic sources have been accessed for this edited volume. In order to address the volume's primary research questions, the volume's authors have utilized a range of primary and secondary source materials. The former includes archival documents, photographs, and films; private family photographs; and field interviews carried out in Zaria, Kaduna, and Kano, and earlier in the Kabba/Bunu Local Government Area (Kogi State). Specifically, the two main archives in Northern Nigeria—the Nigerian National Archives, Kaduna, and Arewa House, Kaduna—have numerous archival files from the colonial period dealing with textiles and trade; Arewa House also holds the field materials on indigo dyeing in Kano State donated by Philip Shea. Photograph collections held in the Special Collections–African Collection (formerly held in Rhodes House), Weston Library, Oxford, as well as the E. H. Duckworth Photography Collection, held in the Herskovits Library, Northwestern University, have also been used to document textile production and dress during the colonial period (1903–1960).

Two other government sources in Kaduna have been very useful: (1) the Photography Archives, Directorate of Public Affairs and Administration, Kaduna, has photographs, contact sheets, and negatives taken during the 1960s and 1970s, as well as a number of 16 mm films from the same era that document the opening and operation of the Kaduna textile manufacturing industry; and (2) the New Nigerian Development Company Ltd., which was involved in the establishment of textile mills and textile printing factories in Kaduna; its records include lists of company participants, trade records, and annual reports. In addition to these archival sources in Kaduna, archival materials (private collections, photographs, and PhD dissertations) at the Ahmadu Bello University Kashim Ibrahim Library, Zaria, and similar materials available at Bayero University were accessed.

Field interviews have been an important part of this study. The chapter authors have conducted interviews with handweavers in the Gwarzo Local Government Area and the Minjibir Local Government Area of Kano State (Maiwada), in Agbede-Apaa-Bunu in Kogi State (Renne), in Zaria City, Kaduna State (Renne); with machine and hand embroiderers in Zaria, Kaduna State (Maiwada, Renne); with Nigerian and British workers at Kaduna textile mills (Maiwada, Renne, Waziri); with Nigerian, Indian, and Lebanese mill owners in Kano (DanAsabe); with textile mill pattern designers (Maiwada, Waziri); and with textile traders in Kano and in Zaria (Hassan, Renne). Interviews concerning digital textile designing, Nigerian-Chinese textile mill collaborations, recent textile mill revivals, and trade have also been conducted (Usman). Additionally, fieldwork photographs document changes in dress styles as well as textile production and consumption. Textile samples from Kaduna Textiles Limited, Kaduna; the Museum of Science and Industry, Manchester; and the Ethnology Department, the British Museum, as well as African textile collections at the Metropolitan Museum of Art in New York, the Museum of African Art, the Smithsonian Institution, and the Kew Museum (Kew Gardens, UK), have also been accessed. Secondary sources include newspaper articles published by northern Nigerian newspapers (*Daily Trust*, *New Nigerian*, and *Triumph*) held at Arewa House, Kaduna, published UN trade records, and numerous books and articles on northern Nigeria textiles and related topics, which are cited at the end of each relevant chapter. An accompanying website for the exhibit, "Textile Trade Ascendancies: Nigeria, UK, China," held in the Clark Map Library, University of Michigan, in 2015 may be found at http://arcg.is/2bkNwSF.

CONTRIBUTORS

Abdulkarim Umar DanAsabe received a PhD in history from Bayero University, Kano, and currently is chief lecturer at the Federal College of Education, Kano, Kano State.

Hannatu A. Hassan is a doctoral candidate in the Department of Industrial Design, Ahmadu Bello University, Zaria, Kaduna State, and currently is a lecturer in the Department of Art, Federal College of Education, Kano, Kano State.

Salihu Maiwada received a PhD in industrial design from Ahmadu Bello University, Zaria, and currently is professor in the Department of Industrial Design, Ahmadu Bello University, Zaria, Kaduna State.

Elisha Renne received a PhD in anthropology from New York University and is professor emerita in the Department of Afroamerican and African Studies and the Department of Anthropology, University of Michigan, Ann Arbor, Michigan.

Dakyes Usman received a PhD in industrial design from Ahmadu Bello University, Zaria, and currently is professor in the Department of Industrial Design, Ahmadu Bello University, Zaria, Kaduna State.

Mohammadu Yahaya Waziri received a PhD in industrial design from Ahmadu Bello University, Zaria, and currently is a senior lecturer in the Department of Industrial Design, Modibbo Adama University of Technology, Yola, Adamawa State.